Working Hard and Making Do

Working Hard and Making Do

Surviving in Small Town America

Margaret K. Nelson
Joan Smith

UNIVERSITY OF CALIFORNIA PRESS
Berkeley • Los Angeles • London

Portions of chapters 5 and 6 previously appeared
as "Economic Restructuring, Household Strategies,
and Gender: A Case Study of a Rural Community," *Feminist Studies* 24, no. 1 (Spring 1998):
79–114.

University of California Press
Berkeley and Los Angeles, California

University of California Press, Ltd.
London, England

Library of Congress Cataloging-in-Publication Data

Nelson, Margaret K., 1944–
    Working hard and making do : surviving in
small town America / Margaret K. Nelson, Joan
Smith.
        p.   cm.
    Includes bibliographical references and index.
    ISBN 0-520-21574-5 (alk. paper).—ISBN 0-520-
21575-3 (pbk. : alk. paper)
        1. Work and family—United States.   2. Family—
Economic aspects—United States.   3. Households—
Economic aspects—United States.   4. Rural
families—United States.   5. Labor supply—United
States.   6. Sociology, Rural—United States.   7.
Rural development—United States.   I. Smith,
Joan, 1935–   . II. Title.
HD4904.25.N45   1998
306.85'2'0973—dc21   98-20758
                                                    CIP

Printed in the United States of America
9 8 7 6 5 4 3 2 1

For Miriam Borgenicht Klein
M.K.N.

For my grandchildren
J.S.

Contents

Acknowledgments

Since we began this book, the economy has gone from bad to good. We suspect, however, that many of those who make their appearance on these pages would not know that from their own personal experiences. They continue to struggle and sometimes, in spite of that struggle, they find themselves falling further and further behind. We remain impressed with the degree of ingenuity, gracefulness, good humor, and resourcefulness these families bring to bear in sustaining themselves, those they love, and, in the long run, their communities. Our first debt of gratitude is to the members of these families for sharing their lives with us.

As this book was written, many things happened in our own families. A dearly loved parent died, and another became progressively disabled and died as we were putting on the final touches. If these losses were in the natural order of things, others were not. A young friend died far before her time, and a deeply cherished sister became ill, as did one of the authors herself.

There were good times as well. Two babies were born, and children married. Others of our children successfully completed college and acquired what we call here good jobs—though some continued to find that bad jobs were their lot for a time. We went on vacations, took sabbaticals, planted several more or less successful new gardens, tried out recipes for low-fat meals, washed more loads of laundry than we can count, and, in general, carried on that life we call family. At every step we were sustained by friendship. Margaret Nelson thanks Emily

Abel, Burke Rochford, Eve Adler, Kate Sonderegger, and Bill Nelson. Joan Smith thanks her entire family, especially Peter, Libby, and Lucas. Each of these individuals was important in his or her own way.

Even in the midst of these relationships, writing a coauthored book turned out to be a curiously insular process. Rather than looking outward to those with whom we could test our ideas and share drafts, we looked to each other. Although the list of specific colleagues to thank is small, our overall indebtedness to the scholarship of, and the personal support we have received over the years from, our professional communities is vast. In particular, at this time we thank Ruth Milkman, Naomi Schneider, the anonymous reviewer at the University of California Press, and reviewers and editors at several other presses (we took their comments to heart as well).

If we did not reach outward for professional advice, we did rely on a long series of assistants of various kinds, some of whom helped in more ways than one. We want to thank those who ably helped conduct our in-depth interviews and who shared in the pains and pleasures of this kind of intense work: Jessica Lindert, Sarah Martel, Joanne Jacobson, and Jennifer Nelson. We are also grateful to Evelyn Holley and Greg Marcus for conducting the telephone survey. For invaluable and invariably cheerful secretarial support, we acknowledge Shelley Roberts and Charlene Barrett. Transcribing was ably, and confidentially, done by Jennifer Nelson and June Fiske. A number of assistants tracked down references and elusive pieces of data, including Gretchen Elias, Elissa Forman, Tiffany Bean, and Priscilla Stanton. Jessica Lindert read and reread final drafts and added insightful comments when we were too familiar with the manuscript to see either the woods or the trees.

We are indebted to the Ford Foundation, Middlebury College, and The University of Vermont for financial assistance.

Last, but not least, we are indebted to each other for much that we have learned, only a small portion of which is presented here. This book was a truly collaborative venture. When we use "we" throughout this manuscript, we are not being either magisterial or authorial; we are merely being plural.

Introduction

This book about the livelihood of working-class families was motivated by an entirely mistaken premise.

As residents of the rural state in which the research was conducted, we were well aware that the region offered considerable opportunity for people to engage in a broad array of economic activities, including employment in a formal labor market, informal or unrecorded work, barter and other forms of nonmonetary exchange, and self-provisioning activities, such as growing one's own vegetables and hunting. We anticipated that the practice of melding a variety of these activities emerged among, and was a major recourse for, those whose participation in the waged labor force was less than optimal because of either inadequate jobs or the lack of full-time work.

We also anticipated that a spate of industrial activity that began in the 1960s and quickly brought the local labor force in line with the rest of the country had led to the creation of a different set of jobs that required *and* enabled families to rationalize the use of their labor. Gone would be the unwaged housewife, to be replaced by the working woman and the local day care center; gone would be the homegrown tomatoes and woodpiles, to be replaced by convenience stores and oil delivery trucks. In sum, we expected that working-class families with members employed in the *new* waged work in the formal economy increasingly would turn to modern forms of labor and consumption, while other working-class families—those who worked for low wages, those en-

gaged in traditional rural activities, those with jobs in the service sector
and especially in the seasonal tourist industry—would have no alternative but to practice forms of labor activity outside the formal waged
market.[1]

We were wrong. We were wrong in part because we had not yet
uncovered a central fact about the changing economy in the area in
which we conducted our research: That area had not just
(re)industrialized[2] and become more "modern" but also had experienced
a degradation in the jobs industry provided. As a result of these two
overlapping changes, not all waged work in the county—and not even
all industrial work—was being cut from the same cloth. Quite simply,
there was good work that offered the benefits and amenities which had
prevailed under what is sometimes called the Fordist regime,[3] and there
was bad work that, though no less "modern," failed to offer those same
benefits and amenities. The emergence of an economy constituted by
this dualism was hardly a local phenomenon. While controversy
abounds about the degree to which bad jobs are replacing good ones
and why, there is now little debate that the growth of bad jobs is widespread and characterizes the contemporary U.S. economy. Neither the
statistically rural Coolidge County* in which we conducted our research, nor Vermont, the state in which that county is located, was im-
mune from this development. Even in the face of economic recovery
during the 1990s, Vermont's Commerce and Community Development
secretary said, "We've created jobs; we've just created a disproportion-
ate amount of jobs in a sector that doesn't pay as much."[4]

It also turned out that we were wrong because, in drawing on the
wealth of studies of marginal populations in "developed" regions as well
as of those in "less developed" parts of the world,[5] we had reversed an
important, and perhaps relatively new, direction of causality between
regular waged employment and the other aspects of a household's survival strategy. Ironically, and contrary to our expectations, we found
that the households with access to decent jobs were also precisely the
households that relied on the combination of very different economic
activities—they used the labor of a second worker, they engaged in entrepreneurial side-work, they depended on friends and neighbors for
access to a broad array of goods and services, and they built their own

---

*To protect the confidentiality of our respondents, we have changed the name of the
county in which we conducted our research. Coolidge County cannot be found in any
Vermont atlas. The details about Coolidge County do, however, accurately represent a
very real place.

homes and grew their own tomatoes. We also found that this combination of economic activities was a source of pride, comfort, and security to these working-class families—as well as the source (and savings) of income. Because much of this work had as its precondition a specific household organization of labor, it also had the effect of reconstituting what at first glance passes for "typical" gender relationships within the household. We were surprised to find, however, that those living in families without at least one good job were considerably less capable of deploying the same kind of complex, multifaceted survival strategy and that in these less well-off households, sustaining customary gender privileges came at a greater cost. These unexpected findings motivate this book.

Although the processes of economic restructuring, as they are enacted in Coolidge County, provide the broad context for this work, neither economic restructuring nor Coolidge County is the subject. We do not seek to explain in depth or in detail the *causes* of economic restructuring. This topic has received considerable attention elsewhere.[6] For our immediate purposes, it is sufficient to note that the effects of restructuring transcend the rural-urban divide (but may be more extreme in the countryside)[7] and the gender divide (although men and women are affected in somewhat different ways).[8] What is most important for this book is how this process has affected the household economy. We do not focus on the effects of economic restructuring that have received the bulk of scholarly attention—declining wages and increased economic inequality[9]—although we offer evidence about these issues. This is a book about a different aspect of economic restructuring—the loss of the *other* advantages working families had come to expect from employment. Though largely invisible in the scholarly literature, these advantages are central to how families live. We have found that the failure of the economy to provide these other benefits—long-term and stable employment, vacations and sick days, regular hours, assured pension plans and health insurance—is an equally (and perhaps even more) significant impediment to the capacity of households to get by and to recreate the so-called traditional household with its complement of gendered activities.

We chose Coolidge County, Vermont, as the site for this research for both practical and conceptual reasons. One practical reason is that it is close to where we live and work. A second, more important reason is that it was subject to a particular version of the economic restructuring that has characterized the U.S. domestic economy for the past two decades. In addition, it is small enough to see close at hand—where, in fact, it is only visible—how families have struggled to accommodate themselves to these shifts in the economic tide.

On the conceptual level, we were all too aware that aggregate studies of economic processes can be profoundly misleading. Lying behind national level data are the significant and important regional differences that are most consequential in shaping the economy of any specific area, and thus of the families whose futures are fundamentally tied to the place in which they live and work. Over the long run, there certainly are trends that influence all regions—there is a world or "global" economy. These trends, however, are always worked out in conjunction with the unique characteristics of specific locales as well as with vast disparities between regions, a hallmark of that world economy.

There are two issues to be noted. First, local economies stand in very different relations to national and international ones. Second, and more important in some respects, different locales have quite different cultures when it comes to how their labor forces will be deployed. As Michael Storper and Richard Walker note, "Community attitudes and practices can also be a medium of political response to the predicaments of work and life. The local population accumulates historical experience of its social condition as labor force and citizenry, and its collective geographical presence eases the tasks of political mobilization around the roles."[10]

Taken together, these two dimensions of local areas have the overall effect of refracturing the same aggregate national and international trends in quite different directions and with very different results. Changes in national average wages, sites of production, or forms of labor control may describe the aggregate but bear little or no relationship to what is going on in any particular place. In fact, there is good reason to believe that far from long-term, widespread trends producing a convergence across regions of the nation (or indeed the world), the specificities of different locales are becoming more rather than less important. Not only is it the case that economic restructuring produces geographically specific results, but the very nature of current economic processes also both heightens and takes advantage of regional differences.[11]

Coolidge County was affected by the current economic restructuring somewhat later than, and in different ways from, other regions in the country. Some of what we describe, therefore, might be considered more relevant to other similar (rural) areas than to urban areas where restructuring occurred at a different time and with some different consequences for a household survival strategy.[12] In addition, Coolidge County may appear unusual (in comparison with the country as a whole) with respect to the particular opportunities it offers for informal economic activity and for making a living off the land. We are less concerned, however, with either timing or the particular content of the survival strategy of Coolidge County residents than we are with two other issues which we believe have widespread relevance: first, that households diversify their economic activities—that is, households combine a multiplicity of activities to get by during a period of change; and second, that the combination that is possible for a given household depends on its specific relationship to waged employment.

Two concepts need further discussion here: household is one; survival strategy is another. We make no distinction between the use of the terms "household" and "family"; in fact, we use them interchangeably. We define a household or family as these terms are used in everyday speech: a group of people who live together, share resources (even if that sharing is not equitable or fair), and (at least at some level) make efforts to coordinate their activities. Having said that, it is the case that we include only certain kinds of households in this study. Because we were interested in how families got along independent of the very real constraints brought against them by virtue of being either single-parent households or households made up of a homosexual couple, we chose to focus exclusively on two-parent, heterosexual families and any children living with them. Also, because Coolidge County in 1990 had a minority population of less than 2 percent,[13] virtually all of our research subjects are white. In short, the data we will be discussing are strictly generalizable only to intact, heterosexual, white families. The apparent limitations of our sample population are, we believe, a source of strength. If even these relatively privileged families face structural barriers to the full use of their available labor supplies, then less advantaged families—single-parent families, gay couples, and families facing racial barriers—are presumably even more hampered. In other words, what we present here is the best case scenario. It will take little imagination to deduce from these data what the worst case may be.

We applied two criteria to narrow further the group of households in this study. First, because from the very beginning we had a special interest in how families with the best employment "chances" were positioned with respect to the practice we initially called "patching it together," we limited our investigation to those families in which at least one person currently had as his or her principal source of income employment in the formal waged labor force. This is a study about families with a link to waged work.[14] Second, because we wanted to see what happened to families that were best positioned to adopt a multifaceted survival strategy, we included only those households in which the second adult partner was *eligible* for employment as well. This is not a book that investigates the lives of families with a disabled or elderly worker, important as such families are. Once again, we limited the population studied not to understate the problems faced by other kinds of families but, in fact, to do just the opposite.

Like our definition of a household, our definition of a survival strategy is quite straightforward. It has an empirical or grounded meaning: a specific set of economic activities families develop to ensure and even enhance their daily survival, including gainful employment (whether in the formal or informal economy), moonlighting or on-the-side employment, self-provisioning efforts, and nonmonetary exchanges with other households.[15] With these considerations taken together, then, we conceive of a household strategy much as Pahl does: "[the] distinctive *practices* adopted by members of a household collectively or individually to get work done."[16] Thus, the strategy is the household's "particular mix of activities or practices."[17]

From its use in historical studies, the concept of a household or family strategy has been picked up by a broad range of social scientists.[18] That use has also aroused considerable debate.[19] On one hand, the concept is lauded by those who believe it can move analysis beyond the classic structure/agency dichotomy and be attractive both to those coming from an interactionist tradition and to those from the Marxist perspective. On the other hand, scholars object to many of the term's connotations, particularly to the implicit assumptions of voluntarism, rationality, consensus, and fairness.[20]

We accept none of these connotations. In fact, we argue that the emerging household strategies take place within a very specific context and that the context (regional resources, labor market opportunities) often shapes and constrains the options households have at their disposal. This is an important point. Although we speak about "tactics" and "choices," and although we use verbs that suggest agency ("send," "develop," "use"), the reader should not be confused by our language. The argument throughout the book makes it clear that some actions represent forced choices.

We also reject the connotation that households are made up of actors whose motivation is purely economic. Instead, we demonstrate that some practices, rather than having any strict economic rationale or logic, are motivated by other kinds of concerns. We show concretely that the practices engaged in by family members sometimes arise from individual choices rather than collective agreement, and that whatever sharing transpires may very well be unfair and inequitable.

Even with these qualifications, we employ the term "household" or "family" strategy because of its connotation of "collectivity," and because that connotation is partly accurate: A household or family is more than a mere agglomeration of individuals going about their business without any reference to the whole. The term thus helps identify a central theme in this analysis: Households are critical units that shape and define economic life, and they do so according to a set of rules that dictate who contributes what, how, to whom, under what circumstances, and with what boundaries.[21]

In what follows, we first provide a context for our analysis by describing economic restructuring in Coolidge County (chapter 1). We then both depict and account for the survival strategies of the households in that county. More particularly, we compare the survival strategies of two different sets of Coolidge County households: those in which at least one member of the household has managed to find and hold onto "good work" and those in which the household members are less fortunate and have recourse only to what we inelegantly, but accurately, call "bad work." This comparison takes place at three levels: as an overall comparison of household strategies, as a comparison of how those strategies affect relationships between men and women within the household, and as a comparison of how individuals within each set of households make sense of their employment.

The first "pass" through the comparison focuses on households as single units with the sets of identifiable goals and aims that we call survival strategies. Whether or not there are differences between family members as to these goals, we assume the members make contributions that maintain the family as a unit. Hence, we focus on what it is the household members do, on how those activities are enabled by the position the family as a whole holds in the labor force, and, to a certain extent, on the motivations that lead individuals to engage in some practices rather than others. We generally ignore here the issue of *who* in the household is engaged in these practices. Our focus in the first part of the book is on *households* and on the comparison between the two sets of households in their access to various elements of an overall survival strategy.

More specifically, in chapter 2 we discuss each of these elements as they occur among Coolidge County families (and among U.S. families taken as a whole), and we provide an overview of the differences between two sets of Coolidge County households—those with good work and those without—both with respect to the extent to which they engage in various survival tactics and with respect to their demography. Chapters 3 and 4 are complementary pieces that look in detail at two broad components of the household economy and at the differences between the two sets of households with respect to each of them. Chapter 3 focuses on income-producing activities (the dual-earner strategy, moonlighting). Chapter 4 explores activities that, even though they do not produce income, meet household needs (self-provisioning, nonmonetary household exchanges).

In the second "pass," we split open the household to consider the implications of these survival strategies for the recreation of gender within the household. No matter how scholars define gender—and no matter how they explain it—two issues stand out. Gender refers to difference, the "social relations that separate people into differentiated gendered status."[22] It also refers to the consequences of those differences, to a social system of inequality in which men generally (albeit not all men and not with respect to all activities) have a status superior to that of women. Joan Wallach Scott refers to both of these when she notes, "Gender is a constitutive element of social relationships based on perceived differences between the sexes and . . . a primary way of signifying relationships of power."[23] These two issues—of difference and of its consequences for hierarchy—will be the focus when we turn our attention to dynamics inside the household. We will explore how it is that the different survival strategies of the two sets of households allow for, or give rise to, the recreation of gender difference (chapter 5); we will explore as well the implications of gender for the division of domestic labor within the two sets of households (chapter 6).

By ordering the book in this way (that is, by starting with the household's overall survival strategy and then looking at its implications for gender and the division of domestic labor), we do not mean to imply that gender occurs only in the household. Clearly, persistent gender differences in the workplace (in both the formal and the informal economy) play a significant role in shaping the options available to men and women alike, and we will briefly examine those issues in chapters 1 and 2. Those differences, however, are not the centerpiece of the analysis. We are interested in how economic restructuring itself plays out its role—not just in the stock market or occupational and industrial reorganization, but also in how men and women relate to each other on a daily basis within the apparent privacy of the home. Finally, we should add that we are not trying to account for the creation of gender in the household; rather, we are interested in showing the very different foundations upon which those gendered arrangements rest (and are *recreated*) in the two kinds of households that constitute the subject matter of this study.

In chapter 7, we turn to individuals to consider how the family's survival strategy shapes the manner in which those with good work— in contrast to those who are less privileged—make sense of and respond to the changing labor force, the very jobs they hold, and the social world in which they have a place. Thus, the focus in this book moves from broad to narrow and then back out again, from an investigation of the context in which the households with which we are concerned are located, through an analysis of the survival strategies of those households themselves, to a discussion of men and women and gendered relationships within households, and finally to a consideration of individual attitudes that on an aggregate level begin to define the public arena of politics (or what passes for politics these days).

Although we are dealing with a very contemporary topic in this book—the consequences of recent forms of economic restructuring— the methods for this study are quite traditional.[24] We employed two different, standard data collection techniques to obtain information about the population. First, using a snowball sampling procedure, we conducted in-depth, face-to-face interviews with a sample of 117 individuals representing 81 different households. Second, we conducted, over the telephone, a random survey of the population from which we drew a subset of 158 households that met the criteria discussed above. (Data collection procedures and measurement issues are discussed more fully in the Appendix.) All the data were collected in Coolidge County, Vermont, between 1991 and 1992.[25]

The notions of good jobs and bad jobs are part of common parlance these days. To operationalize these concepts, we rely on two component features of employment. The first describes the *terms of employment* in a given job: An individual who holds a waged job that is defined as year round, full time, and "regular"[26] is provisionally classified as having "good" employment; in contrast, an individual whose work is part time, seasonal, or specifically designated "temporary" by the terms of that employment is automatically classified as having a "bad" job. This first discrimination, then, gets at what is usually thought of as "contingent" work.

The second discrimination assesses not only the job's stability but also the character of the workplace itself.[27] We include measures of six items reflecting three components of the quality of employment: availability of benefits (health insurance, paid vacation), workplace stability (frequency of layoffs in the workplace, necessity of bringing one's own equipment to the workplace), and "bureaucratization" (number of employees in the workplace, whether or not the employee is related to the employer).[28] Each of these items was scored as a dichotomous variable.[29] A "good" job was defined as one with a score of five or higher; 56 percent of all waged jobs held by respondents were classified as "good jobs."[30]

As noted above, we classify households on the basis of whether or not any of their members currently hold good work. The households in our sample are divided between those in which at least one adult has what we define here as a "good" job (54 percent of the households in the random sample and 52 percent of those in which we conducted in-depth interviews) and those in which all employed individuals hold what we define as "bad" jobs. We make this distinction on the basis of households rather than individuals because we believe—and will argue throughout—that it is the household resources taken as a whole, and not the individual relationship to the labor force alone, that determines how well the members of a given family can put together the various tactics that enable and enhance survival.

Each aspect of a household's survival strategy has its own definition. First, we simply count how many of its members engage in paid work. That is, we distinguish between those households that rely on one earner and those that use a *dual-earner* strategy. Second, we consider whether any individual in the household has, in addition to "regular" or "principal" employment (the activity from which that person derives the greatest income), some form of *moonlighting* activity. Finally, we differentiate between two additional sets of activities. *Self-provisioning* refers to the efforts that household members make to provide, through their own labor (and for themselves), goods and services they would otherwise have to purchase in the (formal or informal) market. We further subdivide self-provisioning into that which is *routine*, and helps to guarantee the daily life of the household, and that which is *substantial*, and helps to improve the family's living conditions.[31] Nonmonetary *in-*

terhousehold exchange, the last set of activities, refers to the efforts household members make to exchange a similar set of goods and services with those in *other* households. We include here a variety of different kinds of practices—informal assistance (the casual and reciprocal exchange of goods and services), barter ("the exchange of goods and services of comparable value or the understood exchange of equivalents"), reduced rates ("the exchange of goods and services for token or symbolic payment"), and moving in with other households.[32]

Although an observer might have difficulty distinguishing among these various practices with respect to their location within the household survival strategy, our respondents could easily make fine distinctions. For example, they could distinguish between the purchase or sale of goods in the market and what we call nonmonetary interhousehold exchange even when the "same" activity was involved in more than one domain and even when the latter involved a cash transaction. Consider the following example. Bruce Sharp* has a full-time waged job; his wife Nancy holds down part-time employment. To the Sharps and any outsider, it is clear that this is a dual-earner family, but that is only the beginning of the story. Bruce Sharp has a plow attachment for his truck with which, on snowy mornings, he clears his own driveway as well as others in his neighborhood. Both Bruce and Nancy discussed this snowplowing in their interview.

INTERVIEWER: Do you charge different rates for plowing for different people?

BRUCE: Yes, it depends on how long it takes me.

NANCY: And how old they are. I'm glad he does, but he wasn't going to tell you. Like [when you plow for] Ted. He's bought you a six-pack of beer. Or a couple of times last winter Bruce would plow and [Ted would] bring him home Friendly's ice cream.

INTERVIEWER [TO BRUCE]: Were you expecting . . . money?

NANCY: No, not for friends. There's an older couple that you've gone down and just, [gotten] $5 or something. Because they want to pay something. You don't make a killing on that.

INTERVIEWER [TO BRUCE]: Why do you do it then?

BRUCE: I started out a long time ago . . . just to give me extra soda money, cigarette money.

NANCY: But you did it a lot of times as a favor when you first started, you just did it to be nice different times. . . . He does one for the apartment house [in

---

*Throughout this book, we use pseudonyms for our respondents. Where we believe that others could identify specific individuals, we change the identifying information while remaining true to the basic portrait.

return for which] Stuart brought you a load of corn. You don't overcharge him. More or less to help out a lot of times. The store, that's a business. That's a different thing. That has to be taken care of.

INTERVIEWER [TO BRUCE]:   And they pay reasonable rates for that?

BRUCE: Yes.

As this conversation, and especially Nancy's interruptions of it, suggests, in addition to taking care of his own family's needs (self-provisioning), Bruce does his snowplowing as an on-the-side business (that is, he moonlights), and he receives an hourly or contracted rate for doing so for "the store." As Nancy says, "that has to be taken care of." Bruce also does plowing as part of interhousehold exchanges: Some he does as part of a casual reciprocity (with Ted), some he barters (with Stuart), and some he does for a reduced rate (the elderly couple). (To make the issue more complicated, in charging the "elderly couple" anything at all, Bruce is freeing them from the burden of reciprocity that is imposed on Ted and Stuart; he is also freeing them from the burden of having received charity. The "fee" in this case is almost a gift. At the same time, the elderly couple might believe that in paying $5, they have purchased a service in the informal economy and not the social economy.) From Bruce and Nancy's perspective—as well as from the perspective of this book—the context clearly differentiates among these separate transactions and among these various elements of their household survival strategy.

In much of what follows, then, we divide households into two groups—good job households and bad job households—and we consider the extent to which each participates in four separate elements of the family survival strategy. The fact that we have to assign idiosyncratic terms—and often clumsy ones at that—to these different components of a household strategy suggests that as a society we have not yet developed an easy language to capture the fact that families need to engage in a wide range of economic activities simply to get by from day to day. This "oversight," we suggest, poses significant problems for policymakers who focus on wage levels alone to determine how families are doing. As we shall see, wages are not enough to sustain families.

Constructing a New Economy

Driving the back roads of Coolidge County, one may get the impression that this is an area that has escaped the last half of the twentieth century. As wrong as that impression is—and it is indeed wrong—it still deserves our attention. History most certainly did not stop at the borders of what appears to be a bucolic place out of time, but it did take advantage of it, in ways that, paradoxically, illuminate a very complex set of quite modern economic processes accompanied by the social and political realities these processes unleashed.

To understand fully what happened to Coolidge County families in recent years, it is necessary to start outside Coolidge County and back in time—in the United States as a whole and the 1960s, when the glue that held the postwar economy together began to dissolve. Industrial overcapacity, along with the saturation of domestic markets, the increased industrial output of Japan and European countries, the two oil crises, and the erosion of Pax Americana had combined to force a profound restructuring of the U.S. economy.[1]

Any number of different measures can be marshaled to describe the resulting changes in the U.S. economy over the past several decades and the terms on which it has recently rebounded. While the mid-1990s witnessed an economic resurgence, the previous declines left an indelible mark on working-class families, both as a consequence of earlier bad times and as a premise for the current good times. Those good times, unfortunately, seem reserved for the upper 20 percent of wealth holders.

Taken as a whole, the present picture leaves little room to doubt that working-class families now confront a labor market vastly different from that of the 1960s. Probably the most striking characteristic of the contemporary labor market is the replacement of good jobs by jobs that fail to offer decent wages, permanent work, and secure benefits.

The feature of the new labor market receiving the most comment is the fall in real wages. As is now well noted, between 1973 and 1997 the average hourly wage—in terms of what people could buy with it— dropped steadily,[2] but the fall in wages is not the only change in what people can expect from their work. Other losses are just as damaging. Consider, for example, the rise in part-time work. Up until the recent past, part-time work was understood to be a feature of the worker, and thus the job held was taken to be a reflection of employee desires rather than the design of the employer. If the 1997 United Parcel Service (UPS) strike did not put that myth to rest, an important piece of data certainly should: between 1970 and 1990, all the unexpected growth of part-time workers—that is, growth beyond that which could have been expected at the 1970 level—was composed of those who said they would rather have full-time jobs. These were the involuntary part-time workers made famous by the UPS strike but who now can be found in every industrial sector.[3]

In addition to this extraordinary growth in part-time jobs is the growth in jobs that require absolutely no commitment on the part of the worker (beyond remaining available for employment) and, more telling still, entail no commitment on the part of the employer. This is exemplified in the extraordinary growth of temporary jobs. Between 1968 and 1992, a period during which the U.S. labor force doubled in size, the temporary workforce exploded fifteen times over:[4] between 1985 and 1995, the number of people working for companies that supply temporary workers tripled, resulting in a total of 2.1 million workers formally employed on a contingent basis.[5] Neither set of statistics, of course, counts those workers who, on a much less formal basis, are in jobs that have short-time employment as one of their characteristics. Where employers had offered stable, year-round work to their employees, they are now increasingly turning to these subcontracted, temporary workers to fill in. Examples abound, but perhaps one of the most striking occurs in what is otherwise considered a bucolic setting in rural Vermont.

One of the country's largest electronics firms, operating internationally and famous for its generous employment practices, has a large plant in a county neighboring Coolidge. (It is Vermont's largest private employer.) In spite of its reputation, this plant regularly employed a temporary workforce made available through another extremely small electronics factory in Coolidge County (about which we will learn more below). Workers were bused up to the larger plant at the beginning of the work day and back at the end. Anyone observing the production process would not have been able to discern the difference between the permanent workers and those who were bused in—the contingent workforce—although their paychecks, benefits, and length of job tenure clearly discriminated between the two.

This example points to a third characteristic of the new labor market: the significant decline in secure, career jobs. Although controversy continues over how to measure job tenure, there is hardly any debate that job stability has decreased remarkably over the recent past.[6] An extensive survey of job tenure carried out under the auspices of the National Commission for Employment Policy reveals that in spite of what appears to be growing prosperity, individual workers face declining economic security.[7]

Of course, the question arises: Is this simply a reflection of a workforce that is more shiftless now than it had been in an earlier period? The answer is no. The changes in job tenure result more from strategies of employers to create a workforce that can be easily hired and just as easily fired than they do from the propensity of workers to quit.[8]

Obviously, as we will discuss more fully in chapters to come, when the organization of work no longer assumes a stable, permanent labor force with strong commitment to an individual firm, conditions are created where workers are just as likely to quit as they are to stay on. Thus, what begins as a management strategy is reinforced by the responses of workers to that strategy. Job instability is then doubled, first because of the management strategy in specific job design and second because of workers' reactions to that strategy.

This doubling up of the causes of job instability significantly exaggerates the effects of the lower wages offered in these jobs. Over a ten-year period, men who changed their employers often earned 30 percent a year less than men with a stable work record, even in the same occupation.[9] One report documents that about one-third of the wage inequalities between otherwise similar workers can be accounted for by job instability.[10]

Finally, contingent, temporary, unstable, and low-waged jobs guarantee few if any benefits by way of either health insurance or pensions.

They are also unlikely to offer vacations, sick time, or paid family leave for emergencies. The irony is that precisely the workers who have lower wages and less job security must find ways of securing on their own the advantages that better jobs had uniformly offered all workers in the relatively recent past.

The effects of these developments, taken in isolation from the rest of the social world in which working people live and raise their families, are dire enough, but they also must be seen in a wider context. Institutions far apart from industrial organizations—schools, churches, day care centers, health care systems—have been predicated on the existence of stable, long-term work histories in jobs that not only pay a "family wage" over a full lifetime but also offer benefits that are guarantees for meeting life's exigencies.[11] Jobs were enough for gaining access to these institutions and the services they provided, but when a growing proportion of jobs no longer offers these securities, there is nothing to take their place in the broader community. When there are attempts to replace what is lost at work with services in the community, the charge is often levied that the fate of workers is a result of their own failures. There is every reason to believe, however, that it is less the character of workers that has produced this bifurcated labor market—made up of very good jobs and very bad ones—than explicit public policies and management strategies.

The attack on unions launched in the early 1980s with the PATCO strike was a self-conscious policy of the Reagan administration. Rhetoric notwithstanding, national policy continues to permit broadly anti-union practices on the part of management. As a consequence, unionization is at a twentieth-century low, half of what it was a mere thirty years ago.[12] Coupled with the deregulation of industries where unions had been strong, this attack on unions was an important contributor to the increase in bad jobs.

Another cause of the growth in bad jobs is the well-noted shift from manufacturing to services.[13] In a context where unions were losing power even in sectors that traditionally had offered protection, the movement of jobs to the under-unionized service sector exacerbated the downward pressure on wages and the deterioration of job-related benefits.[14] Compared to jobs in manufacturing, jobs in trade and services offer fewer opportunities for upward mobility, less job stability, and considerably fewer benefits.

Although the shift to services has been a major explanation for the growth of bad jobs, it is important to point out that almost every industrial sector is now showing signs of moving toward a strategy of bad jobs.[15] These practices of cost cutting and increasing employment of low-wage labor are a function neither of changes in the skill level of the workforce nor of changes in demographics—they are not to be laid at the feet of workers themselves. Rather, they are demonstrably the result of self-conscious strategies of employers in a political context that reinforces these strategies.[16]

Whether they have options or not, employers believe that they need to move toward flexible employment structures to meet the exigencies of globalization and deregulation. Employees who are subjected to the strategies (e.g., downsizing, subcontracting) that result from these beliefs of employers are thus less governed by the individual characteristics they bring to the workplace than they are by the quality of jobs offered to them.

Those less qualified to compete in an increasingly competitive workforce will have even harder times than they might have had before. Recall that under the Fordist regime, even low-skilled workers found secure, well-paying jobs that offered some modest upward mobility through internal labor markets. Even the most dedicated worker now faces an employment situation that is, in recent history, almost unique in its incapacity to offer decent, meaningful work with the rewards workers had come to expect. White workers in every sector have been affected, and African American workers suffer even more from the new labor practices.[17]

Unless personnel offices are more adept at their sorting mechanisms than even *they* would claim, individual worker qualifications such as attitude and likelihood of employment stability have become increasingly irrelevant in acquiring a decent job. In other words, when bad jobs become the prerequisite for economic prosperity, good jobs become unavailable to an increasing share of workers regardless of what they are willing and able to bring to their work.

There is nothing new about bad jobs. What is new is that in the midst of what appears to be increasing economic prosperity, conditions of economic insecurity are growing for a significant portion of the population. In a 1996 article, the *New York Times*, for example, noted the breadth of the problem and outlined the consequences that resulted.

> Nearly three-quarters of all households have had a close encounter with lay-offs since 1980. . . . In one third of all households a family member has lost a job and nearly 40 percent more know a relative, friend or neighbor who was laid off. One in 10 adults—or about 19 million people, a number match-

ing the adult population of New York and New Jersey combined—acknowledged that a lost job in their household has precipitated a major crisis in
their lives.[18]

These points cannot be overstated. The loss of stable employment
and the growth of bad jobs are now systemic features of economic prosperity. There is now a fundamental disconnect between what a significant portion of the working population are told they should be able to
expect of themselves and what they can realistically attain.

The distinction we will be using between good jobs and bad jobs and
the households who have one or the other is no statistical artifact constructed to make an arcane social scientific argument. It represents a
widespread and crucially important phenomenon, the consequences of
which need to be understood.

Although the results of all these shifts—shifts that created an economy based on a radical bifurcation of the kinds of jobs available to
working people—can be studied using large-scale, aggregate data, their
effects on the conditions of working-class households can be gauged
only by closely considering a single area. This is our intention. In what
follows, we place Coolidge County in the context of the shifts we have
just outlined. We will demonstrate that while the county recently experienced industrial expansion (even as urban areas were witnessing industrial decline), this geographic rearrangement was soon overlaid with
changes in the labor process and employment practices that had begun
to characterize industrial production elsewhere.[19]

COOLIDGE COUNTY

In 1960, Coolidge County could not have looked more different from
an urban industrial center or, indeed, from the United States taken as a
whole. Two measures of this difference are especially relevant to the
argument of this book. First, more than a quarter of the population
found employment in the traditional rural sectors of farming, forestry,
and fishing, while less than one-fifth held jobs in manufacturing. By way
of contrast, in urban areas nationally, well more than a quarter of
the population was engaged in manufacturing and only 1 percent
in agriculture (Chart 1).* Second, although in 1960 Coolidge County

*Unless otherwise indicated, statistical data concerning Coolidge County come from
the Vermont Census for appropriate years, and statistical data for the United States come
from the U.S. census for appropriate years.

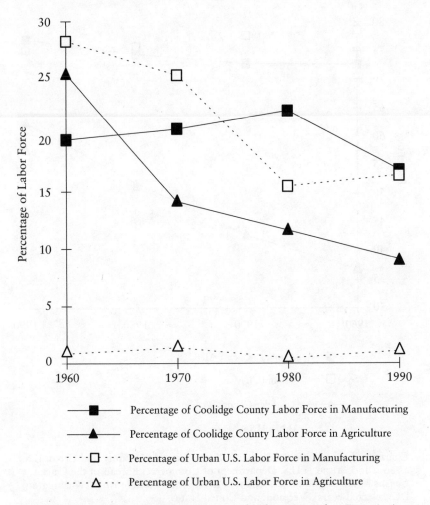

Chart 1. Percentage of Coolidge County and Urban U.S. Labor Force in Agriculture and Manufacturing. SOURCE: U.S. Department of Commerce, Bureau of the Census, *Census of the Population, Social and Economic Characteristics* (Washington, DC: selected years), Vermont and United States.

women were almost as likely as those in urban areas to enter the labor force (presumably to help support the family farm),[20] Coolidge County men not only had low labor force participation rates (72.5 percent) but also demonstrated a relatively strong aversion to wage and salary work (with less than 61 percent so employed). In comparison,

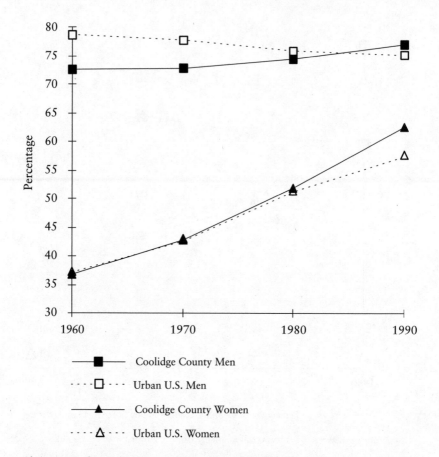

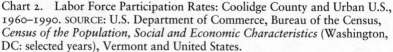

Chart 2.   Labor Force Participation Rates: Coolidge County and Urban U.S., 1960–1990. SOURCE: U.S. Department of Commerce, Bureau of the Census, *Census of the Population, Social and Economic Characteristics* (Washington, DC: selected years), Vermont and United States.

almost 79 percent of men in urban areas were in the labor force, and 78 percent of these men held a waged or salaried job (Charts 2 and 3).[21]

By the 1990s these and other differences had disappeared and even reversed direction. Agricultural employment had dropped to less than one-tenth of the labor force, and the level of manufacturing was almost precisely the same as it was in urban areas. The labor force participation rates of *both* men and women in Coolidge County exceeded those of men and women elsewhere, and the proportions of labor force partici-

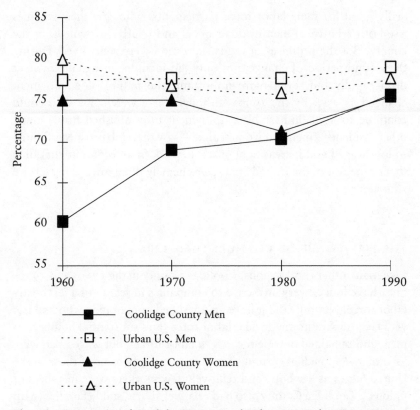

Chart 3. Percentage of Coolidge County and Urban U.S. Labor Force Participating in Wage and Salary Work, 1960–1990. SOURCE: U.S. Department of Commerce, Bureau of the Census, *Census of the Population, Social and Economic Characteristics* (Washington, DC: selected years), Vermont and United States.

pants who were wage and salary workers were quite similar to those elsewhere.

Between 1960 and 1990, then, Coolidge County appeared to be joining the modern age. What appears to be convergence, however, is actually the result of two very different and overlapping waves of change. During the first of these, Coolidge County actually moved in the *opposite* direction from the rest of the country in at least one important respect: Just as urban areas were beginning to deindustrialize, Coolidge County was experiencing a rapid period of industrialization that materialized by 1960 and escalated for the next two decades. This period was a good one for the residents of Coolidge County, and it was especially good for male labor force participants, who saw their incomes rise both relative to men in other areas and relative to women in the county. But the promises of industrialization were short lived. During the second period of change, not only did manufacturing employment drop rapidly but, even more important, the nature of employment changed as well. By the 1990s, although there were some who could continue to hold onto stable employment in established firms, many other residents—men and women alike—saw their job prospects limited to low-waged and increasingly unstable work in an economy that, like that of the rest of the United States, was heavily tilted toward the service sector.

THE FIRST WAVE OF CHANGE: 1960–CIRCA 1980

Like many other rural regions, Coolidge County in the 1960s and 1970s must have looked very attractive to companies in search of a less costly labor force. Not only did it have an untapped pool of men who had not yet been drawn into the formal labor force (and substantial numbers of men who remained outside the *waged* labor force), but wages also were low (in 1960, median earnings for men were 64 percent of those in the United States as a whole) and relatively few workers were members of unions.[22] Coolidge County also had relatively large, stable families (with less than two-thirds the proportion of female-headed families than in urban areas nationally) and more women "willing" to work outside the home (at wages that were but half of those offered to men). Moreover, as a nostalgic image of the rural past suggests—and as confirmed by the high proportion of the working age population outside waged employment—Coolidge County workers could assume that a considerable portion of their needs would be met not only by the family itself (through home-based production of essential goods and services) but also by purchasing the products of informal labor. These workers could thus be "expected" to continue to live on lower wages than those required in more urban areas.

Capital in flight from more urban regions recognized the benefits of this and other rural locations.[23] The number of workers in manufacturing employment increased by 28 percent between 1960 and 1970, and by another 35 percent during the following decade. By 1980, Coolidge County and the rest of the United States had almost precisely the same proportions of their labor forces in manufacturing. That similarity resulted from two quite different, though related, dynamics: industrialization in Coolidge County with simultaneous deindustrialization in the broader United States (see Chart 1).

At first, Coolidge County's new industrialization appeared to be, if not an unqualified boon, certainly a process that produced enormous benefits, including a more diversified economy, a growing proportion of skilled workers among blue-collar workers, employment in larger firms, and rising incomes.[24] These benefits accumulated without a total disruption of the usual way of life within the county; indeed, they probably depended on it.

Between 1960 and 1970, Coolidge County's industrialization created not only many new blue-collar jobs but also a substantial proportion of skilled ones: The number of craft jobs grew both absolutely (recording a 71 percent increase in just ten years) and relative to other kinds of blue-collar work (Chart 4). (In the broader United States, skilled work was also growing, but it was doing so at a much slower pace, and that growth barely altered the configuration of the blue-collar workforce.) Not surprisingly, under conditions of increased industrial production, unskilled jobs were growing as well (just as they were declining in other parts of the country where there was a drop in industrial production). Between 1960 and 1970 in Coolidge County, the number of nonfarm laborers, the least skilled of blue-collar workers, also grew both absolutely and with respect to their share of total blue-collar employment. Thus, there were two strata of labor entering into the new industrial production. One was highly skilled; the other, the nonfarm laborers, formed the backbone of that production. At least in this early period of industrialization, the proportions were heavily weighted toward the former.

The new jobs—skilled and unskilled alike—were being created in firms that, if they were not large by national standards—Coolidge County is not Detroit or Pittsburgh—were certainly larger than previously had been the norm in the area. Between 1958 and 1980, the average establishment size in all sectors increased by 60 percent, fueled by a 90 percent increase in the average size of manufacturing firms. In 1980, the average manufacturing firm was almost twice as large as it had been two decades earlier (Chart 5).

Three of these larger firms remained in Coolidge County well into the 1990s, and a number of those we interviewed had found employ-

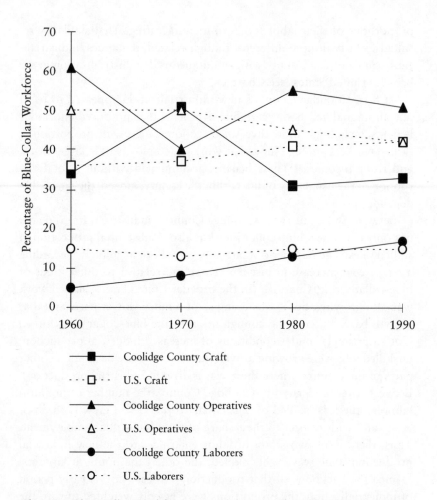

Chart 4.   Blue-Collar Workforce in Coolidge County and U.S., 1960–1990.
SOURCE: U.S. Department of Commerce, Bureau of the Census, *Census of the Population, Social and Economic Characteristics* (Washington, DC: selected years), Vermont and United States.

ment within them.[25]* Until the 1980s, these firms offered stable work with secure benefits to an increasing number of employees. By the end

---

*In this chapter, we discuss five firms in detail. We have provided pseudonyms for these firms as well as for other firms in the area. Information about these firms was obtained from local newspapers, from interviews conducted with managers, and from respondents who worked within them. In what follows, we identify as such information from the latter two sources. We do not refer to newspaper sources explicitly because to do so would be to reveal the location of this study as well as the identity of these firms.

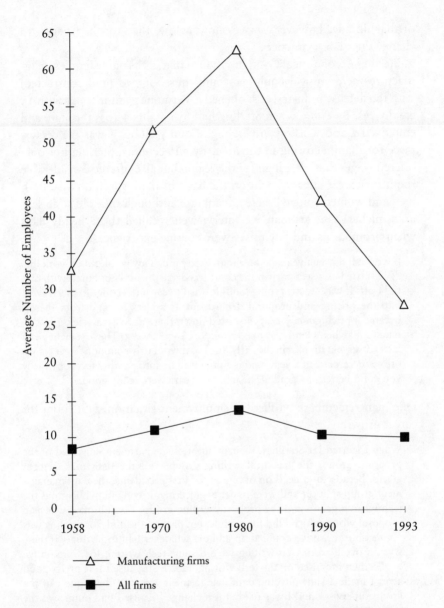

Chart 5. Firm Size in Coolidge County, 1958–1993. SOURCE: U.S. Department of Commerce, *County and City Data Book* (Washington, DC: U.S. Department of Commerce, Economics and Statistics Administration, Bureau of the Census, selected years).

of that decade, however, as we show below, they too had begun to change their labor practices.

Sterling Aeronautical Company, a firm that, as its name implies, manufactures aeronautical equipment and thus boomed (and contracted) with the defense industry, first opened a Vermont plant in 1941 with 33 employees. By 1987, when Sterling had five plants across the state and employed 2,200 workers in Coolidge County alone, it was the centerpiece for manufacturing in the area. By all accounts, Sterling not only offered wages that were high for the region but also offered considerable room for career advancement on the basis of plant-specific skills. Both men and women enjoyed these advantages, although they did so in separate niches. One woman we interviewed recalled those heady days when promotions and pay raises were routine experiences:

> [I worked] thirteen years [at Sterling]. Pretty much my whole adult work life. . . . I started as a secretary in the contracts department; I got bored with that right off. It was mostly typing [and] it wasn't very interesting, so then I went into the pricing and proposal department as a clerk . . . and from there I became a pricing analyst. . . . I started down there at $140 a week as a secretary and when I left I was making almost $600 a week. The first eight years it steadily went up plus in the early 80s . . . it was fairly common to get [raises of] 10 or 12 percent a year, and if you moved up into another level obviously you got a better pay grade. The first few years were really good.

One man remembered a flexible employment situation with room for career growth:

> When I started [at Sterling], their publications department consisted of the proposal group, the technical writing group, and the data management group. Because of a decision of one of the first presidents, the data management group split off and went under engineering, leaving in publications the tech writing group and the proposal writing group. My job offer was as a proposal writer which I did for a while, but back in the mid-70s Sterling was . . . flexible . . . so we doubled up and did whatever had to be done. If there was an overload in tech writing we did some tech writing for six months. . . . So then I focused on the tech writing, mostly, because I was pretty good at it. I made a shift into the data management group at the request of the group supervisor and I was ready for a change because I had outgrown the tech writing. I was at the point where I had gone about as far as I could [and] there was no future growth in it and this guy had promised me the world. That was about 1983.

Ajax, a plastics manufacturer that makes synthetic fibers for use as brushes and brooms, Christmas trees, and bindings, also arrived in Coolidge County during the 1940s and expanded enormously prior to 1990.

Ajax differed from Sterling in three significant ways: Its workforce was much less skilled (in 1991, 100 of its 140 workers were production workers), its wages were considerably lower (workers started at $6.40 an hour and went up to a maximum of $9.70 an hour), and it almost exclusively employed men. Like Sterling, however, Ajax had provided significant benefits for its employees, including health insurance, retirement packages, and paid vacation and personal time.[26]

The third firm, Master Forms Incorporated, represents a corporation with headquarters in Dayton, Ohio. Master Forms owns a number of printing plants that supply standard, printed forms to hospitals and other businesses. According to its manager, Master Forms built its Coolidge County plant in 1965 precisely because it was a low-wage area and fuel and transportation costs were low. In the early 1990s, about one-fifth of Master Forms's 222 employees were women who were largely segregated in that part of the operation that entailed lighter work. Like Sterling and Ajax, Master Forms offered good benefits, rising wages, and secure work to its employees.[27] A woman who worked there for many years, like the Sterling employees quoted above, remembered rising salaries and room for advancement: "When I first entered as a clerk, it was $4.85 or something. . . . The job I have now is a higher classification. The top of that right now is $13.55, which I'm at."

As these examples suggest, men and women experienced this first phase of change in somewhat different ways. Between 1960 and 1980, men's labor force participation rate was slower to rise than that of women (who everywhere were experiencing a rapid entry into the labor force), but among those in the labor force, increasing proportions of Coolidge County men found employment in wage and salary work. The proportion of those men who found that employment in manufacturing increased as well (Chart 6). Given this new employment, not surprisingly, men's earnings rose both absolutely and relative to men in other parts of the country. In 1960, Coolidge County men had earnings that were less than two-thirds of men elsewhere; in 1970, they were earning more than four-fifths as much.

Women's experiences were different. In fact, as a group they were being edged out of manufacturing in Coolidge County: In 1970, that sector had a lower proportion of women than it had ten years earlier. Even though women's salaries rose relative to women's in other parts of the country, between 1960 and 1980 in Coolidge County, the gap in men's and women's wages actually widened. Much of the good work, it appeared, was going to men (Chart 7).

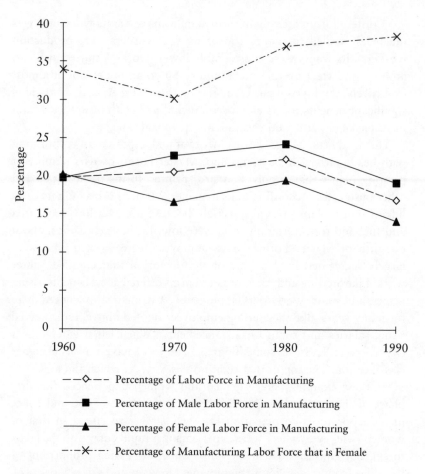

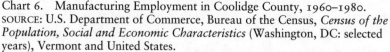

Chart 6.   Manufacturing Employment in Coolidge County, 1960–1980.
SOURCE: U.S. Department of Commerce, Bureau of the Census, *Census of the Population, Social and Economic Characteristics* (Washington, DC: selected years), Vermont and United States.

All in all, however, as industrialization took off, Coolidge County residents were doing much better than they had the decade before. Between 1960 and 1970, median family income more than doubled, and the gap between the income earned by Coolidge County families and that earned by families elsewhere was cut by more than half (Table 1). It is important to make this point. The particular kind of problems working families in Coolidge County experience today were not immediately produced by the influx of industrial activity to the area. When

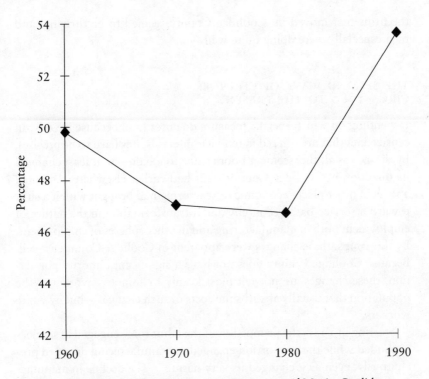

Chart 7. Women's Median Earnings as a Percentage of Men's: Coolidge County, 1960–1990. SOURCE: U.S. Department of Commerce, Bureau of the Census, *Census of the Population, Social and Economic Characteristics* (Washington, DC: selected years), Vermont and United States.

TABLE 1.   MEDIAN FAMILY INCOME:
Coolidge County, United States, and White United States,
1960–1990

	MEDIAN FAMILY INCOME IN CURRENT DOLLARS			COOLIDGE COUNTY AS A % OF	
	Coolidge County	*U.S.*	*White U.S.*	*U.S.*	*White U.S.*
1960	4,242	5,660	5,693	74.9	72.0
1970	8,489	9,590	9,961	88.5	85.2
1980	16,548	19,917	20,835	83.1	79.4
1990	34,561	35,225	37,152	98.1	93.0

SOURCE: U.S. Department of Commerce, Bureau of the Census, *Census of the Population, Social and Economic Characteristics* (Washington, DC: selected years).

the firms first moved in, Coolidge County seemed to be thriving, and men especially were doing quite well.

THE SECOND WAVE OF CHANGE:
CIRCA 1980 TO THE PRESENT

Depending on which specific measure one uses (and because we rely on census data that are offered in ten-year intervals, it is hard to be precise), by the 1980s all this seeming boom came to a halt—or at least changed its direction in Coolidge County, as it had earlier elsewhere. As noted above, in other places economic restructuring had brought with it a shift toward a service-based economy and a transformation in the nature of employment both in manufacturing and in other spheres of employment. By the 1990s, these changes were apparent in Coolidge County as well. Because Coolidge County does not have a significant minority popula- tion, these changes are not felt most keenly by minority workers—the population that usually absorbs the costs of such changes—but by white workers.

Starting in 1980, the proportion of the labor force engaged in services expanded while the proportion engaged in manufacturing dropped pre- cipitously, even as it changed its very nature.[28] The decline in manufac- turing resulted both from movement out of the area and from downsiz- ing among those firms that remained. In the 1980s, there was a dramatic loss of both well-established and relatively recent industry across the state as a whole. To give just a few of the many examples, when Vermont Goodyear closed its Windsor plant in November, 1986, 30 employees lost their jobs; 350 workers lost employment in South Burlington when Digital closed in October, 1992; Rutland General Electric laid off 122 workers in February, 1993; and, in the summer of 1996, Putney's Bas- ketville closed its plant because it could reap a larger profit hiring work- ers in China.[29]

In Coolidge County, the same kind of movement was found. As an area newspaper reported, "Nature's Best Food packed its jars and moved its manufacturing to California to save money. King Foods de- cided it had enough Swiss cheese manufacturing elsewhere and moth- balled its [Coolidge County] plant."

Some of those industries that remained downsized drastically. Sterling, for example, underwent massive restructuring. Ownership changed hands two times (once in 1987 and again in 1991), and em- ployees were subject to periodic layoffs—74 in February 1987, 150 in

October 1987, 44 in October 1989, and 30 in November 1990. Even this constant shrinkage was not enough for the newest owners, who were quoted in an area newspaper as saying they still believed the company had become too "heavily layered" and "too devoted to chasing contracts without enough thought to profitably fulfilling obligations." They immediately cut staff and operations, targeting especially white-collar workers and engineers. An additional 225 employees were laid off in March 1991, and another 110 in February 1992. In 1996, Sterling had but 600 employees (27 percent as many as it had nine years before); in January of that year, unemployment in the town in which it is located stood at 10.6 percent (while the countywide average was 6.4 percent).[30]

Manufacturing employment also was being transformed even as it was being reduced. Changes in labor practices could be seen in both older firms and newer ones. In addition to cutting its workforce, Sterling ceased offering major promotions and healthy wage increases to its employers. One woman who remembered that she had "moved up until 1986" also noted that since that time she "pretty much stayed at the same level" and that the large pay increases had given way to "a lot slower change." Sterling also demonstrated a new inclination toward outsourcing.[31] In 1991, when Sterling was undergoing a major overhaul as part of the deal for its change in ownership, it spun off the print shop and sold it to a former employee. (Even if that new owner rehired the former workers [which rumor suggested was the case], he was unlikely to be able to offer them the wages and benefits they had previously received from Sterling.)

By 1991, although it had not downsized like Sterling, Ajax was no longer hiring a permanent staff. Between 20 and 30 percent of the plant's approximately one hundred production workers were hired on temporary contracts; these newly hired workers had no access to benefits. This greater reliance on temporary workers occurred in conjunction with the new pressures Ajax faced. On one hand, it was being squeezed by the petrochemical industries that were its major suppliers; on the other hand, it was experiencing a new set of demands from the large chains that sold its final products.[32] Just-in-time ordering by retailers had as its counterpart a growing reliance on just-in-time production processes. Like Sterling, Ajax also was increasingly subcontracting its vital services, with adverse effects on its own employees.[33] One man reported that he had started working for Ajax as a machine operator and, after a number of years there, had graduated into the machine shop. When the company did away with the machine shop, he said, he was forced to go back to his earlier position. Even so, he, like other permanent workers, was hold-ing on to his job: The manager with whom we spoke said that the com-pany had recently had no voluntary quits and that one-fifth of the work-force had been there for more than twenty-five years.

Master Forms was under pressure as well, in this case from "mom and pop" print shops that could turn around an order in just a couple of days. Although management had not yet begun to rely heavily on temps (they did use them on occasion), Master Forms had plans both for downsizing (it had already laid off twenty-five people, most of them management) and for revamping their labor force to make it cheaper and more flexible. Master Forms also did some subcontracting for clean-ing the building, snowplowing, and machine maintenance. Like workers at Ajax, Master Forms employees had low turnover rates,[34] but these employees had stopped seeing major wage increases, and they had ex-perienced both cuts in their insurance packages and a speedup in their work. The woman who had started as a clerk said she was no longer getting raises and was increasingly dissatisfied with the insurance policy:

> We just get now—they don't even try to call them cost of living raises any-more—they're called wage adjustments. They haven't met the cost of living in several years . . . We have company-paid insurance, but I don't feel they're very good policies. That's another thing I've noticed that companies have done, they've really cut back on their quality of insurance policies. [For] your day to day, raising a family, it's not that good.

When asked what other changes she had seen in her job during the recent past, she responded:

> Same that a lot of people are seeing in corporate life, I think. As people are leaving they're not replacing the people. The people left are expected to pick up the slack. Just recently they incorporated two jobs. It used to be two departments [but] they've joined them together and now we all do both jobs.

The loss and transformation of good employment in these established industries occurred in conjunction with another change taking place in Coolidge County. Although manufacturing employment (as represented not by the absolute number of workers but by the proportion of the labor force in this sector) declined overall between 1980 and 1990, when looked at from the perspective of the absolute number of manufacturing firms, expansion appeared to continue well into the 1990s.[35] There were forty-two manufacturing firms in Coolidge County in 1980, sixty-two in 1990, and seventy-two in 1993.[36] These two contradictory trends were achieved through a sharp reduction in firm size. In 1993, the average size of manufacturing firms was actually smaller than it had been in the peak year of 1980 (see Chart 5). In fact, in 1990 almost precisely the same number of people were employed in manufacturing as a decade before, but they found that employment in one and one-half times as many firms. Much of this employment occurred in new firms that had very different employment practices from the ones they replaced, even as the older firms were changing their own practices. We provide here case studies of two newer firms that figured largely among the people we interviewed. Both were locally owned, and both offered what we call "bad" work.[37]

Wilson Contract Manufacturing (WCM) can stand as an example of a firm entirely devoted to subcontracting arrangements. The name itself reveals its major mission: WCM contracted with other firms to produce a number of different kinds of electronics component parts. (As we will discuss further below, it also contracted with other firms for workers as well as products.) At the time of our study, its major product was a Nuby Power Pack used with Nintendo games. (The only major competitor for that particular Nuby product was a Taiwanese firm.) Not surprisingly, WCM's production was absolutely market driven: It was "just-in-time" production to meet the orders that Nuby received. This production schedule had obvious consequences for WCM workers, who experienced frequent layoffs. In 1992, WCM had about one hundred employees, of whom eighty-three were production workers. Unlike the situation at Ajax and Master Forms, four-fifths of WCM's workers were women. All employees—men and women alike—were started at minimum wage; the company offered no benefits, no sick days, and no vacations. When asked about health insurance for employees, the manager said, "They don't want it. They would rather have the money." "Besides," he added, "most of them have spouses with insurance or no children to worry about."[38] Both of these claims were hotly disputed by the workers we interviewed. One worker said adamantly, "I think they should offer health insurance for everybody. No matter who it is, it should always be offered."[39]

The second firm, Green Mountain Cuddly Toys (GMCT), can serve as an example of niche marketing.[40] As its name implies, it manufactures stuffed animals, and it does so in rapid response to specialty orders. GMCT is the only one of the five firms discussed here that is located outside Coolidge County itself. Because it employed industrial homeworkers as well as an in-house staff, its employees actually came from a very wide region that extended to one of the most depressed areas in the state, where GMCT hired en masse the former employees of a ski-wear company that had moved its operations overseas.[41] As is true else-where, the homeworkers for GMCT were predominantly women who legally were self-employed contractors: They received no benefits, kept their own hours, and were required to work at a rate that paid at least the minimum hourly wage.[42] In 1994, an investigation by the Department of Labor revealed that the company had underpaid the overtime work of sixty-six of these home-based workers. Eager to dispel what he described as the "unfortunate and incorrect impression" about the re-lationship between GMCT and its employees, the CEO offered his own account of the company relationship with its homeworkers (in an op-ed piece written for an area newspaper):

> Many of the more than 150 individuals who work in their homes for the company work on a part-time basis according to schedules which they set according to the needs of their home lives. Conversations with our home-workers, together with a survey conducted last spring, confirm that these employees value the flexibility and independence this working relationship affords them. Child care and commuting costs are eliminated—the company even pays home-workers for the time they devote to delivery and waiting for and picking up their work. Although our legal relationship bars them from participating in such company benefit programs as paid vacations and health insurance, home-workers do benefit from amenities such as free company events, free tickets, employee prices in our store, and various financial assis-tance programs.[43]

The shape of blue-collar work in Coolidge County reflects these shifts in employment practices (see Chart 4). Recall that between 1960 and 1970, among blue-collar workers the proportion engaged in crafts grew. Although during the 1970s Coolidge County continued to add to its blue-collar industrial labor force at a rate more than three times that of the prior decade (and almost three times faster than the United States as a whole), this *new* blue-collar work consisted not of skilled jobs, which actually lost out, but of operative and unskilled ones.[44] (In the rest of the country, skilled craft workers were now enjoying an increase in em-ployment both relative to the prior decade and relative to their share of the blue-collar workforce.[45]) In contrast to urban areas, where the loss of unskilled work was largely an effect of changes in the configuration of the area's economy, in Coolidge County the increase in unskilled work resulted from an intra-industry restructuring toward more un-skilled jobs.[46] In fact, it was precisely Coolidge County's new labor force configuration that made it vulnerable to this next stage of capital mobility. When the costs of labor become an issue, it is the routine manufacturing jobs that are especially likely to move overseas rather than to a rural area in the United States.[47]

Changes in the gender makeup of manufacturing employment also reflect these shifts. During the "good" years, manufacturing employment had risen more quickly for men than for women. By 1980, as the new companies like Wilson Contract Manufacturing and Green Mountain Cuddly Toys followed different employment practices, women got an increasing share of the shrinking pie. Not surprisingly, as much of the good work for men disappeared, the gap between men's and women's earnings narrowed again, to 54 percent. Although Coolidge County women came close to the national norm (a norm of low wages everywhere) in their earning capacity (93 percent for year-round, full-time work), Coolidge County men still lagged substantially behind men elsewhere (83 percent for year-round, full-time work). While women's concentration in the service sector had been a consistent feature of women's employment, during the 1980s an increasing proportion of men moved into this sector as well.[48]

Just as the deindustrialization of urban areas spurred the recent wave of industrialization in Coolidge County (and continues to do so), that first wave of industrialization spurred the second wave. Once workers had joined firms like Sterling, Ajax, and Master Forms, and once they had shaped their lives around industrial waged employment, they had little to fall back on when they were thrust out. The new firms like Green Mountain Cuddly Toys and Wilson Contract Manufacturing could then take advantage of the conditions necessary for industrialization without offering the same employment benefits. Indeed, at times they could even take advantage of the same workers.

This is not just supposition. There is considerable evidence that the two processes—the disappearance and shrinkage of the older firms and the emergence of a new set of firms with totally different practices—are linked.

Wilson Contract Manufacturing again provides a good example. The firm was begun in 1987 by George Wilson, who previously had worked as a plant manager in Sterling, where he had acquired the relevant management skills and knowledge of electronics production processes. WCM is linked to other major employers by its personnel as well. The sales representative used to work at IBM, and the top manager used to work at General Electric.[49] WCM is only one of many companies that have been spawned by downsizing among upper-level employees. An article in a local newspaper described the new companies started by those laid off from Sterling who, because they were upper-level white-collar employees, were lucky enough to be in a position to start their own businesses. Some of these new businesses appeal to niche markets; several, like WCM but smaller, are production plants; and still others offer services.[50]

The link between this new economic growth and the decline in opportunities at the older firms is evident not only in ownership but also in lower-level employees, equipment, and subcontracting arrangements.[51] The owner of WCM told us that he started his firm in Coolidge County because he knew that workers there had "a strong work ethic" and that "they would work for reasonable wages." In a local newspaper, the owner of yet another new business said, "We were able to pick up the cream of the crop from [a prior industry]. Their skills were very process-oriented." Two of these new businesses are actually located in the buildings formerly occupied by Sterling itself.[52] The most expensive machine at WCM—that is, if it were purchased new—was, in fact, a castoff from Sterling that Wilson purchased in a junkyard.

Most notably, WCM has two different kinds of subcontracting arrangements with a major electronics company, General Machines Incorporated (which is located in an adjacent county). General Machines sends defective circuit boards to WCM, and WCM workers (at WCM wages) identify which chip is not working and why. As noted above, WCM also transports its workers to General Machines plants where, according to the WCM workers, they do work similar to that done by General Machines employees but under the pay scale and supervision of WCM. Through these arrangements, General Machines continues to keep its reputation as an excellent, family-friendly employer—for a much-reduced number of *General Machines* employees.

Local observers put an optimistic gloss on the new industrial activity. For example, the executive director for the Coolidge County Economic Development Commission (and former head of human resources for Sterling before he was downsized) wrote enthusiastically about these new companies and the employment they offer in a local newspaper article: "They have a better feel for what their employees need. . . . The word we get back is this is a great work force and they want their businesses to be successful." There is concrete evidence that this optimism is misplaced. On average, the wages and benefits of the new small, locally owned manufacturing firms do not match those previously offered by the major employers like Sterling.[53] Indeed, one area economist

estimated that in 1994 the wage difference between the older employment and the newer jobs was $7,000—$26,000 annually for those jobs
that had been lost and $19,000 a year for those that had been gained.

As recently as the winter of 1996, when the state economy was sup-
posed to have been improving, the shift toward low-wage work could
still be seen throughout Vermont.[54] Although Vermont's private industry wages as a percentage of those in the United States continued to rise
throughout the 1980s (from a low of 83 percent), they peaked in 1990
(at 87 percent), and by 1994 they had dropped back to 85 percent. As
an acute measure of just how low wages have fallen in recent years in
Coolidge County, take just the short period between December 1995
and February 1996. During that period, a total of sixty-five jobs were
filled in the Coolidge Town Labor Market Area, an area that is basically
coterminous with Coolidge County itself.[55] These jobs offered wages
between $5.28/hour (for nonfood service) and $8.35/hour (for professional jobs), with an overall average of $6.21/hour. If the "average" job
were year round and full time, it would mean a yearly salary of just
under $13,000, or 49 percent of per capita income for year-round, full-
time male workers five years earlier (and 69 percent of female year-
round, full-time earnings during the same period). Even so, on average
there were twenty-two people waiting in the wings for each of these jobs
(Table 2).

The shift toward part-time employment could be seen as well. According to the Bureau of Labor Statistics, 22 percent of all employed
workers in Vermont held part-time jobs in 1995; of those, it is estimated
that approximately 15 percent worked part-time involuntarily.[56] Our
respondents described how, in retail sales for example, part-time work
was all they could find. One woman whose husband had just been laid
off, and who therefore had an enormous incentive to move from part-
time to full-time employment, explained quite simply that this was impossible in the grocery store where she was employed: "They don't hire
full-time cashiers."

In addition, there is much episodic work in Coolidge County. The
tourist industry swells and shrinks with the turning of the seasons. Several of those we interviewed worked in areas that depended on the expanding periods: One woman, for example, worked in retail sales on a
ferry boat; another worked in the laundry of a classy hotel (which ad-
vertises in the *New Yorker*) that was open only during the summer
months. Several of our respondents relied on other occasional, but regular, opportunities to pick up extra income; for example, two women

TABLE 2. COOLIDGE TOWN LABOR MARKET AREA:
December 1995–February 1996

	ACTIVE APPLICANTS (FEBRUARY 1996)	JOB OPENINGS RECEIVED		JOB OPENINGS FILLED	AVERAGE WAGES OF JOBS FILLED (IN DOLLARS)
		Number	*Percentage*		
Total	1474	90	100	65	6.21
Professional	187	11	12	4	8.35
Clerical	206	18	20	10	5.73
Sales	58	4	4	1	8.00
Food preparation/service	111	4	4	5	6.25
Service (nonfood)	158	14	15	11	5.28
Machine trade/operators	71	5	5	5	7.17
Process/benchwork	104	7	7	6	6.13
Construction	316	4	4	7	6.14
Transportation	112	9	10	5	7.75
Package material handler	55	7	7	5	5.30
Farm and other	96	7	7	6	not available

SOURCE: Vermont Department of Employment and Training, *Labor Market Bulletin, Statewide and Labor Market Area; 3rd Quarter, 1995* (Montpelier: March 1996).

plucked turkeys before Thanksgiving. Still others held down jobs for which they were paid on an as-needed basis: lawn mowing, snow-plowing, and janitorial work for buildings that were used only occasionally.

Work had also become increasingly unstable for many state residents.[57] In 1995, Vermont's Department of Employment and Training reported "The placid 2.8% *net* employment growth of 7,000 jobs in 1994 hid the turmoil of an economy undergoing tremendous changes. During 1994, 12.7% of the jobs in 1993 were lost. This constituted over 32,000 positions. At the same time, 39,000 jobs were added to the economy, a growth of 15.5%"[58] (emphasis added). As we shall see later, this turmoil on the level of the economy was more than replicated in the households subject to such significant employment instability.

By the time we conducted this study, some (although by no means all) of the putative advantages of Coolidge County as a site for large-scale capital investment had been undermined by this process. Household size shrank, the proportion of children under the age of eighteen living with both parents dropped, and the proportion of households headed by women increased.[59] Here there is indeed convergence, in the sense that Coolidge County moved in the same direction as other parts of the country, even if it did not quite "catch up." The effects of these changes could be seen in the fact that by 1990, in two-thirds of the Coolidge County families that fell below the poverty line, the household head worked the previous year (in comparison with but half of households in the United States). In that same year, in one-fifth of families falling below the poverty level, the household head worked year round full time; for the United States as a whole, the comparable figure is one-third lower.

The degradation of work—changes in the location, quality, timing, stability, and benefits associated with formal employment—that was affecting workers elsewhere was thus also affecting those we studied in Coolidge County. If there were some workers who were "lucky" enough to hold on to their employment in mature companies like Sterling, Ajax, and Master Forms (even as their working conditions changed around them), many others—those laid off by those kinds of firms and new entrants to the labor force alike—were finding that employment was no longer offering what might reasonably have been expected just a few decades before.

COOLIDGE COUNTY'S INFORMAL ECONOMY

This overview of the changes in Coolidge County has focused almost exclusively on the formal economy, or at least on those indicators of economic activity and of economic well-being that are available in published data sources. An objection might well be raised that because Coolidge County is rural, these indicators are especially crude—that there is a greater chance for informality than in urban areas, and that Coolidge County's residents can therefore live better than wage levels would predict. Indeed, we suggested something similar above when we pointed out that in the early stage of industrialization, the goods and services made available by a substantial number of formally reported self-employed workers (combined with the efforts of unemployed housewives who could engage in home production) might have helped families make ends meet on wages that were substantially lower than those paid in urban areas. Quite obviously, in 1990 these resources were not as widely available in Coolidge County as they had been thirty years before: Nonagricultural self-employment had dropped to less than 6 percent of the working age population, and two-thirds of married women were in the labor force.

Even so, it might still be argued that as a rural area, Coolidge County continues to offer significant opportunities for earning money outside formal labor market employment (e.g., doing odd jobs) and for living off the land (e.g., growing vegetables; hunting).[60] This may all be true; nevertheless, two questions remain: Which kind of families can take advantage of these opportunities? And at what price? These are issues central to this study, and we discuss them extensively in subsequent chapters. Before doing so, it is necessary to explore at some length the features of a modern informal economy and how participation in it has particular prerequisites.

There is significant dispute in the literature about just what constitutes the informal economy.[61] Not infrequently, those concerned with these matters have identified informal work with that sector of economic life that is not systematically recorded and regulated by political units, the only common attribute on which researchers apparently agree.[62]

Precisely because informal activities are in large part flight from formally recognized regulation, it is virtually impossible to actually measure them.[63] There is no question, however, that the informal economy is large and that it forms an important piece of what keeps families alive and thriving and capable of participating in the formal economy as the need and opportunity arise.[64]

Indeed, we found considerable evidence that "shadow work" occurs with some regularity in Coolidge County. Our respondents spoke frequently (if with some uneasiness) about this practice:

> And I do a little side-work—this is confidential, I hope—when I do my side-work, I demand cash. If I don't, I'm not making enough to even go away from here. What I spend in travel or what I spend being away from things I've got responsibilities for—it doesn't pay enough. So I've got to demand cash to make it worth my while.

> Once in a while I'll work with my sister—she works at [a store]—and I'll go over there and help out a little bit. . . . I just go in and fill in for somebody when they're understaffed or somebody is away, things like that. . . . They [*she lowers her voice*] kind of pay me under the table because I'm not there that often. So it's kind of a can-you-help-me-out kind of a thing.

Lest the impression be gained that informal labor market activities result from the lack of formal labor market opportunities peculiar to a specifically rural environment, it is important to note their existence in urban areas as well. Although the kinds of resources and the demand for the goods and services produced in Coolidge County's informal economy are in part unique to a rural area, informality exists elsewhere. Doing "odd jobs" is no less a possibility in urban areas than in rural ones.[65] Indeed, if one were to count the many unreported workers in urban areas, they might well constitute a greater percentage of all workers than a similar count would reveal in a rural setting.[66] We thus suggest, as did Sassen-Koob with respect to cities, it is not a particular landscape that provides the impetus for the growth of irregular labor activities but rather the conditions of advanced industrialization.[67]

Although the recourse to something other than formal labor activities is hardly an exclusively rural phenomenon—or an exclusively modern one—without doubt the *character* of those activities is dictated by the setting in which they occur. First, in rural areas access to land and the products of the land provide different *kinds* of opportunities for non-regular work as compared with more urban areas. When land is cheap and plentiful, much informal work occurs around housing construction. When it is not, informal work is targeted more at renovation and maintenance. Similarly, the existence of large and relatively inexpensive indoor spaces in old buildings is a necessary condition for sweatshop labor. The same sort of labor is carried out in Coolidge County and its surrounding areas, but that labor is carried out in "cottage industries."

Land provides the opportunities to produce and process wood and food products. In contrast, commercially produced goods figure larger in the informally organized labor of city dwellers.

The demands on the informal economy also vary by region. Concentration of population produces one sort of demand; sparsely settled areas another. For example, informally organized day care is much more a feature of rural areas than of urban ones, where the concentration of young children makes commercial enterprises more feasible. Snow removal, a publicly produced service in urban areas, would be economically out of the question for many small towns, thus giving rise to the informal market for the plowing of driveways in the countryside. On the other hand, jitney cab services would be largely out of the question in rural settings but are extraordinarily profitable in densely populated cities. Notwithstanding the nostalgia associated with rural life, informality is a phenomenon with modern aspects and a phenomenon to be found in urban places as well as in the rural countryside.

Although Coolidge County has its own particular characteristics, both other rural areas and urban regions share some of its most significant tendencies, including the fact that in all regions the two sectors of the economy are linked.[68] One obvious link is that these so-called informal activities rely on the products of formally organized markets. A second, and for our purposes more significant, link is that of the personnel involved in these two sets of activities.

Not only do people use goods produced for formal markets for private practices—self-provisioning in the home and as the objects of casual exchange between households—but they also utilize these goods for the *production and sale* of goods and services in an external, albeit informally organized, market.[69] A host of examples can be found in the center of highly urban regions of the industrialized world[70] as well as in the less-developed areas of the world economy—and in Coolidge County. As we will show more fully in subsequent chapters, workers use the tools and skills of their waged workplace after hours for their own earnings. In short, there is a strong nexus between commercial products and the informally organized labor that uses them.

Like the definition of the informal economy, the question of which workers contribute to that sphere and which to the formal economy is an issue of considerable debate.[71] Our data demonstrate that there is considerable overlap between these two. When looked at from the perspective of individuals, we found that many engaged in both, sequentially. A man who held a waged position as a welder also had his own welding shop, and a man who held a waged position as a car mechanic did similar work for his own customers in his backyard. Even if a given individual engaged exclusively in either formal or informal economic activity, almost all *households* transcended that divide.

This brings us back to a central concern. We are making a simple point: Obviously, labor is absorbed in sectors other than those normally associated with a modern, market-based society—sectors that, for want of a better name, have been called the informal or social economy. The task for us is not to determine what to call these sectors or even how to measure them but instead to explore what it is that encourages and enables households to contribute their labor to them. This can hardly be a matter of chance, informality notwithstanding. If these less than formal sectors are themselves a fundamental part of the economy writ large, then there must be systematic means for attracting labor to them. The household and its strategies for preserving its members must serve to bind together the various sources of income the household requires and the various labor activities that are responsible for that income. As we will show below, the transformation of the formal economy has radically undermined the capacity of some households—while substantially enhancing the capacity of others—to make use of their labor in flexible ways and to take advantage of these various sources of "income." It has done so in a fashion that is quite unexpected.

CHAPTER 2

Families Struggling in the New Economy

The fact is that we know very little about how ordinary families put together the activities they count on in their daily lives. We do know, however, that the activities themselves are hardly invented out of thin air. They represent both very contemporary possibilities and older ones put to entirely new uses. Although many families may *want* to engage in activities like sending two earners into the labor force, moonlighting, self-provisioning, and interhousehold exchanges, they are as unequally available as are decent jobs in the formal labor force. This needs to be said for two reasons. First, these tactics are often treated as if they were totally voluntary and available to anyone who cared to engage in them. Instead of being solely expressions of motivation and choice, however, the variable responses of households are as much, if not more, a function of where a family finds itself located in the labor market. Second, the structure of these opportunities makes up a critical part of the "real" economy. If a multifaceted survival strategy is key to the well-being of families and to the economy as a whole, it is no less important to understand the processes by which it becomes available to households than it is to understand how the formal market allocates *its* benefits. To know less is to know only a fraction of that which sustains families during good times and bad.

THE ELEMENTS OF HOUSEHOLD
SURVIVAL STRATEGIES

THE DUAL-EARNER STRATEGY

Although much social science (and, we might add, feminist scholarship) has constructed its understanding of the world by assuming that households are composed of a male breadwinner and a female housewife, now more than ever that model has been proved to be a total fiction for white families, as it long has been for African American families.[1] The majority of all married couple households in the United States send both husband and wife into the labor force. In Coolidge County, where the labor force participation rates of both men and women are higher than they are elsewhere, almost two-thirds of all married-couple households rely on a dual-earner strategy. Furthermore, there is strong evidence, at least in Coolidge County, that in more than three-quarters of married-couple households, when both husband and wife *can* work they both do so.[2] Clearly, whatever the population under consideration, the household with two "workers" is the norm.

This norm has emerged rapidly in the relatively recent past.[3] While some analyses acknowledge that the increased labor force participation of married women is driven by a host of reasons, including women's search for the satisfactions that employment carries, most analyses identify economic need as the critical spur.[4] There is no doubt that the earnings of wives are significant to family well-being. By the early 1990s, one-third of all the income of all U.S. families that had working wives came from their earnings.[5]

This economic benefit is no secret. One man to whom we talked described just how hard it had become trying to survive on his income alone: "It was don't make waves because the water was right up to here [*holding his hand at nose level*]. As a single wage earner it was really getting tight. It was really getting tight. And I was working overtime all I could get, working night, anything I could do just to keep above water." Another man, more simply, conceded to the inevitability of the two-earner household: "I don't think that [living on one income] is possible any more. I think the two-income family is a must."

If the dual-earner household is becoming the norm—and a significant basis for household well-being—it is a notable achievement for families buffeted by growing economic instability. A substantial minority of the households we studied had experienced such instability: In 17 percent of these households, at least one person had been laid off from his or her principal job during the previous year, and more than a quarter of these households had experienced some form of income discontinuity—whether the result of a layoff or not—over the course of the year.[6]

Some research suggests that family fortunes might have snowball effects. In households where men are unemployed, women often withdraw from the labor force as well.[7] Alternatively, households with two labor force participants can help those earners sustain employment over time because access to the earnings of one partner allows the other to evaluate job opportunities more carefully so as to ensure long-term success. Members of two-earner families are also more likely to start a new business.[8] In the face of common economic pressures, then, some families might indeed be better positioned than others to maintain the dual-earner strategy in order to sustain, and even enhance, their well-being.

MOONLIGHTING

Just as the two-earner family has come to be taken for granted, another piece of the story of the survival strategy of households has reached the attention of the popular press. Simply put, what was once the surprising two-earner family has now often become the two-earner, *three-job* family. Though official statistics deny it—in 1992, just 6 percent of employees in the United States *reported* that they held simultaneously two or more jobs—there is reason to believe that holding down more than one job is becoming, if not the rule itself, certainly not an exception to it.[9] Indeed, among the households randomly interviewed in Coolidge County, 39 percent included at least one moonlighting worker, and 23 percent of the *individuals* in those households had at least one form of "side-work."

Nationwide, between 1980 and 1989 the number of multiple job holders increased by 52 percent. The number of women holding more than one job doubled during that decade. The multiple job holding rate among men also rose in the 1980s, although not as rapidly. Thus, not only is there a great deal more moonlighting than ever before, but it also appears to be women more than men contributing to the increase. In 1970, men constituted 85 percent of all multiple job holders; by 1989, men's share of the total had dropped to 57 percent.[10] Still, married men are more likely than married women to hold down more than one job, both in the United States as a whole and in our sample of households.[11]

Not unlike the dual-earner strategy, multiple job holding has been understood to be a response to economic need. A bumper sticker seen on cars in the state—"Moonlight in Vermont—Or Starve"—draws on the romantic image of the region, as memorialized in song, to make a telling comment about current economic conditions. Across the continent, newspaper articles attribute this phenomenon primarily to financial necessity,[12] but there is significant reason to question this connection.

What is surprising about the national level data (the accuracy of which we question as a *count* of moonlighting) is that it is not economically marginal groups (Blacks and Hispanics) who are most likely to moonlight; rather, it is white men and white women.[13] Equally surprising is the evidence that those who are economically marginal and those who are not moonlight for different reasons. More than half of all Black and Hispanic men and women, and more than half of all single and widowed women, report current economic conditions as the reason for holding down more than one job. On the other hand, more than half of married men and women, and more than half of all white men and women say that they moonlight for reasons that are oriented toward improving their life chances—to save for the future, to get experience, to build up a business—or for some other reason altogether.[14] In short, a significant proportion of moonlighters nationally see themselves as using their "off" hours at a second job not so much to meet immediate financial exigencies but as a route out of their current employment situation.

In our interviews as well, some men and some women reported that a second job allowed them not just to meet current expenses but also (and even more important for them) to find satisfactions that their major employment did not provide or to build up a business. These findings stand in sharp contrast to reports that only consumerism and economic distress drive increased work activity.[15]

SELF-PROVISIONING

Objectively, having all adults in the household gainfully employed and holding down more than one "job" at a time are hardly new strategies. Only during the twentieth century did families (and only a small number of families at that) expect that only the adult male would work for wages and that just one job would be sufficient. Nevertheless, the families to whom we spoke experienced both the dual-earner strategy and moon-lighting as entirely new—either as opportunities or as impositions. Not so self-provisioning.

If the families we talked to were any indication of current practices, almost all households regularly engage in some form of routine self-provisioning activities, and a substantial minority rely on a wide range of different ones. In addition, a quarter of those we interviewed had built their own home or extensively renovated an existing one. Rather than viewing these activities as anything new, respondents saw themselves as engaging in *traditional* family behavior.

For example, one woman said that growing vegetables had been a longstanding practice in her husband's family and was now a routine of her own:

> I never had [a garden] when I was a kid. Always wanted one and never had one and ever since [my husband] and I have been together I've had one. . . . His grandfather always had a garden. I used to help him in the garden with it and then I eventually started my own. Had one ever since.

Similarly, one man described hunting as an activity shared with his father and other male relatives:

> I love to be in the woods. I'm a hunter. I was following in my dad's footsteps through the woods. He bought me my first gun. I love to hunt. . . . I haven't hunted since my dad died. My uncle had a camp . . . and all my cousins and my uncle would get together a certain weekend during deer season.

As these examples suggest, although access to self-provisioning—like access to a second earner and moonlighting—is available across regions of the country, the *content* of self-provisioning varies. Different regions offer different possibilities for, and restrictions of, self-provisioning activities. Residence in Coolidge County carries with it particular demands *and* its own particular resources.[16]

Residence in a rural area does not ensure the capacity to sustain "traditional" practices. In fact, access to these practices may well be more limited than it was in the past. Neither those who live in trailers nor those who live in apartments can rely on wood for heating purposes, and neither is likely to have sufficient land on which to raise vegetables.[17] Boiling sap to produce maple sugar requires a large stand of the right kind of trees, and hunting can be done only at certain times of the year, and even then only if one can afford the time away from a job.

Traditional as these activities may seem to those who engage in them, many self-provisioning activities hardly represent an unbroken link with the rural past. As practiced today, they rely heavily on quite up-to-date commodities: The sale of very modern (and expensive), airtight, wood stoves boomed during the oil crisis of the 1970s; much snowplowing is accomplished with snowblowers and modified lawn mowers rather than with the plow attached to a tractor that is primarily used for farming; and green plastic tubing has become a common alternative to the traditional (and labor-intensive) bucket as a way to harvest sap. This may appear to be a trivial point, but it is central to gaining an understanding of how self-provisioning activities function in a formal commodities market as well as within the households that engage in them. The men and women we interviewed may believe they are merely reenacting the roles of their grandparents, but doing so requires a specific location in the economy. In short, what explains these activities is not tradition but the particular and modern circumstances of the practitioners.

Just how these circumstances affect self-provisioning is disputed in the relevant scholarship. Some view self-provisioning as a means by which those without sufficient cash on hand might substitute their own labor to obtain essential goods and services, and as a way households can get by during spells of unemployment.[18] Others argue, however, that what is true of the dual-earner strategy and moonlighting may also be true of self-provisioning—that is, that these activities may not substitute for employment but, in fact, depend on it.[19]

What we learned from families in Coolidge County lends strong support to both positions. Households with two earners were twice as likely to have high rates of self-provisioning as households with just one (34 percent versus 17 percent), and households with a moonlighter were also almost twice as likely to have high rates of self-provisioning as those without that kind of intensive labor force activity (43 percent versus 23 percent). Household income was also a critical determinant of self-provisioning: An extensive engagement in routine self-provisioning was almost twice as likely among those with low earnings than among those earning more (42 percent versus 23 percent). In other words, as was true with adding a second earner or a second job, self-provisioning—even if it is a "tradition" in a rural area—is not equally demanded of, or equally available to, all families.

Nor is it equally practiced by all household members. Although women are becoming increasingly involved in some forms of economic activity—participation in the labor force and moonlighting—their participation in self-provisioning activities is declining. These two trends are clearly linked. The ready availability of market goods has a clear advantage over spending the time to make things oneself, especially when time is less available. In addition, some of these goods might even be more economical to purchase than to make.[20] For example, women can buy clothing as (if not more) cheaply at yard sales or in secondhand stores as they can make it; they need devote less effort as well. Other traditional female activities (e.g., raising chickens for home consumption and for "egg money") have also almost entirely vanished, even from the rural landscape of Coolidge County. Whether from choice or circumstance, however, the same is not true of many activities of routine self-provisioning that customarily have been under the direction of men. Among the households we studied, men still plow their driveways, change the oil in the family's cars, and maintain responsibility for gathering wood for fuel. Only one of the frequently practiced self-provisioning activities absorbed both men and women: Individual households may deviate from more general patterns, but, as a rule, both men and women work in gardens.

NONMONETARY INTERHOUSEHOLD EXCHANGES

Finally, we turn to nonmonetary exchanges found so frequently between households, including informal assistance, barter, reduced rates, and moving in with others as important pieces of the overall household economy. Although in much of the analysis below we consider the first three of these exchanges together, each has its distinct features.

Barter involves the frank and open transfer of goods and services as an above-board trade. The fact that barter is going to take place and the terms of the exchange usually are negotiated in advance. Individuals who participate in these transactions say that for barter to be successful (that is, not to leave ill will in its wake), both parties have to be explicit about their expectations and avoid haggling; the social tie that (often) facilitates barter is jeopardized by the existence of unstated elements in the exchange or by extensive bargaining over prices. Parties also negotiated in advance the terms of an exchange involving a reduced rate for services or goods, yet these negotiations differ from those involving barter at least in part because unstated expectations often do exist. Informal assistance differs from both of these practices insofar as the offer of goods and services comes without any overt discussion of its "fee," because, our respondents said, to discuss the terms of the exchange at all (and not just to bargain) would violate the expectations of sociability.

Each of these practices also has economic costs enmeshed with, and inextricably interwoven into, its more obvious benefits; a price is often extracted for engaging in what appear to be socially and economically necessary interhousehold exchanges. The essence of much seemingly casual reciprocity lies in the unstated, and often unpredictable, obligations that "gifts" carry. Barter can tie up valuable resources (while one waits for the transaction to be completed) and can limit the search for alternative—and cheaper—sources of goods and services. Those who receive reduced rates from friends and relatives are obligated to display gratitude; they also often have to put up with arrangements that are less attractive than those for which they pay full freight. In social networks, as in the business world, there is no "free lunch."

Whether or not they come free, these exchanges play a significant role in the survival strategy of Coolidge County households. Half of all the households with whom we talked said they were the recipients of casual generosity during the previous year—a neighbor bringing over extra vegetables; a friend stopping by to plow the driveway. During interviews, people often spoke about engaging in the practice of barter and about receiving reduced rates for help with child care or self-provisioning projects. A few indicated that sometime in the relatively recent past they had lived with another household for periods ranging from a couple of days to six months.

As is the case for self-provisioning, economic need frequently has been identified as the motivation for interhousehold exchanges. For example, Stack's study of urban African American households argued that the sharing of resources was a response to the poverty confronting the members of that community.[21] We found no evidence, however, that informal assistance is affected by income: If families with acute economic pressures are more in need of these kinds of exchanges than other families, the simple fact of that pressure does not ensure that they will be able to locate others willing to help them out.[22]

Some scholars also view the *gemeinschaft* of rural life as the source of these practices. For example, Levitan and Feldman argue explicitly that "in rural communities and in other areas where the extended family network and social fabric are strong, inter-household social networks are likely to be an economically important aspect of community life."[23] Whether born in the area or not, those to whom we spoke understood these exchanges to be both a tradition and a privilege of small-town life. One woman described how she and her husband helped an older neighbor who had followed customary practices of generosity in the past:

There's a lady down the road—the same one we bought the land from—[my husband] will cut her wood . . . and stack it in her woodshed. And if I have vegetables or different things I'll bring it down to her. . . . They kind of helped us out with land, and when [my husband] was building the house she'd have him down there for dinner, [and to] take a shower and stuff. They were very nice people, kind of like the old Vermonters. . . . They're the type of people that would help other people out and not look to make the big bucks. . . . A lot of people in the area take care of her.

There is also evidence that these patterns may well be disrupted by economic change. Naples writes that in rural communities undergoing restructuring, although the dominant ideology supports neighborliness and community support, many low-income residents "believed that they could not count on most other members of their community for assistance during a crisis."[24] In fact, the woman just quoted suggested that the neighborliness extended to the "lady down the road" was an exception to a more general rule. "Usually," she said, "around here it's kind of like you know who your neighbors are but you don't know them." Support from family and friends, like opportunities for self-provisioning, is not always simply there for the taking.

As was the case for other aspects of a household's survival strategy, men and women participate in nonmonetary exchanges in different ways. For reasons we will explore more fully below, barter, for example, is reserved almost exclusively to men.[25] With respect to informal assistance, gender does not determine participation rates, but it does shape content. Coolidge County residents followed patterns noted by others:

Women are more likely to do routine domestic work (e.g., shopping, housework and washing), presumably largely for elderly dependents. Men, on the other hand, are more likely to do improvements and maintenance work for others (e.g., gardening, decorating, repairs and carpentry). Women are also more likely . . . to provide personal services for others and to care for people and animals in other people's households. Unpaid, informal work outside the household is therefore highly gender-specific.[26]

COMPARING SURVIVAL STRATEGIES OF GOOD JOB AND BAD JOB HOUSEHOLDS

We selected 158 families that closely resembled those in Coolidge County that had at least one member in the modern, wage labor force. Seventy-eight percent of these relied on a second earner as well, 39 percent required at least one worker to moonlight, almost all these 158 families did at least some self-provisioning, and many were enmeshed

TABLE 3.   SURVIVAL STRATEGY OF SURVEY
HOUSEHOLDS

	ALL HOUSEHOLDS (n = 158)	TYPE OF HOUSEHOLD	
		Good Job Households (n = 86)	Bad Job Households (n = 72)
% with two earners*	78	87	67
% with at least one moonlighter	39	35	43
% with high rates of self-provisioning (four or more)*	30	23	39
% with high rates of informal assistance from others (one or more)	49	50	47

*Difference between good job and bad job households is statistically significant at the .05 level or greater.

in nonmonetary exchange relationships with others in their social world. In short, while these Coolidge County families clearly depended on the earnings from waged labor, earning money in the formal market was far from being their sole survival strategy. Wages were not enough. This is true in more than one way—wages were not enough to underwrite the household economy, and wages were not enough to support the members of these households as they planned for the future and searched for meaning and satisfaction in their lives.

In virtually none of the 158 families did the wage work of a single person working at just one job suffice for sustaining the household. Families sent multiple workers out to work for wages and many of those held down more than one job. In addition, families managed a high degree of self-provisioning and, on repeated occasions, families would turn to others for material assistance. Given the apparent availability of these subsidiary activities, it might be expected that families with access only to bad jobs would be more likely to avail themselves of these opportunities. Yet, surprisingly, with but one exception—self-provisioning—families with only bad jobs were no more likely to employ these alternative methods for sustaining themselves than were good job families and, even more surprising, bad job families were substantially less likely to have two earners at work in the formal labor force at the time of our interviews (Table 3).

This first impression of similarity between the two kinds of households does not mean that the activities carried on were the same, but only that subsidiary activities were the rule among almost all families, and among a significant minority, intensely so. Good job or bad, many, many of these families had reason to choose labor activities far outside of the main employment of a single worker. But, as we will see in subsequent chapters, what they chose, and what impact that choice had on the life of the members of these families, were both substantially different. A first glimpse of this difference can be seen in the role played by the dual-earner strategy. It would be a reasonable expectation that families with only bad jobs would be more likely than those with good jobs to rely on the labor of more than one person. Quite to the contrary, families with good jobs were almost one and a third times more likely to have a second worker in the labor force than were bad job families.

What we have here, however, are just initial snapshots of the two different kinds of households which mask much more than they reveal. As we will demonstrate, far from a mostly similar pattern of activities carried on by these families, there are important differences that extend to the forms, premises and costs of those elements that make up the economy of these families and to the implications they hold for gendered relationships within the household.

DIFFERENCES BETWEEN GOOD JOB AND BAD JOB HOUSEHOLDS

Hidden within our broad classification of good and bad job households are the particular labor force experiences and demographic features of each set of families. Because both these experiences and these features have potential relevance for the adoption of various aspects of the household survival strategy, we turn to them next.

Not surprisingly, given our definition of "bad jobs," families that have access only to bad jobs experience considerably more job instability. They were more likely to have had a family member who was laid off from work during the previous year (25 percent versus 11 percent), and only bad job households had experienced two such layoffs. Income discontinuity also occurred slightly more frequently among bad job households than among good job households: During the previous year, in 31 percent of the former and 24 percent of the latter, at least one activity from which the household derived a cash income had been lost. As yet a third indicator of instability, although the proportion of younger workers (those under thirty-five years old) who had located a job within the past six months was the same in both good and bad job households (10 percent in each), among older workers (whom one might have expected had long since found their niche in the world of employment) those in bad job households were six times as likely to have just started a job as were older workers in good job households (12 percent versus 2 percent).

In addition to having different experiences surrounding job stability, the two sets of families differed with respect to the intensity of their participation in the labor force. Although (by definition) in good job households with but a single worker, that individual had year-round, full-time employment, in 11 percent of bad job households the single worker relied on part-time work. In almost three-quarters (71 percent) of dual-earner good job households, *both* workers held full-time jobs. Among dual-earner bad job households, full-time employment was considerably less likely: In 40 percent of these households, both spouses had full-time work, in another 39 percent at least one worked part time, and in the remaining 21 percent, both partners held only part-time jobs.

As one might expect, families with good jobs were much more likely than families less well positioned to have more cash at hand, whether we compare the proportion with total household incomes over $35,000 (77 percent versus 42 percent) or the proportion in which the primary worker had earnings substantially over the minimum wage (61 percent versus 23 percent). Financial resources alone do not explain why one set of families is able to marshal strategies that allow them not only to survive but also to thrive, while the other is not. Even a cursory look demonstrates that what is operating among these households is not money alone, though clearly money plays a part (Table 4).

Whether the primary worker's wages are high or low, there is equal chance for the families *within* each group to send two earners into the labor force and to engage in the moonlighting strategy characteristic of the group as a whole. In contrast, routine self-provisioning is strongly sensitive to income levels and is a strategy employed by families facing economic pressures whether they have good jobs or bad. When family resources are low, routine self-provisioning can help to fill the gap.

Finally, although for the group of households taken as a whole, exchange relationships appear to be unaffected by family income levels, this is actually the result of opposing tendencies within the two kinds of families. As might be anticipated, good job households slightly increase their tendencies to rely on these exchanges when their incomes are low; bad job households, however, do precisely the reverse. In short, for two of the strategies under consideration—the dual-earner strategy and moonlighting—income is utterly irrelevant. Where it is important, it

TABLE 4. EFFECT OF INCOME ON SURVIVAL STRATEGY OF GOOD AND BAD JOB HOUSEHOLDS

	ALL HOUSEHOLDS				GOOD JOB HOUSEHOLDS				BAD JOB HOUSEHOLDS			
	Low Primary Worker Wages (n = 66)	High Primary Worker Wages (n = 68)	Low Household Income (n = 62)	High Household Income (n = 96)	Low Primary Worker Wages (n = 29)	High Primary Worker Wages (n = 45)	Low Household Income (n = 20)	High Household Income (n = 66)	Low Primary Worker Wages (n = 37)	High Primary Worker Wages (n = 23)	Low Household Income (n = 42)	High Household Income (n = 30)
INCOME STRATEGIES												
% with two earners	76	73			86	84			68	52		
% with a moonlighter	41	36			40	33			43	43		
NON-INCOME ACTIVITIES												
% with high rates of routine self-provisioning			42	23			35	20			45	30
% with high rates of informal assistance			52	51			60	47			38	60

TABLE 5.   CHARACTERISTICS OF
HOUSEHOLDS AND HOUSEHOLD MEMBERS

MEMBER CHARACTERISTICS	GOOD JOB HOUSEHOLD MEMBERS	BAD JOB HOUSEHOLD MEMBERS
% of household members below age 40	59% (170)	56% (142)
% of household members with more than a high school education*	59% (170)	45% (142)

HOUSEHOLD CHARACTERISTICS	GOOD JOB HOUSEHOLDS	BAD JOB HOUSEHOLDS
% of households with male primary worker	55% (74)	61% (61)
% of households with children living at home	63% (86)	71% (72)
% with preschool children (among those with children)	29% (54)	29% (41)

NOTE: Numbers in parentheses are the numbers of households on which percentages are based.

* Difference between good job and bad job households is statistically significant at the .05 level or higher.

either operates in the same way for both sets of households (self-provisioning) or in opposite ways from what might be expected (inter-household exchanges). (It is these sorts of surprises that sent us on our way to explore the strategic effects not of high or low wages alone but of good or bad jobs.)

Although the households in our sample differed in the nature of the employment of their members, their overall earnings, and their survival strategies, they were otherwise quite similar with respect to several factors—age, sex of primary worker, presence of young children—that are commonly thought to have an influence on one's chances both to participate in the labor market *and* to be successful therein. On the other hand, they did differ with respect to one significant "supply side" factor that might determine which families *become* good work families and which do not: education (Table 5).

The members of the two sets of households were close to the same age, with good job households being only slightly younger. The two sets of households were also equally likely to have a male as the primary worker: in 55 percent of good job households and 61 percent of bad job households, the husband had either the only, or the better, job. The two sets of households also were similar in their composition: Among both kinds of households, the vast majority had at least one child at home, and equal proportions of the two types of households had pre-school children.

Not surprisingly, households with at least one good job had members who were better educated: Three-fifths of the members of good job households had at least some education beyond high school, in comparison with slightly less than half of those in bad job households. A higher level of education is clearly significant for the *acquisition* of at least some kinds of good work. In recent years, however, education has done little to enable workers to hold onto those jobs. During the 1990s, the calamity of downsizing was not reserved for the "typical" blue-collar worker: "In a reversal from the early 80's, workers with at least some college education make up the majority of people whose jobs were eliminated, outnumbering those with no more than high school educations."[27]

Although a closer and more detailed statistical analysis might help us explain how a particular family *ends up* as a good job or a bad job household, that is not our intention. Rather, we are interested in showing the *consequences* of that status not just for income but also for the full range of tactics (to which we turn in more detail in the following chapters) quite independent of the particular characteristics of the household itself.

Of course, there might also be something more elusive at work with respect to that construction as well. Indeed, a widely held belief is that there are two kinds of people in the world—at least with respect to their economic behavior. There are those who are workers—in the sense that they will always find ways to maintain themselves even in tight times— and those who are not. When an economy offers fewer and fewer opportunities, the former, it is believed, will find ingenious ways of making do, while the latter will either not make these efforts or fail in the attempt. Our analysis rejects this belief, at least with respect to the broader consequences we find waiting for those families that have experienced the worst effects of the restructuring of the U.S. economy.

This is not simply a pious liberal creed. Among the 81 families we interviewed, some (11 percent) were currently bad job households but had in the recent past been much more fortunate—they had had at least one member with a good job and had constructed their lives around that central fact. Shortly before we spoke with them, they were "downsized."[28] Once the members of these families had recourse only to bad jobs, they began to resemble other bad job households far more than they did their former "peers." They too found it difficult to keep both members employed and to continue with the moonlighting that previously had fit easily into their daily schedules. Some had to move and thus were unable to carry through with self-provisioning projects or to maintain ties with neighbors. What changed, then, was not their *propensity* to work (or the human capital that had previously allowed them to find one kind of job rather than another) but rather the way they were tied into the labor market and thus their ability to sustain a complex survival strategy.

To demonstrate this point more fully, let us compare two families, the Riverses and the Dickinsens. In both families, the husbands were about the same age, had about the same level of education, and had held a single job for about the same number of years. Charles Rivers was forty-seven, had two years of technical school beyond high school, and had worked for the same firm for twenty-one years; Bill Dickinsen was fifty-two, had a high school education plus armed forces training in electrical engineering, and had been employed by the same firm for nineteen years. The women in the two families were also quite similar, although, as in the broader sample as a whole, Margaret Dickinsen with a college degree was better educated than Ellen Rivers, who had a two-year associate degree from a junior college. The Riverses had two grown sons who were living on their own. The Dickinsens also had two grown children—a son and a daughter.

As families, the Riverses and the Dickinsens had made similar choices and sacrifices in the past. In both, the wife had remained home when the children were very young: Ellen had waited until her youngest was in first grade before starting to work again, and Margaret waited until both children were in high school. When she started working for pay again, Ellen worked part time in retail sales. Margaret returned to the teaching job she had left when her first child was born.

Before their wives had returned to work, both Charles and Bill had made special efforts to bring in additional income. Charles did mechanical work as a side job, and Bill put in a lot of extra overtime. Even before they were regularly employed, both wives had made financial contributions as well: Ellen occasionally sold quilts to a small company that relied on homeworkers; Margaret babysat and engaged in marketing for a "commission sales" program to help make ends meet:

Once in a while I would sell cards or I sold Amway stuff for a while. . . .
Like you get that Olympic card company and I'd call all my friends and say
do you want to buy some cards and I'd make about thirteen dollars. That
was enough to buy somebody some Christmas presents or something.

When the oil crisis came in the 1970s, the Dickinsens purchased a
wood stove; Bill added chopping and splitting logs to his other self-
provisioning activities. The Riverses also heated with wood, and they
had recently made plans to add a deck to their home. Both families still
grew vegetables and preserved them for use during winter months. Ellen
spoke about the pleasure it brought:

Yes, well, every year I bitch, "I'm not going to have a garden next year. I
don't have time," and I plant one anyway. I like it. It's very therapeutic. It
gets me out of the house. I do a lot of thinking when I'm down working in
the garden. It just makes me feel good to have a garden.

On the face of it, then, the two families seem quite similar with respect
to the kind of efforts they put into survival strategies. When General
Electric downsized four years before we began our interviewing, however, Charles Rivers, at age forty-seven, was laid off from that good job
while Bill Dickinsen, at age fifty-two, survived the numerous layoffs at
Sterling.

After he lost his job, Charles searched for other employment that
would pay as well. He landed a temporary job carrying mail, and he
had dreams of being able to do his mechanical work full time but didn't
have the money to buy the necessary equipment. He had to abandon
plans for completing the deck, and he could no longer stock the gaping
freezer with venison because rather than having a secure vacation to use
for a hunting trip, he had to remain available to take on waged work,
should the opportunity arise. Ellen Rivers stopped working at both her
waged job and her job sewing quilts; she took a job doing contract work
for Green Mountain Cuddly Toys. Because she was then working well
more than forty hours a week, she no longer had time to sew for her
own family, to sell her handicrafts separately, or even to make the occasional gift that could reduce household expenses at Christmas.

The Dickinsens, however, were steadily pursuing both their waged
and their unwaged activities. Bill planned to retire as soon as he could—
"probably in ten years or so"; Margaret, on the other hand, greatly
enjoyed teaching, and she planned to work until they no longer let her.

Each fall, the Dickinsens enjoyed the harvest from their garden, and each winter, they planned for a new round of home improvement.

We do not have to rely on our sample alone. Much has been made about the substantial portion of workers who, once they experienced "downsizing," were unable to replace the kind of good jobs they lost, at least immediately. Some go for a long time without finding equivalent work, and some never find it.[29] The accounts of these workers demonstrate that without the security of a good position in the labor force, they have to abandon a range of practices that rested on that security. They change jobs more frequently, they spend their hard-earned savings, and they move from their comfortable homes to cheaper quarters. What these reports do not highlight is the enormous costs in forgoing other economic strategies that go along with the loss of a good job. Losing his job at General Electric was devastating enough for Charles Rivers; losing the ability to carry on these other strategies not only added insult to injury but also disrupted the entire web of tactics that allowed his family to enjoy a comfortable standard of living.

We too believe that some people are workers and some are not. Personality, background, human capital, and cultural expectations *do* make a difference in getting and keeping good jobs. Unless the labor market is considerably more selective than we believe, however, these characteristics alone cannot predict which workers will have had the good sense and ambition to pick firms or divisions within firms that will escape downsizing and permanent layoffs and who will be so lacking in ambition that they choose to work in jobs that are eventually eliminated. Once a good job is lost, these attributes are of little consequence. When conditions prevent families from finding labor market success, they are constrained in how they behave in both formal and more informal activities. In the next two chapters, we explain why this should be the case.

Naturally, there are and will always be some "deviant" families within each group—whether by virtue of unusual "motivation" or because of unusual circumstances. Bruce Sharp—the man who put his snowplow to such imaginative uses—was extraordinary on both scales. He engaged in a variety of activities that were usually beyond the means of bad job households. As we talked with him, it became apparent that he had considerable energy and determination. Yet, even in its "deviance," a case like Bruce's can be instructional. Bruce lived next door to his parents, who owned a farm. He thus had access to their land and their equipment. If he were to move—or what is more likely, given the state of agriculture in Vermont, if his parents were to lose the family farm—Bruce's situation would be quite different: He would no longer have room to plant a garden, and he would have to buy his own tractor. No degree of energy or determination could substitute for those substantial losses.

Naturally, as well, neither the good job nor the bad job households are homogeneous groups. Although roughly similar in the average age of their members, each set of families contains those who are new labor force participants and those who are later in their careers. Each set also contains some who have always had the same status as well as those— like the Riverses—whose fortunes have changed with time. Downward mobility is a common phenomenon in a community in which work is being degraded. We interviewed only a very few families that had experienced upward mobility. Even in those rare cases, good luck was sometimes short lived. After years of struggling to get by on bad work, Frank Lawrence, for example, finally found a job on the Sterling Aeronautical Company assembly line. A year before we spoke to him, he had been laid off from that job, and he was working instead at Wilson Contract Manufacturing. The tractor for sale outside his home eloquently told of his family's current plight.

Both age and mobility in status—and the interaction between the two—are important determinants of many of the tactics under consideration. Take their effects on self-provisioning as an example. The Shorts are a relatively young good work family. They did not yet have enough money set aside to renovate their kitchen, although, Jane and Paul said, they would begin this project in three years, *if*, they added, they were both able to keep their jobs. As noted above, during the good years, when Charles Rivers was employed at General Electric, his family had purchased a home, land, and tools. Hence, Charles could still plow the driveway, plant a garden, cut firewood, and make necessary repairs to keep his aging cars on the road, and Ellen could still grow a garden. The goods accumulated during the years of stable employment helped this family through some of the dire consequences of its current misfortune. In contrast to both the Shorts and the Riverses, those households in which no one had ever had a good job utterly lack the resources with which to build up a base of self-provisioning activity. Missy and Larry Stannage survive through a combination of Larry's waged work as a car mechanic and Missy's two part-time jobs—babysitting in her home and being a clerk at the local library. Although Larry invests heavily in tools and can repair his own aging car, they live in a trailer that cannot be heated with wood, and they do not own land that can support a large garden.

As economic restructuring extends through Coolidge County, fewer and fewer households will be able to achieve the accomplishments of their predecessors. The dichotomy we employ in this book now probably underestimates the full degree of difference between good job and bad job households not only because each group combines families of different ages but also because the group of bad job households contains a number of those that have only recently experienced misfortune. Over time, we predict, the dichotomy will become even more rigid and even more telling.

CHAPTER 3

Earning a Living Means
More than a Job

By and large, good work households are very busy places. The dual-earner strategy is the norm, and men and women both work long hours at their principal jobs. Busyness is intensified for the substantial minority of households in which at least one individual moonlights. As we will see in the next chapter, many also engage in self-provisioning activities which range from the substantial (and time-consuming) endeavor of home construction to routine home maintenance. Finally, especially among the busiest of these households, individuals engage in a variety of nonmonetary exchanges with members of other households; they thus incur obligations to others that take time and effort to meet. What is striking about the good job households is that the various pieces of this complex survival strategy mesh well, creating an overall stable pattern. This coherence is no small achievement: Family members work hard at their individual activities; they also expend considerable effort in maintaining the whole. These efforts are extended because not only do these various pieces provide important measures of economic support, but they also enrich the lives of household members.

Judged by their many activities alone, bad job households are not entirely different. They too can be extremely busy places with two workers, various moonlighting activities, active engagement in routine self-provisioning, and maintenance of interhousehold networks. Without the centerpiece of stable, good jobs, however, their survival strategies confront barriers that make it impossible to construct the kind of predictable, orderly pattern of family life enjoyed by those with labor market advantages. Even when they *could* be maintained, the activities fit together less coherently: The effort expended by those in good job families paled in comparison to the constant juggling required of members in bad job families. Sometimes, the juggling pins tumbled with a crash to the floor. Like Tolstoy's happy families, among those households fortunate to have at least one good job, there was a remarkable similarity in the way they went about sustaining themselves. Among families not so favored, there was little commonality. They were forced to adapt their strategies to constantly changing circumstances. What was true today could be entirely different tomorrow.

THE DUAL-EARNER STRATEGY

If we consider the most obvious new labor strategy taken up by families—the use of two earners rather than the traditional, single male breadwinner pattern—the two kinds of households are significantly different. It is not just the quantitative difference that impresses. Much more important, the direction of these differences goes in exactly the opposite direction one would normally predict. Households with a hold on at least one good job are much more likely to send more than one earner into the labor force than are households with only a bad job.[1]

Not only do most good job households have two earners, but in the vast majority, both of those earners also hold down full-time employment. The situation is quite different in bad job households, which have twice as many *second* workers with part-time employment as do good job households (60 percent versus 29 percent).[2] This difference in the intensity of the second worker's employment is even more substantial than the difference between the two sets of households in the reliance on two earners.

There is another difference as well. The overall quality of waged employment held by the *second* worker is also significantly higher in good job households than in bad job households;[3] in fact, two-fifths of good job households are "doubly good" insofar as *both* earners hold down good jobs. Thus, even when bad job households have second earners, that feature of their survival strategy has a quite different meaning than that same tactic does among good job households.

Not surprisingly, when young, both sets of dual-earner households experience considerable job instability: In each set of households, approximately a quarter of the labor force participants had acquired a job within the last six months. Good job households apparently settle down rather rapidly, while bad job households remain unsettled. Among dual-earner households in which both partners were over twenty-five (and thus presumably out of school for a number of years), three times as many of the labor force participants in bad job families had started a job within the past six months than was the case in good job families (18 percent versus 6 percent). In other words, the difference in the frequency with which the two sets of households rely on two earners at any moment (and enjoy the benefits of full-time employment) masks a third distinction: Among bad job families, the group of dual-earner households undergoes constant change, but among good job households, that group not only is larger but also is consistent over time. In effect, when we consider bad job households, we have snapshots of families frozen against a background of changing employment. If we took the picture earlier, we might well have found two workers among any bad job family that now has only one, or we might have found precisely the reverse.[4]

Some of the shifts bad job households endure result from losing good work. When Michael Johnson was laid off from his decent job, he was unable to replace it with another that was equally good. In fact, he signed up as a "temp" with a local agency that supplies workers to area businesses. Now, when the agency locates employment for him, both Michael and his wife, Martha, work outside the home. When the agency comes up empty-handed, the family relies on Martha's work alone. Previously, the Johnsons had been a solid two-earner family.

Because it might well be assumed that differences between the characteristics of good job families and bad job families determine the difference in the frequency with which they rely on the dual-earner strategy, this issue is explored in some detail (Table 6). Interestingly, a significant difference remains between the two sets of households in the likelihood that they will rely on the dual-earner strategy even when we control for the characteristics of their members and for their composition. Although that difference is more pronounced under some conditions than others (when the second worker is a woman, when the household includes at least one preschool child), as a general rule that difference between the two sets of households cannot be attributed to the privileged character of the individual members of good job households or to a specific kind of household composition. In fact—and this is particularly surprising given the easily drawn conclusion that the lower educational achievements of the members of bad job households might account for the

TABLE 6.   PERCENTAGE OF HOUSEHOLDS
WITH DUAL-EARNER STRATEGY BY HOUSEHOLD
CHARACTERISTICS

HOUSEHOLD CHARACTERISTIC	GOOD JOB HOUSEHOLDS	BAD JOB HOUSEHOLDS
% of households with dual-earner strategy by age of second worker		
Younger workers*	82% (38)	50% (28)
Older workers	88% (36)	72% (21)
% of households with dual-earner strategy by education of second worker		
High school or less	86% (28)	67% (28)
More than high school*	85% (46)	56% (27)
% of households with dual-earner strategy by sex of second worker		
Female*	81% (48)	45% (44)
Male	92% (16)	81% (16)
% of households with dual-earner strategy by presence and age of children		
No children at home	88% (32)	52% (21)+
Older children only	93% (29)	83% (30)
Preschool children*	80% (25)	67% (21)

NOTE: Numbers in parentheses are the numbers of households on which percentages are based.

* Difference between good job and bad job households is significant at the .05 level or higher.
+ Difference within a set of households is significant at the .05 level or higher.

greater tendency of these households to reserve a second worker—the difference between the two groups of households is *more* substantial when they both have better-educated second workers than when those second workers are less educated.

It might also be assumed that within each set of households the characteristics of the family and of its members determine the use of the dual-earner strategy, and we explored this possibility as well. There is a striking difference between families that enjoy a labor market advantage and those that do not with respect to the manner in which individual and family attributes shape the likelihood that both adults will be employed. In good job families, traditional barriers to employing a second worker have been all but eroded, while in bad job families they remain effective. No matter whether we consider the characteristics of the household itself or the characteristics of the would-be second worker, in good job households that second worker likely took a job.

Not so in bad job households. In these households, the traditional barriers to families utilizing the labor of a second worker still had an effect. Younger would-be workers were somewhat less likely to hold down a job than were those who were older (50 percent versus 72 percent). If the second worker was a woman, she was almost twice as likely to stay home than if that potential worker was a man (45 percent versus 81 percent). If there were younger children at home (or if there were no children at home), families were less likely to send that second worker into the labor force than if there were older children in the household (67 percent and 52 percent versus 83 percent). Indeed, education is the only factor that not only does not operate the way that would be anticipated—that those with lower educational levels would be less inclined to be in the labor force—but functions, if at all, in the reverse manner: Those households in which the second worker had more than a high school education were somewhat less likely to have the second worker in the labor force than those in which the second earner was less well educated (56 percent versus 67 percent).

In their own right, these are important differences in the circumstances under which bad job families deploy two earners; they guide our analysis below when we turn to an understanding of how bad work shapes a family's labor force strategy. These data also tell us something striking about our assumptions concerning labor force behavior. In good job families, those individual and household characteristics that are normally thought to influence labor market behavior—age, level of education, gender, and the presence and age of children—have virtually no effect. In short, in good job households factors that might act as barriers to full participation in the labor market are, apparently, quite easily overcome. Among bad job families, they make more of a difference. Even there, however, these factors do not have precisely the impact that would normally be predicted: Education in particular works in the reverse direction. Taken as a whole, these findings demonstrate that what remains most predictive in terms of the most salient difference between the labor market behavior of families is that one group has access to at least one decent job and the other doesn't. The character of that job makes the difference. The question is how.

THE NATURE OF EMPLOYMENT AND THE CAPACITY TO SUSTAIN THE DUAL-EARNER STRATEGY

A close look at families and how they survive reveals something quite striking. Good work underwrites the employment of a second member even if that second worker's earnings are relatively small; good work also protects the household's workers during periods of family stress. Bad work offers neither of these advantages and thus inhibits the use of a dual-earner strategy, particularly when there is a preschool child in the family.

Although the usual understanding of employment starts with the need for earnings, as every new entrant into the labor force knows, a job costs money. Travel, appropriate clothing, and child care can consume and even outweigh the advantage of earnings.[5] Among good job households, the second worker did not always earn wages sufficient to make employment financially advantageous, at least in the short run. Nevertheless, these family members worked. They did so in many cases for reasons other than immediate financial gain.

To see how this happens, it is important to remember that because the good job household has one secure income and, presumably, a stable economic future complete with secure pensions, it can tolerate an occasional negative cash flow. For example, both Lois Donahue and her husband, Eric (who had a good job working for a municipal water system), indicated that the cost of child care almost entirely negated the financial benefits of *her* part-time employment with a real estate appraiser. Lois, as the second worker, still placed enormous value on her job. Working outside the home gave her freedom from the routine of the household, created financial autonomy, and secured her place in the labor force. That Eric Donahue might also be subsidizing his wife's *employer* had not occurred to him. Nor, it seems, did it occur to Lois:

> I make good money. [My employer] pays me well. I don't get any other benefits. It is a real borderline thing. I just don't want to lose my job. It's a good break. It gets me out. When I wasn't working, it got to the point where, if I bought something [my husband] didn't approve of, he would say so: "You shouldn't buy that because I earn the money." [I responded], "I can fix that. As a matter of fact, I just got offered a job yesterday!" So, it does work, it's just enough.

Of course, Lois's comments appear to feed directly into the argument that women work for "pin money"—Lois's work supports her own consumerism, and her husband tolerates her efforts. Lois was hardly unique among second workers in good job households in locating the motivation for employment in enhanced purchasing power, but before we simply dismiss these second workers—as Lois does herself—three points should be noted.

First, women are not the *only* "second" workers in good job (or even in bad job) households. In more than two-fifths of good job households, men have work of lower quality than that of their wives. When men are "second workers," they (sometimes) acknowledge as much and speak about *their* jobs as being the "optional" ones. Philip Menard described his decision to become a logger in this way: "I just picked up a chain saw and went to work. It isn't really much of a business but it was something that I enjoyed doing. And with [my wife] teaching I didn't really have to bring in that much money. And I enjoy it."

Second, there is no reason to accept at face value Lois's own implicit suggestions that her salary goes toward "extras" while Eric's is used for necessary household expenses. How women view their work is as much a function of how they—and their husbands—see themselves in the social order as it is a function of their actual role in the household.[6] The differentiation of household expenses into tidy but separate categories of "extras" and "essentials" more often reflects who is paying the bills— and from which paycheck—than it does any intrinsic difference in the significance of those expenses. In some families, when *her* paycheck covers the mortgage and groceries, those become "extras"; when *his* paycheck covers the same items, they miraculously are transformed into "essentials."

Third, even if it were true that Lois made little contribution to the well-being of her family and frittered away her earnings on consumer goods of her own choosing, we should heed well the rest of what she has to say. Lois does not want to lose her job; by holding onto one with marginal utility, she is securing her place in the labor force with the prospect of better pay in the future. Moreover, she has a job she has chosen. She enjoys the work (as Philip Menard did *his* job), and it meshes well with other household demands. From her point of view, it is "desirable" work secured by the good work of her husband.

The important, indeed crucial, point is that even though bad job households may well have greater financial incentives, they cannot afford to send into the labor force (or continue to carry) a second worker who does not make an immediate, significant contribution to the household's well-being. Gender may determine which person will work—men are more likely to hold down a job than are women—but it is the costs of employment, when weighed against a worker's real or apparent labor force opportunities, that preclude the dual-earner strategy itself.

Child care is one of those costs, and it is particularly relevant to the finding that bad job households are especially likely to abandon the dual-earner strategy when they have young children.[7] Many women in bad job households pointed out that they would be unable to earn enough to cover that expense, particularly if they were limited to low-wage work: "We were finding, for what I was making, I couldn't pay a sitter and pull out any extra money. It just wasn't worth it, and that's why I'm doing what I'm doing today—being home with the kids."

Child care is not the only constraint. Because there is no public transportation in Coolidge County (as in most rural areas), families with two workers usually need two cars (especially if children have to be transported to and from day care). The expense of purchasing and maintaining those cars can be prohibitive. A woman married to a carpenter employed in a small contracting firm, when asked what she considered the barriers to her employment, replied "Just the one car and he has it so we would have to get a new car." Good-paying jobs, especially for women, mean hefty investment in very work-specific wardrobes which can be very costly when weighed against the wages offered by the job. In sum, bad job households can neither develop the infrastructure to support a second worker nor tolerate even the short-term job-related costs.[8]

In addition to securing important financial resources, good work can help prop up a second worker's labor force participation and thus allow the household to sustain the dual-earner pattern over time. Because good work ensures sick leave and paid holidays—paid time off that is crucial if both adults in a family (and especially one with young children) are going to remain employed—the primary worker can meet his or her family obligations without fear of being fired, and the "other" worker (regardless of the quality of his or her own work) does not have to jeopardize a job when crises arise. One woman with a good job reported that she could draw on paid vacation time to remain home during a week when her children were sick and could even reserve time for the anticipated hospitalization of her toddler:

> One day [when my daughter was sick] I came home from work early. Of course I have vacation time. . . . I usually keep a week to two weeks [of vacation] for a day here if I want to take it or half a day there. . . . My youngest is supposed to be going in [for surgery] and . . . so I [have] kept extra time for that.

Her comments were echoed by others with good jobs who explained how they parlayed benefits into an ability to cover unanticipated illness within the family. Even if the second worker in the household does not have similar benefits, the primary worker has the necessary flexibility to sustain the labor force participation of *both* of them.

Without these amenities, bad job families have a difficult time keeping both adults at work, especially when there are very young children. Jake Dwire received a warning from the Wilson Contract Manufacturing management when he stayed home to rest after being up all night with a sick child; this same management fired his sister when she chose to tend to her son rather than go to the plant:[9]

> I just got a written warning a couple of weeks ago because [my daughter] was up all night and I was up all night with her, and . . . I couldn't go to work the next day and I got a written warning for missing too much time at work. . . . [My sister's] son was sick one day so she stayed down at my house . . . and when I came home she said that [her employer] had called down there and asked her to come up to the plant for a while, and they fired her.

Because bad job households do not have the benefit of protected employment during times of family crisis (a sick child, a new baby), families frequently must respond (either voluntarily or involuntarily) by at least one member leaving his or her job. In contrast to those who would argue that unstable workers produce bad jobs, we would argue that bad work produces an unstable deployment strategy.

There is a circularity here that is important to note. The jobs held by members of bad job families offer few benefits, and there is little if any incentive built into the reward system to keep employees at work. Under conditions of domestic stress, workers have no choice but to do things that eventually lead them to leaving their jobs either by choice or because they are fired; the cost of "managing" a family crisis without quitting work is simply higher than the cost of leaving the job itself. Because the cost to bad job firms of losing an employee apparently is low—these are firms that regularly lay off people—then it is clearly the case that managers are far more willing to respond to an employee's irregular hours by a dismissal. Thus, for both these reasons—low cost to management and low relative cost to employees—workers presented with the domestic demands of very young children or a shift in the work arrangements of other household members are much more likely to leave their jobs, either through dismissal or "voluntary" action, than are workers in good jobs.[10]

Having one earner drop out of the labor force is not the only solution to the pressures on the dual labor force pattern among bad job households. In the absence of job flexibility, twice as many dual-earner *bad* job couples than dual-earner good job couples rely not only on part-time work but also on staggered work schedules (33 percent versus 16 percent).[11] These arrangements are selected for a number of reasons that should be true for both groups: Couples can save on the expense of child care in this way; some prefer to raise their children by themselves; and, for some, being together as a couple does not outweigh the benefits of the staggered schedule. It is precisely those couples most at an economic disadvantage that are more frequently required to deal with the kind of marital instability that staggered hours bring. Insult is added to injury.

Furthermore, the instability of bad jobs directly undermines the intricate and often elaborate strategies these less-fortunate households have to devise to keep a second worker employed. Carla Griffin had been providing child care in her home before her husband lost his job. Robert Griffin soon found a new job, but it was out of state. When the Griffins arrived in their new home, they decided to wait until they were certain that Robert's job would last before Carla too sought employment. Eventually, Carla found a job, and she held it for just under a year before Robert's new employment evaporated and they decided to try their luck back home. When they returned to Coolidge County, Robert found a new job and Carla "started job hunting again." The Griffins' alternation between the single-earner and dual-earner strategies thus emerged directly from the instability of Robert's employment. Carla always wanted—and needed—to hold down a job; sometimes circumstances made it impossible.

Patricia Slater is another young woman with preschool children. She spoke of job changes that occurred with dizzying speed, as well as constant change in the family deployment pattern:

> The summer after [my second child was born] I worked at Blueberry Meadows, made blueberry jam—actually my sister and I did that together—we did that. . . . [T]hen I went back to work at [a beauty parlor] and after I left there I've been [working from] home. I've sold Tupperware, I've done that nights, and I've been in a networking firm—Amway Corporation—buying direct wholesale from a distributor through this corporation and getting other people into the network. . . . MCI is in this network so we get our phone service cheaper. . . . And I did a paper route. . . . I got up at 2 in the morning and I was done by 5:30 depending on the day. That was seven days a week. . . . I did day care, I forgot about that. I had three children in my home. . . . I did that from September until June. When [my husband] lost his job there was just my babysitting income and . . . from September to November we were both employed. . . . From November until March my babysitting was the only income. In March I started the route, so in March I was doing the paper route and day care. . . . When school got out I finished day care

and just did the paper route. . . . [Now] my husband's been back to work about three weeks and the company he's working for is a federal company so he's making $20 an hour instead of $10. And that's temporary. Because he's working he leaves at 4 in the morning, and there is only the one car and no one to take care of the children, [so] I can't do my paper route.

In short, bad job households find it especially difficult to initiate and sustain a necessary survival tactic. In contrast to second workers in good job households, second workers in bad job households lack financial support to underwrite their labor force participation; neither worker in a bad job household has job flexibility to call on in the face of common family crises, and thus either one or the other quits a job or they try out the stressful practice of relying on staggered schedules. A change in one person's job—a not infrequent occurrence among bad job households— undermines the employment of the other.

Because these problems have as much to do with the character of bad jobs as they do with wage levels, it is surprising that when the primary worker has *higher* wages, bad job households are actually slightly less likely to send two earners into the labor force than they are when the family's immediate financial situation is more difficult: 68 percent of those with low incomes rely on a dual labor force strategy, in contrast with 52 percent of those with higher incomes (Table 4). At first glance, what seems to be paradoxical behavior indicates the real costs of bad jobs quite apart from low wages. The utilization of a second worker comes at an extraordinarily high price. When they can afford to, it appears that bad job households sacrifice an extra income to avoid paying that price.

Under two sets of circumstances, however, bad work households "overcome" these difficulties and deploy a second worker at approximately the same rate as good job households: When there are school-age children in the household, and when the second earner is a male. Families with children to support have an obvious incentive to increase their labor force activity. Bad job households can respond to this incentive only when employment does not have to compete with the expense of child care; once children are in school all day (and may even be able to remain alone during illness), the second worker can more easily be sent into the labor force. Male pride is an additional "spur" (one to which we will attend more fully in Chapter 5) that drives a second worker to seek employment even if, as is sometimes the case, that employment comes at a cost to the household economy.

MAINTAINING STATUS

If the difference between good work households and bad work households is a function of the *kind of work* held by the members of those households (rather than their demographic characteristics), it is also possible to switch the direction of causality, or at least to suggest a second kind of circularity. Bad work itself is often a consequence of the single-earner strategy; conversely, good work can be a consequence of the dual-earner strategy, not only because two earners increase the statistical likelihood of finding that better employment but also because good and bad job households are "trapped" in entirely different cycles.

Imagine a good work family in which both adults work in the formal labor force, then consider what happens when one of those two earners is laid off from work. If that hypothetical worker held a good job, she may well receive severance pay and unemployment insurance and thus have some cushioning that diminishes the immediate impact of that loss. She can spend a little extra time searching for a replacement position, and she can even be selective about that replacement. If that worker is the only good job worker in the family, she can thus attempt to preserve the family's status as a "good job" household. (She can also seek to maintain her *individual* status.) Of course, the primary worker may not be able to replace a lost good job with another good job, and the family (if it has relied on but a single good job) might become a bad job family. This, in fact, is what economic restructuring produces for many of its "victims," like the Riverses and the Johnsons. At least initially, the response to loss is shaped by what is lost. Households that have been firmly anchored in good work might drift for some time, but at least, for the short duration, they drift within sight of the promised land.

In his discussion of what happened when he was "downsized" by the Sterling Aeronautical Company, Rick Martin made both of these points. He explained that his good job provided a benefit package that enabled him to be selective about a replacement position *and* that, even so, some of his former coworkers might find their futures drastically altered:

> We had an excellent [severance package] and I think—not I *think*—I *know* it would have been terrifically hard [otherwise] and I probably would have taken *any* job at that point. So I'm actually still being paid by [Sterling] while I have another job. . . . And for people who are still unemployed it means you don't have to panic. It means that you can pay attention to the job hunting without going crazy worrying how you are going to make it week to week. And for people who were there a long time—obviously they may

have a harder time finding a job, or . . . finding something comparable to what [they] left. But they have the support of the severance package. It does mean, at some point when that runs out, a lot of people are finding lesser jobs, so your income is [cut]—you have to do with less.

Even if the laid-off worker does not hold a good job, the fact of membership in a dual-earner family provides its own kind of cushioning. Here, for example, is how a husband spoke about how comfortably they could live until his wife (who had just lost her job) found a new position (which she did within two weeks): "So there wasn't any time frame, there wasn't any limit, and she could look for whatever she wanted without feeling pressured. I think that helped a lot. That worked very well." Although his wife responded that she "still felt that sense of panic," her husband insisted, "but it was not real. We could easily survive on my salary."

The members of good job families do not go without work for long periods (and still retain that status): The dual-earner strategy is the good job household's usual *and* stable pattern. The combination of good work and the dual-earner strategy itself takes the immediate "edge" off the experience of job loss: They don't have to "panic" or take just "any job." Members of these households also have an educational level that promises a wider range of jobs from which to choose. By virtue of their location within good job households, they also have access to networks of colleagues and friends who can help them locate other good jobs.[12] Although the woman we quote below exercised selectivity in her job search and viewed the success of that search as the result of luck, her luck was clearly conditioned by social factors:

> I've really never applied for many jobs. The only jobs I've ever applied for I've always gotten. . . . From people I know I've always heard about jobs. I've always had good luck. I don't know what it would be like not to. In my lifetime I've only had three jobs. [After I was laid off] I was probably facing a commute . . . and much less pay and I didn't know how I was going to do that because we just make it as it is. So then, I was just out there beating on the doors—not every door because I didn't want to do just anything—and then just by a sheer stroke of luck somebody called and gave me a lead about another job and that turned into something. So it was sheer unadulterated luck in my opinion.

By way of contrast, consider the job loss scenario in the bad work family. First, that lost job is considerably less likely to carry benefits like unemployment insurance or severance pay to carry the family over the rough spots. Second, that lost job is already more likely to be the *only* job in the household. *Each* member of the family is now under enormous pressure to do precisely what Rick Martin could avoid—to take the first job that comes along. Sue Jencks described how her husband's unemployment (he was the only wage earner at the time) left him so desperate that he pounced on an entirely unsatisfactory opening: "He just went back to work a few weeks ago. But he still is looking [for work] because what he took is just something to get us by until he finds something better. He's selling vacuum cleaners door to door." Because she was not at all certain that he would be able to find any job at all, Sue began looking for work as well. She located employment first, and she began working at Wilson Contract Manufacturing. "If he finds something better," Sue said, she will drop out of the labor force again. When measured against the costs of day care for her toddler, Sue's job is of little value *if* Bill's job can cover their bare expenses. Within a few short weeks, then, this family went from being a single-earner family, to a "no-earner" family, to a dual-earner family. In all likelihood, it will soon become a single-earner family once again. Earlier in their working lives, *both* Bill and Sue had been employed, and both of them had held good jobs. Downsizing had sent them on this new course.

Like their more fortunate peers, the members of bad job families also rely on members of their networks to locate opportunities during stints of unemployment. These networks provide information about a very different kind of job from those described in the good job networks. Furthermore, there seemed to be an impenetrable wall, so that in one relatively small community, information about jobs went two separate rounds—good jobs in their networks, bad jobs in theirs. Jake Dwire had originally heard about WCM from his sister; Sue Jencks learned of openings there from a neighbor. Each and every respondent who sewed at home for Green Mountain Cuddly Toys told us about learning about that option through word of mouth. We heard nothing from respondents in bad job households about employment opportunities that would improve their prospects.

If a good job family can enhance its members' workplace advantages, it cannot always protect those members: The loss of a good job (as was the case with Sue and Bill Jencks) can result in a downward spiral. Bad job households do not so readily move in the opposite direction. In the previous chapter, we introduced the Riverses as a somewhat older bad job household that had previously had good work but was now caught in the cycle of bad work. A younger bad job family—the Badgers—vividly illustrate many of the points made above. Their history dem-

onstrates the reasons for job loss, the consequences of staggered schedules, the absence of infrastructure support for a second worker, reliance
on networks, and the hope such families often pin on temporary employment.

Barbara Badger described her family's employment situation over the
course of the previous year. Twelve months before we spoke with her,
the Badgers had a dual-earner strategy. Ernie, who was employed at his
father's printing company, was the family's primary worker. Barbara
did child care in her home. When his father closed his shop, Ernie lost
his job. Without his earnings, the Badgers were unable to meet rent
payments on their apartment, and they had to move in with relatives;
they stayed there for almost six months. Barbara thus lost the infrastructure that enabled *her* to work (much as Carla Griffin had when Robert's
employment ended): "We didn't have enough money to stay in our
apartment. I was doing day care in our home, and because we couldn't
stay in our home I had to give that up." For almost six weeks neither
Ernie nor Barbara had a job. Then Ernie found temporary daytime
work, and Barbara found a job she could do evenings. Barbara did not
like hers at all: "I first took a job as a hostess at the Prime Beef Restaurant, and I didn't really like it. I didn't like the atmosphere there, and I
really didn't enjoy it." She also minded that she never saw her husband
and was away from her child at bedtime: "When I was working at night,
when [Ernie] got home from work he was keeping the baby and I was
going to work, and I wasn't there for [the baby] or for Ernie. I didn't
like that either." Eventually, she quit and looked around for something
better. She located yet another job—which paid less—through a chance
arrangement facilitated by her parents (good job household):

> My parents were members at the fitness center. They bought a family mem-
> bership, while Ernie and I were living there, so we actually were involved in
> the membership, and I saw the nursery there so I guess I was just looking for
> a job, so I stopped by to see if the nursery needed help. They did and that's
> how I ended up there.

Because Barbara works only twenty hours a week, she cannot support
the family on her earnings alone, nor can she cover the rent on their new
apartment. With a second child due in four months, she knows she will
have to take some time off. She hopes the fitness center will hold the job
for her. Ultimately, however, the Badgers are counting on Ernie's new
job working *at* but not *for* General Machines Incorporated (he is employed by a "temp" agency), which pays better than others considered
during his bout of unemployment:

When my husband was out looking for jobs, I know people wanted to pay him minimum wage and $5 an hour, and he's trying to support a family, and that was really hard for us, so General Machines worked out. . . . He's making around $6 an hour, but he works twelve hour days and so he gets a 28 percent differential so he is really making about $8 an hour. . . . We are doing better than we have ever done.

But, as Barbara said, that job is temporary.

They take them three months at a time. They either extend it or let them go. When he was there a three-month period, they extended him six months. I think that is up in September, so hopefully, they will extend him some more. . . . But we have also heard that they haven't hired a permanent person from a temp in years. We don't want to depend on it, in a way, but we don't want to throw it away, because if he looked for another job . . . or if he was offered another job, he would be afraid he was passing up a chance there.

If things don't work out the way Barbara hopes, they may well end up back in her parents' home—this time with two children and no jobs.

SELF-EMPLOYMENT

We have tacitly assumed that in each kind of family, both the primary and secondary worker are engaged in waged work. As the example of the Badgers indicated, such is not invariably the case: Barbara spent at least some time as a self-employed family day care provider. Indeed, in a substantial number of each kind of household, at least one worker is self-employed in his or her principal job (18 percent of good job households and 25 percent of bad job households). This pattern is even more common among dual-earner bad job households than it is among dual-earner good job households (37 percent versus 21 percent). There are two additional differences.

First, the quality of self-employment in good job households is somewhat higher than the quality of self-employment in bad job households.[13] Why this should be the case has to do, once again, with the ability of the family member with a good job to underwrite a spouse's enterprise—whether that be waged work or self-employment. Consider Ellen Woodward, who, like Barbara Badger, does day care from her home. Ellen's family day care is a substantial business: She is licensed by the state and therefore gets supplementary training, food, and free advertising. Because she cares for nine children (six preschoolers all day and three older children before and after school), she can hire an assistant and still generate a substantial income. Ellen did not do all this on her own. Her husband Frank's steady wages provided the credit rating that enabled her to borrow $12,000 to renovate their garage for use as the day care space, and Frank's job also secured their health insurance. Ellen acknowledged that she would have to give up her occupation if Frank lost his employment: "The day care wouldn't carry us. It is not enough."[14] In this dependence on her husband's earnings, Ellen is little different from Barbara, but there were more significant differences. Barbara did not have the resources to renovate a space to be devoted exclusively for child care, or even that "extra" space itself. As an unregistered day care provider, she had to remain small enough that she would not be noticed by state officials: Barbara cared for only three children.[15] Also, as noted above, Barbara's husband *did* lose his job, and she *did* have to give up her day care.

The relationship between the waged job and the coexisting self-employment is different in the two sets of households. In good job households, the waged work of one spouse supports the household and often steadies the self-employment of the other. We spoke with Susan Lee just after she opened a fabric shop. Although she had not yet made a profit, her household could survive on her husband's income alone; she thus had the luxury of building up her business without immediate financial pressures:

> I don't think [I've made a profit yet]. No, it doesn't show too much in the books but I'll know more at the end of July. I have a bookkeeper that will come in and she'll sit down and figure it out and find out if I'm making a profit—which I'm not. . . . They say the first six months are nonprofit anyway. . . . I'm hoping, I'm keeping my fingers crossed. I want to try to get through to fall because I think that's when business will pick up. . . . It hasn't been [a struggle] yet. There's been times where we wondered where we were going to get the payment for the loan, but it hasn't been that bad. We manage. We cut back on groceries one week or another bill will get shoved aside. . . . I don't think it's been that hard. . . . But as far as making it—well, we'll make it.

In this case, the unsteady earnings that are almost inevitable with self-employment meant, as Susan said, a "cutback" here or a bill "shoved aside" there, but not a shift overall in the family's labor force configuration. No member of a good job household told us that a waged worker had entered the labor force or shifted jobs to accommodate the self-employment of another.

In bad job households as well, waged work helps support the household, but it cannot steady (or subsidize) self-employment directly. Because bad work is unlikely to bring in reliable enough (or substantial enough) wages to underwrite the added expense of a flagging business, the uncertainties of self-employment have a greater impact. Financial distress is measured not just in a "cutback" here or a bill "shoved aside" there, but in radical shifts in the family's well-being *and* in its employment practices. Pete Ayer and Jeff Blair, for example, are trying to expand their small-engine repair shop. Because they are still struggling, Pete's wife has returned to full-time work even though she preferred her part-time job. Jeff's wife now provides day care in her home because it pays more than her part-time jobs.

Although waged work is the central focus of this book, we make these points about self-employment for a reason. Increasingly, self-employment appears to be an attractive option.[16] Many of those we interviewed, as we will see below, had aspirations to turn side-work into full-time self-employment. In Chapter 1, we described the businesses started by former (upper-level) employees of the Sterling Aeronautical Company. Some of the downsized lower-level employees were headed in precisely that direction, albeit on a smaller scale. One man we spoke with was going to start a business doing reupholstery for vintage cars, another had launched a sign-making business, a third was drawing his wife and children into a landscaping business, and a fourth was planning to purchase a van to provide sightseeing tours to affluent visitors. But, *caveat emptor*: Without the balance, security, and fundamental support of a good waged "companion," self-employment can turn a household economy on its head.

MOONLIGHTING IN VERMONT

When he was describing the jobs he had held before he started his good job working on a road crew for the Vermont Department of Transportation, Eric Donahue mentioned that he had once been employed in a garage that did body work on cars. He then added, "I have always done body work. I still repair cars." Eric also told us that although he had been accumulating the tools that underwrote this side-work for much of his life ("I started body work when I was fourteen years old. I just kept picking [tools] up"), the previous year he had made some significant investments that enabled him to get the job done more easily and to make a bigger profit at it. Eric, however, was not actually doing a lot of car repair in the months before we interviewed him. That activity competed with the other demands on his time: The Donahues own a duplex that they rent out, and Eric does all the repairs there; he also builds up his woodpile each year, and he makes sure that he has the time and money to take a long hunting trip in the fall. Still, car repair is always a possibility. ("When I get short of money and want some money, I just do one.")

Like Eric Donahue, Paul Currier is also employed full time—in his case, however, in a bad job. Like Eric, Paul also has work he does on the side: Each weekend, he is employed as a laborer for a logger. This arrangement originally began as an informal one, but now Paul is paid recorded wages:

> It used to be [under the table]. When I first started . . . it was [under the table] and the hours got longer and the pay got more, [my boss] kept giving me a raise, giving me a raise. He finally said, "I hate to do it but I'm going to start writing checks and claiming some of this." But he was real nice about it. He raised my pay to make up the difference so I brought home [the same amount].

Even though working weekends is hard, Paul appreciates the extra income: "Everybody says you're crazy to work seven days a week but if you change what you're doing . . . you get used to it and it helps. The money has been awful handy."

Paul's wife, Joan Currier, also has "regular" employment in a bad job. She works part time in a doctor's office. "I'm only paid for the hours I'm there working, I don't have paid vacations or anything. It's between fifteen and twenty hours a week." She is about to start another job as well: "I'm going to start answering the phone here. A friend of mine has his own business, and three afternoons a week I'm going to be sitting here waiting for his phone calls to come through and then give him the messages and he's going to pay me by the hour for that. This is under the table."

"Moonlight in Vermont—Or Starve," the local bumper sticker reads. Surprisingly, given the greater economic stress in bad job households, moonlighting is only slightly more common among these families than among good job households (43 percent versus 35 percent). As is the case with Paul and Joan Currier, moonlighting is only slightly more often the status of *two* workers there as well (21 percent versus 10 percent). Moreover, in good job families moonlighting is an equally likely practice whether there is but one earner or two; among bad job households, those with the dual-earner strategy are much more likely to have at least one of those earners moonlighting than is the case in households that rely on a single earner alone (48 percent versus 33 percent). In short,

TABLE 7.   MOONLIGHTING IN GOOD JOB
AND BAD JOB HOUSEHOLDS

	GOOD JOB HOUSEHOLDS	BAD JOB HOUSEHOLDS
All households: % with any moonlighter	35% (86)	43% (72)
% of households with at least one moon- lighter that have two moonlighters	10% (30)	21% (31)
% with a moonlighter by type of house- hold		
One-earner households	36% (11)	33% (24)[+]
Two-earner households	35% (75)	48% (48)
% of dual-earner households with two moonlighters	12% (75)	26% (48)
% of moonlighting that is unwaged*	61% (38)	36% (28)
% of dual-earner households with a moonlighter by presence of children		
No children	21% (28)	45% (11)
Preschool children	35% (20)	61% (24)
School-age children only	38% (27)	17% (24)
% of moonlighting jobs acquired in last six months	9% (38)	22% (28)
Patterns of moonlighting		
Two full-time jobs	17%	13%
One full-time job and one (or more) part-time jobs	52%	38%
Two or more part-time jobs	30%	49%
Total	100%	100%
Total N	30	31

NOTE: Numbers in parentheses are the numbers of households on which percentages are based.

*Difference between good job and bad job households is significant at the .05 level or higher.
+Difference within a set of households is significant at the .05 level or higher.

it would appear that once the barriers to intensive work activities are overcome by bad job families, they become no less busy than good job households—but that busyness has a much higher entrance price. (For an overview of these differences, see Table 7.)

THE PREMISES ON WHICH MOONLIGHTING DEPENDS

As was the case with the dual-earner strategy, moonlighting in good job households does not depend on member characteristics. Whether they have just one earner or two, and whether they have young children or not, good job households do not vary their pattern of moonlighting. This constancy suggests that among good job households, moonlighting is *sometimes* an optional activity chosen for reasons other than sheer economic need. Although these findings come as something of a surprise, the situation in bad job families is even more unexpected. It would normally be assumed that families with but a single worker (and that worker holding down a bad job) would make an effort for that one worker to augment income by adopting some form of moonlighting. In that case, moonlighting could act as a *substitute* for the second worker. Paradoxically, this is exactly the reverse of what bad job families do.[17] Equally paradoxically, moonlighting among bad job households occurs at an extraordinarily high rate among those households that have enormous constraints on their members' time: In three-fifths of the bad job households in which both parents are employed and in which there are preschool children, at least one parent holds down two or more jobs. No other group of households relies so extensively on the strategy of moonlighting.

These unanticipated findings strongly indicate that bad job households are not lazy households but households that are missing the necessary ingredients to solve their economic problems. When they come upon those ingredients—a second car, a grandmother or neighbor who can watch the children for less than the market cost, work schedules that permit coordination, a network that can help family members locate employment—they are quite willing not only to send a second family member into gainful employment but also to multiply the number of jobs held by at least one of those workers.

Don Dwire, for example, has many of the necessary resources even though, as an employee in a bad job, he is otherwise disadvantaged with respect to his position in the labor force. He holds a full-time job in retail sales from 9 A.M. to 3 P.M., and his wife, Judy, works the swing shift at Wilson Contract Manufacturing from 3 P.M. to 11 P.M. Because they are both working (and because Don is good at repairing cars and has a keen eye for trading them), they have been able to purchase and keep on the road two (relatively reliable) vehicles. Don and Judy schedule their jobs so they do not *need* to pay for child care. Even so, Don *can* also ask his mother to look after his children from time to time; hence, he is well prepared to accept supplemental work when the opportunity arises. He also has a network of friends and relatives who can help him find that extra work.

Another bad job family, the Bushes, face a very different situation. They too have young children, and they too need the income from more than one job, but they have only one car and they have no relatives in the immediate area to help keep down the costs of child care. From time to time, Ron Bush tries to moonlight. When he does, his wife, Janet, is left alone from early morning until late at night. She has no way to shop or to get the children to doctors' appointments. In this household, the tensions that accumulate quickly erode the benefits of Ron's supplemental work.

This is not to imply that the Dwires have it easy. For better or for worse, Don and Judy spend little time together. Understandably, Judy finds it tiring to put in eight hours of paid work after a full day of caring for the children. Understandably as well, she complains that Don takes the children to his mother during the time *he* should be watching them and thus depletes the savings they could reap from staggering their work hours. Don's position is no easier. He feels that between responding to his own family's needs for money and to the obvious needs of his mother (because she is watching grandchildren, she cannot hold down a full-time job[18]), he is always working. If, at the moment, this household can take advantage of multiple employment opportunities, the stresses that accumulate might soon prove disruptive.

Indeed, these disruptions occur quite often in bad job households. Like the principal employment of the members of bad job households, moonlighting activities also prove to be unreliable. Among the bad job households, 22 percent of all moonlighting jobs had been acquired within the past six months; in contrast, among good job households only 9 percent of all moonlighting jobs were begun so recently. This should come as no surprise: The instability of moonlighting is part and parcel of the larger picture of instability among bad job households. Each shift in a job situation resonates throughout the household. At one moment, the household members can juggle a number of pins in the air; at the next moment, there seems to be one pin too many.

VARIATIONS IN MOONLIGHTING

For members of good work households, moonlighting involves a distinctly secondary activity: Like Eric Donahue, they work full time at their waged work and then spend considerably fewer hours at a second job. This view of moonlighting as distinct from, and subordinate to, one's regular job derives from good work. To even speak this way about some individuals in bad work households involves a kind of conceptual distortion. Like Joan Currier with her two part-time jobs, many moonlighters in bad job households do not begin with full-time employment in their principal work but rather hold a couple (and occasionally more than a couple) of jobs, no one of which could be defined as the "supplemental" job much less the central one. Almost half of the moonlighters in bad job households had two part-time jobs; by way of contrast, all but one-third of the moonlighters in good job households worked full time in one job and part time (or occasionally even full time) in the other.

Shortly before we interviewed her, as a member of a bad job household, Martha Blair held *three* part-time jobs: cleaning the town hall, driving a school bus, and working as a cashier in a drugstore. The Blairs also had a foster child in their care and, as Martha knew well, being a wife and mother are jobs too.

> We're kind of unique. We always have something in the works. We've had a foster child for the last year, that came a year ago July and just left in June. So, we had income from that and I also was driving a school bus, a small one, which I drove two days a week, during the school year, plus the drugstore, plus I take care of the town hall. So, I guess I had four jobs, besides being wife, mother, etcetera.

On an hourly basis, Martha earned the most from her cleaning job, but this job was episodic—when the town hall was needed for a community event, Martha would be called in to tidy it and set up chairs. When the event was over, she would be called in again to mop the floors and put the chairs away. The other jobs occurred at predictable intervals, but (with the exception of being a wife and mother) they too were highly unstable, particularly because as a slightly experienced worker she could be undercut by someone willing to work at minimum wage.

> Everything ended when school ended. Our foster child went back to live with his mother, the school bus ended, and the job at the drugstore ended because of the economy. [The owner] can't afford to keep the help that he has got. [During the school year he had] one high school kid who was working part time. He now has him full time. He didn't need me anymore.

Dottie Seeley, in another bad job household, was in much the same position. She regularly held two part-time jobs. Like Martha, she worked as a store clerk, and also like Martha, she had the same kind of episodic responsibility for her town hall. Dottie also "regularly" worked full time cleaning and packaging turkeys for the three weeks leading up to Thanksgiving. If we had interviewed her at that time, we might easily have said that she processed turkeys as her principal job and "moonlighted" with jobs as a cashier and cleaner. Over a longer period of time, it is the turkey processing that becomes moonlighting. In both these cases, the very term "moonlighting" becomes problematic; sequential, multiple job holding may, in fact, often be a more accurate description.

Eric Donahue, in contrast to both Paul and Joan Currier, can illustrate the other significant difference between moonlighting practices in good job and bad job households: Eric moonlights through an entrepreneurial activity; Paul and Joan have second "waged" jobs. This is a difference in control over the terms and conditions of moonlighting, and it does not arise by chance: Whereas 61 percent of the moonlighters in good job households are "self-employed" for that supplemental work, only 36 percent of the moonlighters in bad job households moonlight through self-employment.[19]

This difference derives from the very different kinds of opportunities good work and bad work supply. Just as individuals in good work households have steady and predictable wages that can support a second worker, so can they afford to make long-term investments in an on-the-side business. Eric Donahue has provided one example. Once he had located good work, he began to spend heavily on tools. Another good job worker, Jack Curtis, similarly invested heavily in his landscaping enterprise. His accounting of those financial arrangements indirectly hints at the fact that he both drew on his salary to subsidize large investments and made commitments that he believed would pay off some years later:

> I probably [earn] a couple of thousand a year [from lawn mowing]. Give or take, it depends. Last year was a good year because it stayed wet and I mowed a lot of times. This year it has stayed dry . . . so it has been flexible. I can't say that I'm going to earn $1,800 every year; I could go way down as low as $1,200 and I could go up to $2,000. . . . I've had to buy a truck. I've had to buy *two* trucks in order to get my equipment around. I've had to build a trailer, and I had just one lawn mower but now I bought two and a weed whacker and a couple of push mowers. I've probably invested some money. It's a very bare bones investment but it's still an investment. . . . I probably would have bought a truck anyway . . . I have $6,000 in that, I bought a secondhand lawn mower this year, that was $1,500, and a couple of pushers at a couple of hundred [dollars] apiece, and I got a trailer at $300, and my old lawn mower was $3,500, so you're talking close to $10,000, $12,000.

Few members of bad job households have sufficiently steady incomes to enable them to commit to entrepreneurial moonlighting. Nor do they have benefits like health insurance that can protect them from unanticipated debt. We spoke with the franchise/owner of a Handy Tools truck. He drives around the region selling tools directly to consumers. He told us that the accumulation of unpaid medical bills was the primary reason for bad credit and thus for an individual's exclusion from the practice of building up equipment necessary for an on-the-side business.

In bad job households, individuals who experience special circumstances can maintain practices of entrepreneurial moonlighting. This was the case for Bruce Sharp, who drew on the machinery available on his parents' farm to underwrite his snowplowing business. Those who have previously been in good work households also might have accumulated those resources some time in the past and thus can engage in these practices even when other aspects of their lives are crumbling. Pete Ayer, for example, lost his good employment as the result of an accident. As the co-owner of a repair shop, he continued to do heavy construction jobs (under the table) with equipment he bought during better times, but his hold on that equipment was precarious. He had recently lost to his creditors his family's second car and the boat used for summer excursions. Even as we spoke with him, he was making arrangements to refinance his truck before it too was repossessed.

Those who have never had good work experience the dilemma in which Jake Dwire found himself. His employment as an assembler of circuit boards (on a Wilson Contract Manufacturing subcontract with General Machines Incorporated) pays two dollars above minimum wage. When the contract ends, he may be laid off; at best, he will go back to earning twenty-five cents above the minimum. His wife is unemployed, and they have a new baby. His family clearly needs a secure, second income from him, yet unlike Jack Curtis, Jake cannot take the risk of an investment that may not pay off. Nor can he assume that the summer will bring opportunities to earn a little extra cash. Because he cannot develop his own landscaping business, he has to rely on a friend who might—or might not—need his assistance: "I used to help [a friend] mow lawns, but this summer he hasn't needed any help."

Other bad work respondents made this point about resources explicit. Ricky Jones works as a carpenter for a cabinet-making company. He can use its equipment in the evening. His wife explained, however, that the company then puts restrictions on what he can charge:

> The only thing that Ricky gets is the use of a shop if he has a side job. But that kind of hurts too because he can't charge his customers anything less than $30 an hour because they don't want him undercutting them. . . . If Ricky was charging people 10, 15, 20 bucks an hour we would still be making good money. But now he can't if he uses the shop out there. The pro-

duction he could do out there would be a lot more because they have so much more bigger machinery, it cuts the time in half with the things you can do with it.

Once an on-the-side activity is off the ground, the entrepreneur's waged work can further help bolster a business by providing skills, contacts, and reliable clients. Because the members of bad job households cannot launch an on-the-side business, they cannot take advantage of these "benefits."

Occasionally, entrepreneurial activities draw on specialized skills developed in (waged) employment. The training and experience in George Kemp's current good job welding aircraft engine parts feeds into his own on-the-side business as a welder. Another man we interviewed was being sent, by his employer, to night school to learn plumbing; he was also doing some on-the-side work that drew on this new skill.[20]

Waged work also provides important contacts for on-the-side entrepreneurial activity. Moonlighting entrepreneurs draw on workplace colleagues for access to necessary commodities and for assistance with aspects of their businesses that they either cannot, or choose not to, do themselves.[21] Because Doug Hill works for a car dealer, he knows wholesalers and mechanics. He relies on both of these to make a little money on the side: "Once in a while . . . I buy cars at work for what the wholesaler would buy them for and get some of the guys at work to fix them up for me . . . and then you sell them and you ought to make money."

Contacts available at a waged job also provide an easy source of a *reliable* clientele.[22] Some respondents used the work site as a place to engage in commission sales.[23] In this way, they cut down on expenses of travel, and they do not have to use their "leisure" time for moonlighting:

> The Popular Club, I run that. . . . It's a catalog that you are secretary for and you have members and they take orders and then you get dividends. Like last Christmas I got about $700 worth of free merchandise from the catalog and that helps buy presents for the kids. . . . I do it at work. I put the catalog out there and they give me the orders and I collect the money from them and then send the payment in.

Others use the workplace to gather a clientele for their *own* businesses. Molly Collins explained how her on-the-side knitting business grew from her contacts at Sterling Aeronautical Company: "[I find clients at] work. Friends. They know I have the machine and I'm just getting so that I've made some sweaters that I've worn myself and I think it's self-advertising, basically." Her husband, Dick, located clients for his body shop in the same way (and in the same workplace):[24] "He hand picks them basically. Well, most of his customers come from work [at Sterling], word of mouth, and of course there's a lot of people there. He likes to do the little jobs."

There are other perks as well. One man who worked at Sterling drove a commuter van. Although he did not receive pay for his efforts, he did have his own commuting expenses covered, and he had use of the vehicle during nonwork hours. Dick Collins did not rely on Sterling only for his clients: When the company was renovating its building, Dick also was able to take, for free, lighting fixtures to use in his own shop.

In short, a good job can underwrite the entrepreneurial side-work of its employees. A bad job cannot be counted on in the same way. Ricky Jones would like to have his own on-the-side business making furniture, but his day work is not steady enough to permit his making a long-term investment in tools. If he could get his own business off the ground, his waged job might very well offer some of the same advantages enjoyed by those who hold down good work. Like George Kemp, Ricky's waged work teaches him skills that he could use in his side-work, and, like Doug Hill, he works with others with complementary skills. But Ricky cannot afford to make that important first step.

The difference between the *entrepreneurial* moonlighting in good job households and the *waged* moonlighting in bad job households has a significant consequence for the capacity of a household to manage its time. Important as side-work may be for individuals in good job households, it can much more frequently be contained so that it does not interfere with other activities.[25] Moonlighters in good job households (like second workers in those households) can be selective about the "jobs" they will take and the amount of time and energy they will devote to those jobs. Eric Donahue exercised this option: "If somebody comes in with a car and they want it fixed, I look at it and if I want to do it, I'll take it. If it's something I don't want to deal with I'll just say no." Jack Curtis gave up clients when he believed they were not worth the effort:[26]

[The lawn mowing has] been very stable ever since I grew it up to the size I wanted it. I have lost only one customer and that one I didn't lose, I *wanted* to discontinue him because it was such a small lawn and so far to travel that I wanted to find somebody else. It's been very stable. I've got one, two, three, four and the town—I've got five. And with the town I've got the school and three sites for the selectman.

Such time management is not a possibility among moonlighters in bad job households. Waged jobs have to be done at specific times and in specific places. If the family relies on the income from on-the-side work, the job holder does not have the option—that Eric Donahue and Jack Curtis exercised—of choosing not to take on more work than can be handled comfortably. A "casual" attitude toward a waged second job can jeopardize that employment altogether. Paul Currier could not choose whether, or even when, to show up for his job working for a logger.

In the absence of flexibility, the coordination of diverse activities can become an overwhelming task, especially when households already stagger their "regular" work schedules. Jeff and Martha Blair are lucky in this one respect. As noted above, Martha has several part-time jobs, and Jeff is trying to get his own business repairing small engines off the ground. Because he has not yet been successful, like his wife and co-owner, he "moonlights" extensively. Because Jeff's shop is adjacent to their home, the Blairs can make accommodations: When Martha needs to attend to one of her jobs, she can leave Jeff in charge of their preschool child; if Jeff is called to one of his, he has several options—he can close the shop altogether, he can rely on his partner, Pete Ayer, to carry the business, or he can ask Martha to greet customers for him. Tom and Carla White confront similar problems of competing demands, but no element of *their* survival strategy is flexible: They need to coordinate with precision his two jobs (one full time, one part time, both waged), her two jobs (both part time, both waged), and day care arrangements for two small children. When the demands of coordination become too great, something has to give. Having more than one individual engaged in moonlighting may be a more common practice among bad job households than among good job households, but it is also an uncertain and rapidly changing one.

TRADING AS THE BAD JOB FAMILY'S
ENTREPRENEURIAL ACTIVITY

Although the members of bad job households cannot develop entrepreneurial moonlighting activities but are compelled, should they need that additional income, to find waged work, they do engage in a kind of "ersatz" entrepreneurial activity that we call "trading." Members of bad job households—and especially husbands in these households—buy and resell goods to generate extra cash.[27] Most of this is quite informal. Don Dwire, for example, offered this description:

> I buy and sell cars. I buy and sell anything I can sell to make money on. Cars, guns, motorcycles, whatever. I just drive along; if I see something I like I buy it. I don't usually pay that much for [anything I buy]. A couple of hundred dollars. A lot cheaper than that a lot of times.

His brother Matt said much the same thing:

> If I happen to come across a cheap car I try to pick it up and try to make money on it selling parts or the whole car, but again it's not something we count on. If it's there and we can make the money, a dollar on it, we'll try it.[28]

If the Dwire brothers actually make purchases solely for the purpose of resale, like other members of bad job households they occasionally find themselves in the situation where they have no option but to sell something originally acquired for household use. In bad job households, the ownership of expensive items like guns, snowmobiles, and boats is provisional.[29] Men and women alike recalled possessions that had been sold during hard economic times. (One woman even said that without moving the dishes from the table, her husband carried it out to the porch and then put a "for sale" sign on the "whole kit and caboodle.") Members of these families also explained that a failure to be able to engage in impulse buying was to them a measure of just how very hard times had become. After Sarah Hayes was laid off from her job at Wilson Contract Manufacturing, she commented on the ways in which her husband had been forced to cut back: "[Before] if my husband wanted to get a junk car and work on it, it was no problem, the money was there." Later in the interview, she emphasized that the buying of junk cars was a significant activity for her husband—but not one that had a positive economic value:

> Like I said, if he wanted an old car, to work on, he'd go and buy it. He'd work on it and end up selling it for less than what he paid for it. But . . . now . . . he doesn't go out every time he sees something that he likes and buy it.

Walt Seeley accepted with equanimity that he was better off not getting attached to worldly goods. When asked why he was selling the snowmobile displayed on his front lawn, Walt responded,

I could use the money more than I can the fun right now. I figure, I'm the type of guy that luxuries mean nothing to me. I can always sell a luxury today and when things get better tomorrow I'll buy another one. I'm not attached to anything.

In Chapter 5, we will argue that the pattern of economic activities available to bad job households has an effect on the dynamics of the household and on how men and women view themselves. What is most important at this point is that the "ersatz" entrepreneurial activity of trading stands in sharp contrast to the "real" entrepreneurial moonlighting done by individuals (albeit also mostly men) in good job households. Although the latter activities do not necessarily reap substantial earnings, they do *not* have the same kinds of negative consequences for the household.

MOONLIGHTING'S REWARDS

No matter what form it takes, moonlighting produces valued supplemental income. In good job households, the "extra" money is treated in a special way. Sometimes, as Jack Curtis suggested, it supports luxuries, or "extras": "[The lawn mowing is] more or less for extra things that we want to do—keeping a good car, things in the house, buying Christmas presents for grandchildren, things like that—things that we probably really couldn't do out of my everyday check." Even more commonly, because by consensual agreement income from moonlighting constitutes one spouse's discretionary spending money, it does not enter the general household accounting at all. The private uses to which it is put should not obscure moonlighting's economic significance for the family as a whole. Members of good job households use their on-the-side entrepreneurial activities as opportunities to build up a business that could provide the basis for self-employment down the line or act as protection against future unemployment.[30] Entrepreneurial moonlighting also represents a form of "saving." Even if deep investments preclude "profits," moonlighters acquire tools and equipment that embody a lifetime's work and that can be passed on to children or sold to pay off debts. Finally, the moonlighting activities of men and women in good job households often become the site for the creation of rich networks that, as we have shown, can be crucial when they go about their search for work.

The picture is quite different among bad job households. Quite sim-

ply—and quite obviously—in these households the income from moonlighting is needed to keep up with rising expenses:

JOAN CURRIER: When he started [moonlighting] that money was extra. [Now]
we use it to live on. . . . And when I started working that was extra and now
it's still extra but it's necessary every two weeks that I got that check to go pay
for certain bills or whatever and that's why I'm looking forward to starting this
other little part-time job answering phones three afternoons a week because
that's going to be a little extra cash.

PAUL CURRIER: The new extra.

JOAN CURRIER: Yes, the new extra.

Occasionally in these families as well, men and women hope to reserve
moonlighting income for discretionary spending, but equally often this
income *must* be directed toward meeting ongoing household needs.
Bruce Sharp initially claimed that money from his on-the-side work
snowplowing supported his "habit" of buying guns and motorcycles.
He also acknowledged that he spent some of that money to purchase a
kitchen stove when the hot plate they had been using broke down and
that he keeps some in reserve in case the furnace goes on the blink.
Because bad job households need moonlighting jobs to sustain a cash
flow, individuals in these households have to weigh carefully the costs
of moonlighting jobs (like the costs of their "regular" ones) against their
benefits. When the scale tips toward the former, they are quickly
dropped: "I [had a second job] last year. I worked at a pizza place just
for fun money. But it ended up I was spending more on gas than I was
really making so I quit." No piece of employment in bad job households
is stable and secure; because of the problems of coordination and cost,
the supplemental pieces that constitute moonlighting appear and disappear at an especially rapid clip.

This chapter has demonstrated how the character of the primary
worker's employment shapes the possibility that a household can initiate
and sustain income strategies that supplement that worker's earnings.
Not only is the capacity to support the dual-earner strategy directly tied
to the kind of employment held by the primary worker in both sets of
households, but among bad job households that fail to have a second
earner, moonlighting also becomes considerably more problematic. We
have also seen that neither the dual-earner strategy nor moonlighting
has the same meaning in the two sets of households. In good job households, the second worker is more profitable and moonlighting takes
place as an entrepreneurial activity. The stable and coherent income

activities of a good job household offer possibilities for personal enrichment. The sporadic income activities of bad job households, on the other hand, mesh less easily and often produce as much stress as satisfaction. These kinds of differences between the two sets of households are not limited to those activities through which they earn a living. As we will see in the next chapter, similar patterns are found among the nonincome components of their survival strategies.

CHAPTER 4

Making It at Home

It is easy to romanticize the nonmonetary aspects of a household's survival strategy. Most certainly, locally made products in more cosmopolitan markets trade off a sentimental vision of Vermont residents with sufficient resources at hand to "make do" on their own. It is this image of small-town life in which residents know each other, trade their products, and maintain their economic independence through their own nonmarket labor that lurks behind the popularity of Vermont's "niche" products. But all is not so simple. Indeed, Vermont families do engage in nonmarket activities, but whether they are able to do that and how, depends not on some traditional values incorporated into the "made in Vermont" seal but on where these families stand with respect to the formal, quite contemporary economy.

In this chapter, we abandon nostalgia for a close examination of how self-provisioning and nonmonetary interhousehold exchanges become elements in the household economy. The first half of this chapter describes self-provisioning, beginning with the more substantial form of this strategy—building or extensively renovating one's own home—and then turning to engagement in more routine activities such as changing the oil in the car or growing vegetables. The second half of the chapter examines nonmonetary exchanges between households. We thus turn from the household in isolation to its location in a community of family and friends.

SELF-PROVISIONING

SUBSTANTIAL SELF-PROVISIONING

Almost half (47 percent) of the more advantaged households we interviewed either had built their own homes or had recently engaged in *major* home improvements. In striking contrast, no household without a recent history of good work had done either of these.[1] What is it about households with at least one good job that enables them to engage in these activities? The answer is as self-evident as it is paradoxical: Self-provisioning consumes enormous resources before it can even begin to justify its expense.[2]

What is true of gardens and household repairs (and we will discuss these issues shortly) is even more the case for *major* construction projects.[3] The family must be able to negotiate zoning and building permits;[4] it must be able to make an initial investment for the purchase of land, equipment, and raw materials; and because home construction is a long-term project, its members must anticipate that they will *continue* to have secure incomes and the capacity to manage their own time.[5]

Take the example of Curt Shaw. Drawing on his savings from eleven years in the same good job at Sterling (and occasional on-the-side car repair), Curt purchased a lot and constructed a basement apartment on that site even before he and his wife, Colleen, were married. After he had carried her down—rather than across—the threshold, he got back to work. Slowly, he built the house above and around themselves—first the ground floor, then the garage and decks, and eventually the second floor as well:

> After a year in the basement we moved up here, this first level was done. . . .
> Well the garage came a year later. . . . Then after the garage was done we
> put the decks on. Then we still hadn't done the upstairs and we weren't in a
> big hurry for it because we had [our first child] in that room there. But then
> we wanted to have a second one. This was . . . two years ago or so. We
> started working on the upstairs little by little. . . . The upstairs is just done.
> We just had the carpets put in yesterday as a matter of fact. And this part's
> [*motioning to the area on the ground floor*] been done for four years.

In contrast to the assumption that self-provisioning can serve as a substitute for decent employment, the good job households engaged in long-term projects (much like families that want to buy a home) sometimes add a second worker to secure the necessary earnings. In this case, the second earner is a means to an end, a *consequence* of the desire to ensure home construction. Betty Hutton returned to work shortly after her son was born even though both she and her husband would have preferred the more "traditional" one-earner family: "I just found that we had bought this [land] and [we were working] on getting this house built so I had to go back to work to get that going." Colleen Shaw, who was already employed when she and her husband married, said that she held onto her job through three separate pregnancies because she relied on anticipated tax returns—her way of saving—to move on to the next building phase:

> See, what we started doing was every time we got income tax money back, that's what we'd do with the income tax money. I don't know how or why or whatever or however we were doing our W4's but we would get like $4,000 back every year. So it's quite a bit of money. . . . And then we had a baby in April which we lost . . . so we kind of put the upstairs off for a while. Then I got pregnant again so we had to work on it again. So then this year's income tax came around and that's just how it works. With income tax money.

Ironically, substantial self-provisioning (like engagement in an on-the-side entrepreneurial activity) not only depends on additional formal labor market activity but also requires having time that can be bracketed and defined as discretionary. With two earners, time becomes a valuable family resource. It is the ability to *control* that time which is so important in extensive self-provisioning. This is a privilege reserved to those who have at least some good employment and, as a consequence, do not have to resort to *waged* moonlighting or staggered work schedules.

Colleen Shaw told us that her husband worked all day at his job (as she did at hers) and then came home to put in another full "day's" work on the house "until eleven or twelve at night." Although he had previously spent some evening time on his side-work (car repairs for pay), he now dedicated it entirely to getting the house finished. Susan Drake said her husband followed much the same practice. Neither woman implied that domestic life was easy: Exhaustion and discouragement were ongoing features of their daily lives, and tempers often flared. The possibility for even these hard times, however, grew out of the family's attachment to *good* waged employment.

A number of bad job households had also engaged in substantial self-provisioning projects. On closer examination, however, these all turned out to be households that quite recently had been among those more fortunate but had since experienced downward mobility. They used resources generated from those earlier good times to accomplish home renovation projects. In the majority of these cases, and this is the important point, downward mobility brought these activities to a halt. Recall that the Riverses were unable to build a deck for which they had made extensive plans. Another woman said that after her husband lost his good job, they had to stop building for the future: "We still have the garage to do, but we can't do that at this point. We have mainly got to concentrate on taking care of bills right now." Others wondered whether they would be able to continue to enjoy the comforts for which they had saved and scrimped in the past: "I hope we don't lose the house. It's a great joy to us."

For most bad job households, these expensive (and profitable) self-provisioning activities are simply beyond reach. Even if, at a given time, they have an income sufficient to support such projects, unlike their more fortunate counterparts, bad job households cannot assume that their resources will remain adequate over the long haul. Even if, at a given time, the members of these households have sufficient time to devote to self-provisioning projects, these individuals know full well that a drop in income can send each of them scurrying to find new sources of earnings. Under these conditions, home construction disappears entirely and extensive home renovation transmutes into home repair. Enhancement turns into maintenance. When bad job families find themselves stretched in all directions, maintenance finally gives way as well. Good job households like those of the Huttons and the Shaws build their own homes and thus eventually live better than their wages would otherwise allow; bad job households like those of the Badgers and the Slaters purchase doors and windows to keep out the cold and repaint rotting wood, but the difference in their living conditions as a result of these maintenance activities is slight. A good job family like the Donahues can extensively renovate an old house and then rent out apartments; a bad job family like that of the Seeleys lives in one of those units, and (unless special arrangements are made whereby rent is reduced for maintenance[6]) they find activities of home improvement a simple drain on already limited resources of time and money.

ROUTINE SELF-PROVISIONING

With this understanding of *substantial* self-provisioning, we return to the patterns that give rise to the more ordinary activities of "routine" self-provisioning. Common as these activities are among good job households, they are even more common among bad job households: 23 percent of good job households but 39 percent of bad job households have high rates of routine self-provisioning. The difference between the two sets of households emerges most clearly with respect to the single activity of gathering wood for fuel: Bad job households are twice as likely as good job households to engage in a practice that, in a cold climate like that of Vermont, can ensure quite significant savings.[7] The story of the difference between the two sets of households does not end there. Within the two sets of households, self-provisioning takes place in different circumstances and rests on different preconditions.

Among good job households, routine self-provisioning sometimes competes with those substantial self-provisioning projects that are designed to improve their lives rather than simply to sustain them. Some good job families engage in a wide variety of projects, and some choose among alternatives. Some are generalists, and some specialize. When resources allow, some routine self-provisioning becomes altogether voluntary. Jack Curtis, for example, takes care of most of his car repair himself. From time to time, however, he hires a friend to do some of that work for him: "I change my own oil, I rotate my own tires and I change my own plugs and air filters and things such as that but I have [on occasion] hired a friend who knows how to do this stuff."

Like most choices, that of deciding how much self-provisioning to do is frequently conditioned by earlier decisions. Households engaged in large projects like home construction find it difficult simultaneously to pursue minor activities like growing vegetables. (When Colleen Shaw was asked about gardening, she gestured toward mud that would someday become a rolling, green lawn. "I can hardly grow lettuce there," she said.) Others clearly consider what they enjoy—and what they find worth their time and effort. Some individuals view hiring others as a well-earned recompense for a lifetime of hard work. Most good job families, however, hold on to at least some of these activities; as with home construction, they find therein rich rewards that extend beyond the material value of the finished products.

Because substantial self-provisioning is out of their reach, if individuals in bad job households are going to substitute their own labor for commodities, they can do so only through the more commonplace activities. As we showed in a previous chapter, among both sets of households, those with lower income engage in this kind of self-provisioning at a higher rate than do those with higher incomes. Indeed, household income is a *more* significant determinant of self-provisioning practices than household type (see Table 4). Among low-income households—whether those with good jobs or those with bad—necessity does not *invariably* create opportunity. Two other factors, each important in a different set of households, shape self-provisioning practices in a more definitive way than either income (within each group of households) or household type (within each income level). Among bad job households, the number of earners has a dramatic effect: The more earners, the more self-provisioning. Among good job households, the presence of moonlighting is more important: When there is moonlighting, self-provisioning is more likely.

Bad Job Households, Number of Earners, and Moonlighting   As in much of our story, there is a paradox in the finding that bad job households with two earners are more than twice as likely as bad job households with but a single earner to have high rates of self-provisioning (48 percent versus 21 percent). When these families fail to maintain the dual-earner strategy as an accessible, ongoing achievement, they are also unable to develop other tactics that might *substitute* for employment. What is clear is that the capacity to provide for oneself (by cutting one's own wood, for example) rests squarely on whatever else allows the maintenance of two workers in gainful employment and on what those two workers can contribute to these practices. Herein lies the catch—at least for bad job households. As we have seen, bad job households have a hard time establishing the conditions to generate that second worker. Paradoxically, then, there is now a "leisured" housewife (or sometimes househusband) in exactly the households that can least afford that "luxury."[8] Yet these housewives differ from those housewives described by Marxist feminists, whose unwaged labor subsidized the capitalist wage costs. Although the modern housewife may continue to be responsible for stretching the paycheck (by shopping at yard sales or in bargain basements for inexpensive clothing and household necessities) and although she may do the work of getting public assistance for her family, she can no longer use her time at home to engage in the productive labor of self-provisioning.[9]

   At first glance, then, it might appear that motivation and effort are significant issues. There are some families that, no matter how unfortunate in the labor market, are eager to use as much of their labor as possible to provide for themselves. In these households, not only do all the adults work for wages (albeit in bad jobs), but they are also willing to engage in substantial work at home to guarantee for themselves a decent standard of living. Then there are those other families that are unwilling to send everyone into the labor force and equally unwilling to convert that "leisure" into unpaid labor that would add to the comforts of the family. Nevertheless, on closer inspection this interpretation fades, replaced by a deeper and more profound understanding.

First, there is reason to believe that the second earner is not the direct cause of self-provisioning or even a reflection of an underlying motivation. Rather, having a second earner itself rests on the underlying preconditions that allow families simultaneously to use that labor in paid work *and* in self-provisioning projects. When these preconditions are absent, the family can do neither. Recall that in the previous chapter we saw that a set of conditions (e.g., having a second car, being close to a grandmother or neighbor who could watch the children for less than market costs, work schedules that permitted coordination, and being able to sustain geographical stability) stood behind the capacity of bad job households to allow at least one worker in a dual-earner bad job household to moonlight. The same set of preconditions underlies the propensity of bad job households to maintain a second earner and simultaneously to sustain high rates of self-provisioning.

Take, for example, the issue of what accompanies the privilege of geographical stability. Carla and Robert Griffin, discussed in Chapter 3, served as an example of how the dislocation of one worker unsettled the employment pattern of the second. They had to move, and that mobility interrupted self-provisioning efforts. Knowing that they were moving in the middle of the summer, Carla and Robert quite reasonably decided it made little sense either to plant a garden or to split wood for the following winter. Once settled back in Coolidge County, they hurried to restart a familiar round of self-provisioning projects. Matt and Patty Dwire had much the same kind of experience. As long as they were living with relatives, they could neither sustain two jobs nor begin alternative activities. Once Matt was established in his relatively long-term position and Patty in hers, the Dwires could anticipate making efforts to improve their situation. Matt said proudly:

> I am going to do everything that I can, like this weekend coming is my designated weekend to start painting the trim on the house and just whatever. We moved in late so I don't have a garden here this year but I am going to have a garden next year. Whatever I can do myself I am going to do.

As these examples suggest, whatever causes disruption in a household will have an increasingly negative effect. As the dual-earner strategy unravels, so does self-provisioning.[10]

When a bad job household has low earnings, it is highly "motivated" to cut corners, but it can do so effectively only when conditions also permit it to generate that second worker. Among bad job households with low incomes, 56 percent of those with a second worker have high rates of self-provisioning, in contrast with only 29 percent of low-income households without a second worker. (The number of earners is relevant to self-provisioning among those with high incomes as well: One-third of the households with high incomes and two earners have high rates of self-provisioning, in contrast with none of those with high incomes and but a single earner.[11]) Once again, there is good reason to believe that the limited economic strategy of bad job households rests on real constraints rather than the personal predilections of its members: When bad job households have both need *and* the necessary preconditions, they engage in routine self-provisioning at an extraordinarily high rate.

Second, extensive labor force attachment, as measured by the degree to which bad job households use a dual-earner strategy, has another, perhaps even more direct, link to the capacity of households to engage in self-provisioning projects—by providing access to job perks.[12] These perks are available to the employed members of both kinds of households. One man, as a result of his good employment (working for the State Highway Department), gets free wood:

> My husband works for the state, so when they cut trees down the guys are able to take [them] home. So if it's winter time—during the day when they don't have to plow the roads—they're cutting trees. So they've got a lot of trees and they just split it up for the different guys. [They] put it in the woodshed and they can bring it home.

Two men in bad jobs moonlight for a logger and thus also get free wood. So does a man employed as a caretaker for a large estate: "During the winter when we get bored with other stuff, we cut wood around the estate and [my boss] brought me down a couple of loads. That was cheap. I paid him for gas to bring it down and that was it." A man with a good job knows where and when his company throws away the wood pallets that make excellent kindling:

> He gets pallets from Sterling, that we both cut up out here. We have a little electric chain saw for that. . . . They throw them away. They stack them next to the dumpster waiting for the garbage man to take them, if the people don't take them.

A worker with a bad job in a grocery store can use the garbage thrown out at the end of the day to feed a pig being raised by a friend for half of the profits. Another works for a car repair shop and can use the shop's equipment to fix his own car; although he pays for these parts out of his take-home pay, he has access to essential tools:

> I've got a truck I just bought from my father-in-law for a couple of hundred dollars, and I'm getting it ready. I've got repairs. Luckily [my boss] lets me put the parts on account and then what he'll do is he'll take so much out of my pay. That's the only way I can afford to have another vehicle. I can't afford another vehicle. But I can't afford to be without it.

Because the members of good job families *can* afford alternatives to these perks, they play a lesser role in their self-provisioning efforts than they do among those with less adequate work. Those in bad jobs need these specific resources, even when their use competes with, rather than supplements, income: The mechanic who uses the store's "parts" to repair his own car jeopardizes his earnings. The more jobs held in the family, the higher the probability that these necessary perks will be available.

Because self-provisioning in a bad job family depends directly on a *specific* job, if that job is lost, self-provisioning vanishes as well. Rather than being a detached activity that enables survival in spite of bad work or even being an alternative to waged work, self-provisioning builds on employment, and the more employment, the better. It is this modern status of self-provisioning—not as a substitute for money income but as its companion—that produces a new kind of poverty, quite different from before. Bad jobs limit self-provisioning, and without the ability to engage in that activity, bad work households with but a single earner are even poorer than wage levels would suggest.

Good Job Households, Moonlighting, and Self-Provisioning   Among good job households, by way of contrast, self-provisioning is more likely to continue independently of the second earner.[13] However, the self-provisioning of more advantaged households is an outgrowth of their entrepreneurial moonlighting: 13 percent of good job households without a moonlighter had high rates of self-provisioning, in contrast with 43 percent of those in which there was a moonlighter. (By way of contrast, having a moonlighter was irrelevant among bad job households: 37 percent of households without a moonlighting worker and 42 percent of those with a moonlighting worker engaged in routine self-provisioning at a high rate.)

In good job households, most moonlighting is entrepreneurial in nature, and it depends on tools and equipment, the availability of which is a function of the advantaged position these households hold. Once those tools and equipment are at hand, the households produce marketable products and products for self-consumption. These arrangements exist regardless of income. Among good job households with low incomes, those with a moonlighter are two and a half times as likely to have high rates of self-provisioning as are those without a moonlighter (25 percent versus 10 percent); among those good job households with higher incomes, those with a moonlighter are four times as likely to have high rates of self-provisioning as are those without (32 percent versus 8 percent).[14]

Perhaps as important, self-provisioning may also serve as a justification for expenditures on this kind of capital equipment by making it serve household—as well as individual—purposes.[15] (Alternatively, but to the same end, an "indulgence" in the tools of self-provisioning might lead to an attempt to make money off this same equipment.) Thus, we are looking at a set of linked activities—entrepreneurial moonlighting joined with self-provisioning—the total of which is anchored in the household having at least one good job.

The benefits of a good job go far beyond that which is predicted by wages alone. The quality of life experienced by these families is denser and richer than that of those not so privileged. Nevertheless, it is both the side-work *and* the good job that constitute this extra benefit and not just the good job itself.

Bad job households do not have this privilege of turning income from moonlighting into optional practices, and the waged moonlighting activities of bad job households—working an evening shift in a pizza parlor, driving a truck for a cheese factory—do not create similar possibilities for "double dipping." Patty Dwire is highly unlikely to start making pizza at home; Don Dwire does not own the truck he uses for deliveries for the cheese factory, and he cannot (openly) haul wood in it.

THE VALUE OF SELF-PROVISIONING

Why do people work so hard at self-provisioning? The eventual savings that ensue are certainly one reason why the members of both kinds of families so extend their labor time. For those engaged in substantial self-provisioning projects, these savings *can* be immense. George Kemp calculated that his home "would have cost double" the $60,000 he spent if he had hired others to complete the work. George Cornell, looking proudly at part of his family's construction project, said "We raised the roof and I hired to do that. But *I* built the sun room and the deck and renovated pretty much the whole house. That's $20,000 to $30,000 saved."

Even so, households with good jobs and good incomes could, perhaps, forgo the extra savings and instead purchase the goods they produce for themselves; they are in a position to exchange wages for leisure, or in this case, self-produced goods for commodities. There is even some question whether self-provisioning always saves money: Some projects might, in fact, require tools and equipment that outweigh the benefits they reap (as was true of the finances surrounding a good deal of entrepreneurial moonlighting and even some second earners among the good job households).

There are two other benefits to self-provisioning beyond the value of its products, albeit not as easily calculated.[16] First, as we discuss further in Chapter 7, self-sufficiency secures a definition of self that is frequently undermined by an exclusive reliance on waged work. Second, and almost in contradiction to the first rationale, self-provisioning is also often a means whereby households tie themselves to, and forge alliances with, other households. When households exchange vegetables, tools, skills, and time, self-provisioning turns out to be a highly sociable endeavor rather than a solitary pursuit.

The members of bad job households also value savings, opportunities to enact self-sufficiency, and occasions to forge links with others, but both the balance among these motivations and the "size" of the rewards are different. Limited to routine activities, self-provisioning among bad job households carries smaller material and lesser "psychological" benefits. In this context, self-provisioning is compelled more by the need for its material rewards than by an interest in its intrinsic satisfactions. Rather than representing an *ability* to manage on one's own, self-provisioning becomes *having to* manage on one's own. In an already overburdened life, it can simply become an additional responsibility: "As far as myself, I never have any leisure. Neither of us does. . . . There's always something else to do, especially this time of year. Now it's canning vegetables. Tomorrow it will be something else."

In short, the nostalgic idea that workers with less than adequate wages can fend for themselves by patching together a life sustained by venison and homemade tomato sauce holds no truth for households whose terms of employment (even self-employment) methodically subvert the conditions under which deer can be hunted or a garden can be planted. In addition, workers with bad jobs are positioned differently from workers with good jobs with respect to the extent to which they can rely on those in other households to support them during hard times.

NONMONETARY HOUSEHOLD EXCHANGES

BARTER, INFORMAL EXCHANGE, AND REDUCED RATES

Good job and bad job households rely equally often on the members of other households to share goods and services like surplus vegetables or to offer a hand in changing the oil in the car.[17] We did not count the frequency with which household members received reduced rates from others for ongoing needs or bartered with others as an "informal" way to make transactions. The interviews reveal, however, that if not equally common, these exchanges occurred with some regularity within both kinds of households.[18] Similar as the practices appear on the surface, like many other strategies they actually differ depending on whether they take place in good job or bad job households. Three subtle yet profound differences in the conduct of these arrangements provide that contrast: the relationship between exchange practices and other aspects of the household survival strategy, the manner in which exchange relationships are established, and the risks attendant on making exchanges. These three differences are themselves interrelated.

Superficially, independence and interdependence appear to be in contradiction. At the very least, there is a contradiction in these separate moral stances or self-images: Individuals cannot simultaneously proclaim themselves to be entirely self-reliant and totally tied to others.[19] As practical approaches to the world as well, the two can compete: Obligations to others can impinge on and disrupt attempts to maintain one's position in society or to achieve upward mobility.[20] In practice, however, at least among good job households, these two aspects of household strategies often reinforce each other. For example, good job households with two earners are three times as likely as those with but a single earner to have high rates of interhousehold exchanges (55 percent versus 18 percent). The achievements of waged work, self-employment, and self-provisioning thus occur within the context of reciprocal exchanges; in fact, sometimes these achievements depend on and even serve to create that series of exchanges.

It is precisely the households one would least expect to add to their

burdens—the very busiest good work households with two earners and
one moonlighter—that most actively seek out interdependence: 62 percent of these households have high rates of exchange, and no other kind
of household has equally high levels of engagement in this practice.
These busy households vigorously opt for the acquisition of goods and
services through exchanges in which sociability is expressed rather than
through the more impersonal exchanges of the formal economy. A deep
reliance on wages (or other forms of income) has not made these informal kinds of arrangements disappear.[21]

These busiest households were also the most likely to be engaged in
substantial self-provisioning projects that carried with them, and indeed
often demanded, occasions for various kinds of interhousehold exchanges. Respondents explained how they relied on the availability of
less-than-market costs for the services of a friend or relative:

> [The house] was a contemporary which came like in two halves but all the
> inside, the painting and stuff like that, we did ourselves, and then the siding
> on the outside, my brother has his own construction company so that works
> out good, so he did that for us for less than it would cost.

Because they were likely to have at least one person with an on-the-side
entrepreneurial activity, the busy good job households were also well
positioned to engage in the more structured practice of barter:[22]

> The guy that built [the house] took firewood, he's a friend. And another
> friend that did the sheet rocking we paid him in money but he also took some
> of it in firewood. We bartered whenever we could.

In sum, the good work held by at least one family member enables
these households to initiate substantial self-provisioning projects and to
engage in entrepreneurial moonlighting; nonmonetary exchanges with
other households enable them to make flexible and cost-effective arrangements for the enactment of both tactics.[23]

When we turn to bad job households, something strikingly different
emerges. Among bad job households, the rate at which a family engages
in informal assistance varies neither with the number of earners nor its
members' participation in moonlighting. Moreover, among bad job
households, it appears that a choice must be made: either self-
provisioning or making exchanges with others. Among bad job households with low rates of self-provisioning, a slight majority (59 percent)
engaged actively in interhousehold exchanges, but very few (29 percent)
of bad job households with high rates of self-provisioning followed that

practice of sharing with other families. Whereas good job households increase the likelihood that they will have access to the resources of *other* households by becoming more productive themselves (and especially when they have two earners), the survival strategies of bad job households either do not have the same effect or, in the case of self-provisioning, have precisely the opposite effect. Bad job households protect their scarce resources of time and money by either self-provisioning or engaging in interhousehold exchanges; good job households have the luxury of being expansive with both.

Underlying these differences is the capacity of households to sustain exchanges that simultaneously serve economic and social ends. Good job households accomplish both goals with relative ease; they achieve a truly social economy.[24] Bad job households behave much more like conventional economics would predict: In their exchange relationships, the two goals often conflict.

Among good job households, exchange relationships take place in conjunction with self-employment and self-provisioning. Households that engage in nonmonetary exchanges (which, as noted above, is not the case among *all* good work households) solidify the relationships on which those other activities depend. When individuals wait long periods until they have paid off their debts or until their barter partners complete their obligations, the gap is filled by trust that simultaneously creates and reinforces the social bond.[25] Take the following example of two members of good job households who work in this way as they exchange the products of their entrepreneurial endeavors—fuel wood for truck repairs. Tom Hubbard described the arrangements in this way:

> All I did was just keep track of my hours on his vehicles, figuring, last year I was getting $20 an hour and every so often I'd just figure the hours and take it off the total of the wood [I got from my friend], that kind of thing until it was paid for and then we either went the other way. He would pay me or put it down as credits toward next year's wood, that kind of thing. It was whatever he wanted to do. Because it didn't really matter to me, I knew I had to get the wood anyway. So it didn't matter if he wanted to do it with credits or he wanted to pay me once we got done paying off for the last batch. And most of the time it's been just credits toward the next year's wood supply. I think it works out pretty well.

This reinforcement of relationships, like that between Tom and his friend, might not be possible if either party urgently needed to be paid in full. In that case, they might each need to settle accounts at the moment of exchange. If they relied on cash itself rather than bartered services, they would find themselves bound to the more impersonal norms of a market exchange, norms that might be disruptive to the friendship itself. Within the context of long-standing social relationships, however, a nonmonetary exchange (like barter) is the ongoing assumption of both parties because it serves them equally well.

The picture of nonmonetary exchanges is quite different in bad job households, which can rarely afford to wait for reimbursement while they build social ties. Nevertheless, barter is a common practice here as well, but rather than an occasion to build and reinforce friendships embedded in employment or self-provisioning projects, barter becomes the occasion simply (or not so simply) for goods and services to trade hands. Jeff Blair barters goods from his self-employment on the spur of the moment with, as he describes them, "a gentleman" and "a logger." His arrangements are short term and resolved on the spot. Unlike the long-standing relationships ensured when Tom Hubbard and Philip Menard exchange car repair for firewood, Jeff Blair's "deal" neither cements an existing friendship nor creates a new one:

> The gravel you see in the driveway was one thing I [bartered for]. The gentleman bought a saw and I said, "You give me $285 cash and you bring me two loads of gravel and you can take the saw." So basically what I was doing was getting my costs in cash and the profit was the driveway. But he didn't have to pay nearly as much for the gravel so it helps out both parties. I got my woodpile [through barter]. I said to a logger who was building his log truck to haul loads of wood, I said, "Do you have anything I got that you could use?" "Well, I could use some files." I said, "Okay, how many do you want?" . . . Thirty-six dozen is what it worked out to be. He told me a price on the wood—cash—and then I figured it out with my price with a discount and I said, "Well it comes up to thirty-six dozen." And he ended up saving himself $100 on the files and I ended up saving myself $100 on the wood so both parties went away happy. And I'm not opposed to doing that at all when I need something.

Members of bad job households believe in the same set of rules for nonmonetary exchanges as do members of good job households. Both groups understand that reciprocity should be a norm in informal exchanges, that reduced rates should be repaid with gratitude, and that fairness should prevail in barter. Because individuals in bad job households face more urgent needs, however, they cannot always abide by those rules. Bad job households with low incomes receive *less* assistance from others than do bad job households with high incomes. Greater economic pressure does not occasion greater assistance; in fact, it has just the reverse effect. Social relationships that are *secured* through exchange among good job households are *jeopardized* among those households that might need these relationships the most.

After too many demands have been placed on them, the members of other bad work households may be unwilling to contribute toward the welfare of those who fail to reciprocate. For example, Marshall Rondeau (bad job household) believed he had overextended himself in assisting family: "My sister has used us so hard in the last five years that it has gotten to me." Similarly, Matt Dwire (bad job household), as he tries to get his own life in order after years of casual employment, hopes to put a lid on the free assistance he offers his brother Jake (also a bad job household):

> I had it happen when they've asked enough. Just, I don't know, when you feel like you are being used. . . . I have a brother that lives right next door here. A couple of weeks ago we gave him a bill for a few services that he neglected to offer us any money for and since then he hasn't asked for too much. You hate to be that way but you can't. . . . He comes over to use our washing machine and our telephone. It all costs money.

Even if bad job households have good job households in their networks, the latter might be unwilling to share their resources with friends or family members who constitute only a drain. Kathy Hastings spoke bitterly about those in her extended family:

> We both have siblings that have sponged off parents for years and we don't think very much of it. . . . [They] don't ask us for help any more—they did at one time and when we didn't get it back we stopped. And they were very angry with us. They see that we have more than they do but they don't see how we got it.

Some bad job households recognize these potentials and protect their pride: They withdraw before others close the door on them. Others withdraw because they fear the consequences of entanglements.[26] Ellen and Charles Rivers described a history of deep connections to a broad community of family, friends, and neighbors. Now their economic situation is quite precarious, and they seem to be choosing isolation instead. Ellen denied feeling obligations to anybody (although she accepted the requirement to return a favor):[27]

INTERVIEWER: What do you think people owe their families?
ELLEN: I don't feel I have any obligation to anybody, really. When my sister has her baby in September, yuh she's watched my kids a lot, for me for no pay

or anything. Yes, I will return the favor to her. . . . But as far as owing anybody anything—no.

INTERVIEWER: How about neighbors and friends—the same thing?

ELLEN: Yuh, no I don't. Both Charles and I feel the same way about this—we don't really like to owe anybody anything including favors because they can always come back on you in a negative way. So, whenever things are done it's usually been an exchange for pay.

Others shift their networks so that they now rely more on family than friends.[28] Still others—especially younger bad job households—enter relationships of support with parents in which dependence is more socially (and personally) acceptable.

The good job households that participate in nonmonetary exchanges also do so on occasion to satisfy real needs. Some receive child care from friends or relatives for a reduced rate. Some make arrangements to barter for vital household requirements such as wood for heating or car repairs. Some rely regularly on a neighbor to plow their driveway or know they can count on a friend to bring over vegetables to fill the supper pot. Even when need compels, however, good job households exercise two forms of self-protection. First, whatever income the family relies on to meet its ongoing expenses—whether it is derived from waged work alone or from a combination of waged work and self-employment—remains untouched or unaffected by these practices.[29] Second, these practices remain associated primarily (albeit not exclusively) with activities of self-provisioning and often in pursuit of items that constitute luxuries.

Even with the accommodations of shifting alliances, the economic orientation that propels bad job households into these exchange relationships eclipses the protections that good job households make a strong priority. When individuals in bad job households engage in barter in conjunction with an activity on which the household relies for significant income (rather than in an activity which provides discretionary income), that practice can threaten household stability. Barter is not a straightforward substitute for transactions in a formally organized commodity market because individuals can never be certain that they will be able to depend on it for a specific purchase. Jeff Blair regularly tries to barter for the goods and services his family needs (gravel for the driveway, wood for heating purposes). He is successful only some of the time, and he cannot readily predict when those sometimes will be. Although barter eases the pressure to come up with cash, it does so at the cost of making the commodity flow entirely unpredictable.

This unpredictability compounds the stress of survival within bad work households. In fact, some individuals withdraw from barter arrangements (as from other kinds of nonmonetary exchanges) not just because they fear entrapment or assaults on their pride but also because they cannot manage uncertainty. Walt Seeley said,

I did [barter before], and it seemed like all of a sudden, you were down and you needed a job or you needed some money, some bills were coming, and everybody that you bartered with it was their turn to collect. They all wanted it at the same time. So I found it's better, you pay them, and they pay you. You start getting into that with too many people, eventually you're not making any money. You're spending too much time swapping.

Gerry and Sue Danyow made much the same point:

GERRY: Really to be honest with you I'd rather stay away from [barter]. It can get into a messy situation. . . . It doesn't put the money in the bank.

SUE: That's the problem, it doesn't pay bills. You have bills to pay and that doesn't pay bills.

GERRY: I'd rather have the cash, I'd rather have the money.

As used by good job households, nonmonetary exchanges meet significant needs: Reliance on an informal network of friends and family members helps in the construction of a life well worth living. Rather than being at odds with self-sufficiency, reciprocal exchanges complement it. The members of good job families can maintain balance in their networks and can carefully circumscribe the use to which they are put.

Nonmonetary exchanges also abet the survival of households that have to make do without the benefits of good work, but they cannot be counted on to do so. Each kind of exchange, in its own way, includes an element of unpredictability and the possibility that one's obligations will expand intolerably. In households that live close to the edge, nonmonetary household exchanges are especially problematic practices, hardly cause for nostalgic celebration.[30]

These practices can also rest on "luck" (the willing partner to the barter relationship, the family member or friend with the service that is needed, the parent [or child] with extra cash to tide one over). In a community undergoing rapid economic change, luck is an increasingly scarce commodity. When members of the older generation lose their jobs, assistance to their children dwindles. In Chapter 3, we described the job instability confronting the families of two sisters—Patricia Slater and Barbara Badger. Patricia and Barbara were each in the habit of relying heavily on their parents (for favors, a handout here or there, and, as we will see below, even housing). Now that their father has been laid off by Sterling, he can barely help himself, much less his children. In fact, he is calling in some of his chips as he struggles to set up his own business. In some families, a downward spiral into a new set of relationships means diminished resources.[31] As one member of a bad job family said,

> Brothers and sisters, they can take care of their selves, and we have to take care of ourself and they have to take care of their selves—*unless you got a rich family and everybody helps each other somehow. But [then] the money always comes back to the guy who gives it to you. In a poor family it don't.* (emphasis added)

Sentiment aside, interhousehold exchanges are not reliable substitutes for the traditional bases of economic security. They cannot be counted on to fill the gaps left by solid wages and secure benefits, and households with the greatest need often pay most heavily for relying on them.

LIVING WITH OTHERS

Studies of the Great Depression reveal that doubling up on housing was a common response to that economic crisis; in contemporary times as well, there is evidence that families join together during periods of economic stress.[32] Quite appropriately, Levitan and Feldman view this kind of "reconfiguring the constituency of the household to include non-family or extended family members" to be an extremely significant form of nonmonetary household support. Among our questionnaire respondents, this type of household reconfiguration not only was relatively rare but also was limited almost exclusively to bad job families.[33]

Some interview respondents in bad job households experienced a history of moving in with other families or of having others move in with them. Usually, that doubling up was the end point of a process: First someone lost a job, then someone lost housing. For example, since they were married four years ago, Barbara and Ernie Badger have had several intervals, amounting to a total of about eight months, during which they lived with one or the other's parents. The loss of employment figured heavily in the reason for this pattern:

> When we first got married we lived with my husband's parents, until we moved to Oklahoma, then we had our own apartment there. Then, when we came back we had to move back in with family because we didn't have jobs. So we lived with my parents for about six months, I would say. Then, we had an apartment and my husband had a job. Then, he got laid off from his job, slow economy, I guess and then we were back with family again. So, we

have been back and forth in the family. . . . In the long run, it really helped us because we had a chance to save up and get back into our own apartment, and pay off some bills. We didn't have a job for a while so they were really helping us out a lot. We'd get part-time jobs. . . . Actually, one time when we were out of work, my husband got called for jury duty, he was on jury duty most of the time he was without a job, so that helped us pitch in for food and expenses for our parents when we were living there.

Like the other exchange practices we have discussed, these arrangements have the potential for being enormously problematic. Barbara knows that her family would have suffered even more if they had not been able to turn to family; that knowledge does not relieve the remembered pain of overcrowding and unwanted advice:

> [Our parents] have always been there to help us, but it was hard for them. It was usually pretty crowded, because we would have one bedroom that the three of us were in, and all of our stuff that we needed to bring. It's stressful because parents are more involved and you have little fights and stuff, they are always trying to put in their two cents, so that's pretty hard.

Some respondents assumed formal obligations in lieu of free rent. Matt Dwire lived in housing provided by his in-laws in exchange for working for them at a time when he could find no other employment. His memories are no more positive than Barbara's. What originally seemed like a straightforward arrangement soon became considerably more burdensome:

> We moved into a house that Patty's father owns in Carterville. We lived down there for two and a half years. . . . The house in Carterville, he let us have it at reduced rent and I worked part-time for him in, like a family business. . . . I was involved with their exotic animals. They raise miniature donkeys and such. . . . I mostly worked on weekends. I helped do the weekend chores like cleaning the barn. I did do some feeding, but then the other responsibility was when they went away for a weekend we would do all the chores. Or like they would go away for a week at a time in the spring and we would have to do that. . . . It was hard. They say never rent from a family member. They expected more than what they told us when we moved in as far as work that should have been done. It was a real hassle because sometimes they would go at the last minute. I'd get out of work Friday afternoon and they would say, "We are leaving in an hour to go to New Hampshire. We'll be back tomorrow night." You know, then we're stuck there. If we had plans it was too bad. That didn't happen a lot but it did happen.[34]

Even more generous arrangements carry potential risks. Tiffany Farrell and her fiancé, for example, live in a trailer in her parents' backyard.

Although theoretically they are buying the trailer from her parents, they are benefiting from a flexible payment schedule:

> We pay my parents rent—sort of. We're supposed to pay them $100 a month. Sort of it ends up being paid off in work, sometimes it gets paid off in groceries or you know, it's nothing standard. Part of it we just take advantage of the fact that they're my parents.

If Tiffany openly accepts dependence (taking "advantage of the fact that they're my parents"), one man with whom we spoke found that "taking advantage" could go both ways. He and his wife lived in a trailer, and on the land, owned by his in-laws. He recalled that even though there were no stated obligations, because it was "their trailer, their property," unstated expectations were numerous: "It was basically if they needed a hand they'd holler. It was just part of the farm."

The findings about self-provisioning and interhousehold exchanges lend depth and texture to the conclusions drawn from the investigation of income activities, especially with respect to the issues of the cumulative advantage of good job households and its contrast, the cumulative disadvantage of bad job households. Among the former, both substantial self-provisioning and interhousehold exchanges build on and even reinforce the dual-earner strategy and moonlighting. Good job households do not have to make choices among competing alternatives because the various components of the survival strategy articulate well. Although bad job households with two earners are more likely to have a moonlighter and high rates of self-provisioning, those that engage in the latter practice cannot count on social exchanges. As is true among good job households, certain components of the survival strategy are found together among those less fortunate: Both moonlighting and self-provisioning are more common when the household has two earners. Rather than suggesting interdependence between these aspects of the survival strategy, these links emerge from access to underlying resources that bad job households find it hard to secure. In the absence of these resources, bad job households are often forced to make choices among conflicting options.

Although we have emphasized the issue of conflicting priorities among bad job households, we do not mean to imply that they alone have to make choices. As we turn to the internal dynamics of households, we will see that many of the practices in good job households are sustained even though they benefit some members rather than others.

Just as good job households can easily sustain collective practices, so too can they absorb the different goals of husbands and wives. Among bad job households, where making choices about collective goals is itself more problematic, the attempt to meet individual goals has more devastating consequences.

CHAPTER 5

Gendering Strategies

In the previous chapters, we described how households in Coolidge County responded to significant changes in the economy of the region in which they lived. Quite simply, our task was to explain how a degradation of jobs, one hallmark of the restructured economy, affected the survival strategies of these families. Thus, for the most part we ignored the way that men and women are differently attached both to the restructured labor force and to the less formal components of the family survival strategy. We also slighted the reality that because of those differences, men and women (or, more accurately, husbands and wives) have unequal privileges and burdens as well as competing goals and interests. In short, we ignored the vital question of whether, and how, gender is constituted *within* the household in an area undergoing economic change.

Now it is time to rectify that omission.

Because women's lower status *in the family* has often been explained on the basis of their relatively marginal status in the workplace,[1] it is frequently assumed that a change in women's position in the labor force will have a measurable effect on gender relations inside households. What we found was a much less straightforward scenario—one that takes into account both labor force participation and the other kinds of efforts families make in putting together their survival strategies.

In both sets of households, gender differences and gender hierarchies are sustained, but they are sustained on grounds considerably different, and considerably more complicated, than the conventional models would suggest. Moreover, depending on the fortunes of the families in question—whether they have a hold on at least one decent job or not—gendered relations are enacted on different grounds and require very different kinds of vigilance in order to be constantly secured.[2] Although they never completely disappear, what they take to be maintained and the price of that maintenance are considerably different depending on where these families find themselves in the broader economy.

GOOD WORK HOUSEHOLDS

At first glance, gender appears to rest on a fairly traditional base of male superiority in the labor force among good job households. In approximately half of these families, husbands can rely on better-quality work than their wives, even when those wives also work full time (Table 8, section B). Many men can also count on usual patterns of sex segregation in the workplace to provide them with jobs that are decidedly dissimilar to those of their wives. To take one of many examples, Molly and Dick Collins both work full time at the Sterling Aeronautical Company. Molly is an administrative assistant, and Dick is a craftsman.

The formal labor force participation of wives undercuts these sorts of "conventional" supports for gender. Most good job households do rely on a dual-earner strategy. In 71 percent of these households, both husbands and wives work full time (see Table 8, section C).[3] In 59 percent of the households, husbands and wives have approximately equal hourly earnings, and in 71 percent their earnings are valued equally by family members (Table 8, sections D and E). Moreover, this erosion of gender props has occurred *not* because the workforce engagement of men has shifted (most men in good job households have stable, full-time employment; 76 percent have good jobs) but because their wives have also begun to develop their own stable, full-time work histories (38 percent of women in good job households have good jobs themselves).

If the "normal" underpinnings of gender have been eroded, members of these households have found ways to replace them with other structural supports. Rather than employment in the formal labor force alone, it is the full range of household survival strategies that plays a central role in regaining for men whatever status they might have lost when their wives went to work—but only among good job households.

In good job households, men are almost twice as likely as are women (25 percent versus 15 percent) to moonlight, but the difference between

TABLE 8. HOUSEHOLD CONFIGURATIONS:
Comparisons of Husbands and Wives

HOUSEHOLD CONFIGURATION	GOOD JOB HOUSEHOLDS	BAD JOB HOUSEHOLDS
A. Comparative employment patterns (all households)*		
Households with only men working	9%	28%
Households with only women working	3%	6%
Dual-earner households	87%	67%
Total	100%	100%
Total N	86	72
B. Comparative quality of employment (dual-earner households with both in full-time employment)		
Men have better quality work than women	53%	31%
Women have better quality work than men	26%	27%
Men and women have equal quality work	21%	42%
Total	100%	100%
Total N	53	19
C. Comparative intensity of employment (dual-earner households only)*		
Only men work full time (women part time)	24%	29%
Only women work full time (men part time)	5%	10%
Both work full time	71%	40%
Both work part time	0%	21%
Total	100%	100%
Total N	75	45
D. Comparative wages (dual-earner households only)*		
Men earn more than women	37%	32%
Women earn more than men	4%	30%
Men and women earn same wages	59%	39%
Total	100%	100%
Total N	72	44
E. Comparative valuation of earnings (dual-earner households only)		
Men's wages are considered more important than women's	24%	25%
Women's wages are considered more important than men's	4%	6%
Women and men's wages are considered equally important	71%	70%
Total	100%	100%
Total N	75	48

*Differences between good job and bad job households are significant at the .05 level or higher.

men and women in rates is only part of the moonlighting story. As we saw in Chapter 3, individuals in good job families generally moonlight in order to engage in entrepreneurial activities, while the moonlighting among individuals in bad job families is almost always just more waged employment. The "extra" work taken on by men in good job households sets them off not only from men in bad job families (to which we will return below) but also from their wives.

In good job households, women who moonlight are less inclined to do so through an engagement in an entrepreneurial business than are their husbands (39 percent versus 52 percent). Moreover, when they do, their pattern of activity is quite different from that of their husbands in several ways.

First, on closer inspection, at least some of *women's* entrepreneurial moonlighting activities (and this is true of the few women in bad job households with this kind of work as well) turns out not to be genuine self-employment but an engagement in commission selling for programs like Tupperware and Amway. These programs restrict women's earnings to in-kind discount purchases.[4] Darlene Hubbard, who held down a full-time job at the Sterling Aeronautical Company, explained how her moonlighting worked:

> And Christmas time I do toy parties to bring in [extra income] . . . friendly home toy parties. Depending on how much stuff you sell, you get a percentage for toys for the kids. . . . The majority of my stuff comes from there.

By way of contrast, the entrepreneurial moonlighting activities of men are under their ownership, and they more often result in unrestricted income. This difference is crucial. Men's entrepreneurial moonlighting provides access to cash; women's activities, on the other hand, replicate their already highly gendered activity of "keeping the bills down." Whether they actually do so in fact, men's activities *appear* to expand the family's horizon; women's merely meet it.[5]

Second, the content of *entrepreneurial* moonlighting (like the content of self-employment generally) remains deeply differentiated by gender. Men and women who develop entrepreneurial moonlighting activities draw on the skills they have acquired over the course of a lifetime— from vocational education, from jobs, and from their parents and their peer groups. Each of these facets of men's and women's lives confers different skills. Men learn how to make machines work and how to repair those machines when they fail to operate as they should; women learn how to use (some of) these machines (they sew and knit), but they do not repair them for pay.[6]

Third, because entrepreneurial moonlighting among men in good job households often entails subcontracting with formally organized private and public enterprises, there is the strong guarantee of a steady flow of work in spite of that work's "informality." Even when men do not have contracted work, the jobs done by them (e.g., car repair, snowplowing, and lawn mowing) are in high demand in Coolidge County. Thus, men not only have reason to justify the enormous capital investments their businesses require but also can be certain of generating a substantial cash income on a steady basis. Women can be less certain of securing a profit because they sell goods and services (e.g., handicrafts) for which there is less of an ongoing demand; they thus have less reason to make deep investments in their activities.

In good work families, by consensual agreement, husbands and wives enjoy the rewards of their own entrepreneurial activities. They are each free to use that "extra" money to further their individual goals (including reinvesting in the business if they so choose). As one man said, "The money I earn from doing car repairs [on the side] is *my* money." One woman spoke similarly about the income from her side-work: "That's my *play* money." Even if each spouse has the same attitude toward this extra money, as a consequence of the differences discussed above, husbands have access to a substantial discretionary income to spend as they wish.[7] In contrast, women are less likely to have an entrepreneurial activity at all; if they do, their earnings are usually quite small. In addition, as noted, when that activity takes the form of commission sales, women have limited choices. As Darlene Hubbard suggested, toy parties promise "a percentage for toys for the kids" rather than an income that can be turned to her own personal needs.

In addition, men's after-hours businesses articulate with domestic life in a way that guarantees their relative freedom and even, on occasion, control over women's labor. These activities are almost always physically separated from domestic life, even if this means no more than a business carried on in the attached garage. Even more striking, these on-the-side businesses frequently demand the contributions of a wife, who is called on to answer phone calls, take orders, and wait for supplies to be delivered. George Kemp, who worked in his on-the-side welding shop during the day, tried to secure his wife's labor:

> I told her [it wasn't worth it for her to work outside the home] and we tried to—I tried to get her to work in the shop here and I said, "Well you do all

my running for me and try to do that stuff." That didn't work out. She had cabin fever. She had to get out and be with people.

By way of contrast, when women do develop an entrepreneurial business, their activities more often keep them at home and subject to the incursions of family members. But they rarely require men's labor.[8] Hence, even when women do find the time to develop side-work, that work carries relatively small benefits.

Molly and Dick Collins can illustrate these gender differences within a single household. As we noted above, Molly and Dick both hold down full-time (but quite different) jobs in the same firm. Although Molly has the greater prestige of being a salaried worker, Dick's hourly pay adds up to a higher income (especially when he opts for overtime). Together, they earn approximately $50,000 from these two jobs alone, but they do not stop there: Each has entrepreneurial side-work as well. Molly knits sweaters, and Dick does body work on cars in their attached garage. Molly recently bought a new knitting machine, and Dick owns a wide array of expensive tools. Dick's investments overshadow Molly's ($3,000 versus $750). He also reaps larger profits. Each year, Dick earns $5,000 to $6,000 "extra." Over the course of the previous twelve months, Molly earned about $400, more than three-quarters of which immediately went toward the loan on the knitting machine itself; in fact, because she also spent $400 on yarn, she was operating at an overall deficit. As she says, "You find with craft-type things you can't make the kind of money that you make on other things."

Like many women who do "craft-type things," Molly produces her finished goods and then seeks a market for them (either at craft fairs or through the casual interest of workplace colleagues). In contrast, Dick responds to a pre-existing demand: "He handpicks [his clients] basically. Well, most of his customers come from work, word of mouth, and of course there's a lot of people there." Dick renovated the garage to provide himself with a workplace that is entirely separate from the rest of the house. Molly uses the guest room as her work space. While we were speaking together, we were interrupted three times as Molly fielded phone calls about Dick's business.

Although on-the-side activities are a function of opportunity, skill, and necessity, there is strong reason to believe that they also function explicitly to restore eroded gender props in good job households. Two pieces of evidence point in this direction. In those dual-earner good job households in which wives have full-time jobs, husbands are almost seven times as likely to have entrepreneurial side-work as they are in those dual-earner good job households where wives only work part time. (Put differently, 88 percent of men's moonlighting in dual-earner house-holds occurs when their wives work full time and only the remaining 12 percent when their wives work part time.) More striking still, and equally paradoxical, among households in which both husband and wife are employed and both work full time, men are more than twice as likely to work two jobs when their wives have employment that is as good (in quality) as theirs than when their work is better than that of their wives.[9] (Put differently again, two-thirds of men's moonlighting in dual-earner families with two full-time workers occurs when women's work is equal or better in quality to that of their husbands and the remaining one-third when wives have work of lesser quality.)

In short, these patterns clearly indicate that moonlighting among hus-bands in households with access to decent primary employment can be a way of "righting" the balance between themselves and their wives when the employment of their wives threatens a kind of rough equality. Once these husbands develop on-the-side businesses, they get a kind of hegemony vis-à-vis their families that they may not otherwise claim. The privileges associated with being a husband—long thought to be a func-tion of being the only, or at least the main, breadwinner—are recreated not through their principal jobs but through their side-work.

Of course, not all good job households have an individual engaged in moonlighting. Others engage in substantial self-provisioning. The vast majority (82 percent) of good job households in the snowball sample included either moonlighting among men or substantial self-provisioning; often they included both. Like moonlighting, self-provisioning is equally relevant to the recreation of gender.

With the exception of gardening, the kinds of self-provisioning that previously had been women's province have been all but eliminated in favor of market commodities, while the substantial self-provisioning that is unique to good job households and the routine self-provisioning that is common among both kinds of households turn out to be male preserves (see Chapter 2). Even if self-provisioning does not always pay off in objective rewards, like on-the-side entrepreneurial activity, it gives men special opportunities to enact a customary gender role. This is so for two reasons that extend beyond the "mere" fact that these practices secure opportunities for men to engage in activities that have been coded "male." First, self-provisioning offers men opportunities to work with other men and thereby to build up their networks of solidarity; these networks often reinforce a traditional masculinity.[10] Second, self-

provisioning involves tools and equipment that appear to be of particular *symbolic* importance among rural men—a pickup truck, a John
Deere tractor, a chain saw. In fact, many men focus as much on the tools
they have acquired as they do on the savings they reap in self-
provisioning. When Eric Donahue talks about gathering wood for fuel,
for example, he first explains the process, then he gloats about his equipment: "We got [the wood] cut and delivered in blocks for the same price
we get log lengths. We just had to split it and stack it. I have all that
equipment too. I have chain saws, tractors, handsaws, trucks . . . I have
it all." (His listing is interrupted by his wife, who calls his equipment
his "toys." In this way, perhaps, Lois Donahue reveals her interest in
subverting the gender hierarchy Eric believes he creates through his self-
provisioning efforts.) Much like entrepreneurial moonlighting itself,
these symbols—the tractor, the chain saw—might be especially important when women's paid employment threatens men's preeminence in
the household. (While all men may have similar payoffs from these symbols, it is only men in households privileged with good jobs who can
find a legitimate justification for purchasing them.)

Moreover, by virtue of their special skills, men often took leadership
in large-scale self-provisioning projects and required that their wives
"work" for them.[11] This requirement, even if it resulted in an opportunity for wives to expand their own range of skills, also resulted in occasions when they were instructed, and criticized, by their husbands.
When Susan Drake was asked whether she had the appropriate skills
before they started their home construction project, she said:

> No and I still don't [have those skills]. [My husband] will tell you that. It
> was mostly, "Here hold this board." And I used the nail gun and got yelled
> at for not doing it quite right. It was mostly when he needed another hand.
> I think anybody can lift a beam and put it here and that kind of stuff. He
> didn't allow me to do any [trim work]. He did every bit of the trim work
> himself, because he didn't trust anybody else to do it the way he wanted it
> done. So I was allowed to help him cut boards and sand the rosettes and do
> some staining, but that was about it.

As we saw earlier, there is yet another possibility to improve the
household situation that apparently is available to both kinds of families. Both good and bad job household members engage in a range of
nonmonetary exchanges with the members of other households. Here
too, much like entrepreneurial activity and self-provisioning, gender
shapes who does what: Men barter, women don't. Men and women
participate differently in casual exchanges: Men assist others by engag-

ing in time-limited, concrete tasks; women do more of the caregiving work that extends over weeks, or even months and years.

To some extent, the roots of these patterns can be found within the other aspects of the survival strategies of households. We turn to barter first. In general, individuals barter goods and services produced in self-employment. Because men have more self-employment than do women (21 percent versus 16 percent), they are better "positioned" to engage in this practice of barter. Although husbands have more self-employment than their wives in both sets of households, among men in good job households this self-employment comes in the form of moonlighting: Two-thirds of the self-employment among good job men occurred as on-the-side work. This pattern can be contrasted not just with that found among men in bad job households (where only one-third of self-employment was on the side) but also with patterns among women in good job families (where, as well, only one-third of *their* self-employment was on the side). The difference is crucial for how the work is treated inside the family. As a rule, family members are reluctant to interfere with earnings from their principal jobs—these belong to the household as a whole. On the other hand, recall that in good job households people indicated that, as an agreed on practice within their families, the earnings from moonlighting constituted an individual's discretionary and personal income. Hence, among the good job households, men more often than women find themselves with the freedom to turn to barter; women, more often, have to turn their self-employment earnings over to the household unit—in cash.

For example, compare Ellen Woodward with her husband, Frank. Both Ellen and Frank have income from self-employment. Ellen's self-employment constitutes her principal job (she is a family day care provider), whereas Frank's self-employment takes the form of occasional on-the-side plumbing jobs (a skill acquired through training paid for by his employer). Ellen's income from day care regularly figures into the family budget, and she is reluctant to take it in the form of barter; Frank's income from plumbing jobs constitutes his "spending money," and he is free to take it however he chooses.[12] Men in bad job households are more likely to be in the same position as Ellen. They cannot engage in barter without risking the security of the family's income; when they do so, they are not adding new responsibilities to the ones they already have but instead transforming those that are already in place.

The gendered patterns of caregiving are also partly the consequence of different patterns of labor force involvement. Women who work part

time or are out of the labor force altogether are especially likely to be
drawn into obligations of caregiving.[13] Alice Desrosiers spoke about the
obligations to the extended family that flourished when she was unemployed: "My husband's grandparents used to [need help] and of
course with my being at home, I was the one chosen. Of course it was
my choice—but I was the one chosen to go and check on them and make
sure they got their meals and stuff." Jennie Smith works outside the
home full time, and she too ends up doing the ongoing work of trans-
porting her mother-in-law to doctor appointments and buying her groceries. As Alice's comments and Jennie's experience make clear, these
patterns are not *just* a matter of availability—or of free choice—but
rather rest on gendered expectations about the kind of help it is appropriate to ask for from men and women and the kind of help men and
women are obligated to offer.

There is yet a third set of gender differences that has to do both with
the balance between barter and casual reciprocity and with the kinds of
activities that become elements of each type of exchange. As has been
noted frequently, women's skills are often "naturalized." This "naturalization" affects women's pay in the global economy. It also affects
women's "pay" in interhousehold exchanges. Even when they are highly
developed, women's abilities are not regarded as real skills to which a
price can be—or should be—attached. This is especially true of babysitting—a skill that (because it is perceived as available to all women)
is not considered a skill at all.[14] Hence, babysitting is "traded" or
"swapped." It is never referred to as barter among individuals bound
by social ties. Sandra Peters is a highly skilled woman who had risen far
within the manufacturing firm in which she was employed. After she
had described her husband's deep involvement in barter, she was asked
whether she did any bartering herself. She responded, "No. I was just
thinking. . . . I guess I don't feel I have any real skills to bargain with.
Babysitting we trade back and forth."

Although this difference might appear to be just a matter of terminology—exchanging like for like being called trading or swapping, and
exchanging unlike for unlike being called barter—there is more to it
than that. The exchange of these services among women is incorporated
into casual reciprocity rather than the more explicit and carefully delin-
eated procedures of barter *even when* these services constitute a means
whereby women earn a living (or part of that living). That is, women
are expected more often than are men to engage in an easygoing give
and take with respect to the provision of goods and services for which

they might otherwise be paid. Whereas men are "allowed" to charge a fee for their skills (and even to collect that fee from friends and relatives), women are "encouraged" to exchange these skills in the gift economy.[15] Many women who knew how to sew and knit (and even those who had an entrepreneurial moonlighting business that developed from that skill) suggested that they rarely bartered their products, but that they did give them to others as gifts.[16] Molly Collins, for example, spoke about the seasonal variation in the effort she devoted to her on-the-side knitting business and the fact that she often spent much of that time on gift preparation for friends and family members: "I get real busy in the fall because I do a lot of stuff for Christmas [gifts]." Barbara Lattrell, who did sewing on the side as her entrepreneurial activity, made the dresses for her niece's wedding for free:

INTERVIEWER: Did you help out with your niece's wedding?
BARBARA: I made all the dresses.
INTERVIEWER: You didn't get paid for that though?
BARBARA: No. That was her wedding present. Many hours of hand sewing.

Like women who engage in commission sales programs, women save their households enormous amounts of money through these practices. In the process, they also significantly reduce their *own* "earnings." When the labor of self-employment is given away as a form of sociable exchange, it reinforces gendered patterns of women as gift-givers rather than women as workers whose activities constitute a crucial aspect of household survival and thus deserve to be subject to close protection.

In sum, good job households are almost invariably dual-earner households, and in these households women's employment is decidedly *not* marginal. Even so, gender is recreated there. That recreation stems not only from men's superior (and different) employment—a preeminence which is fast disappearing in a good portion of these households—but also from the different ways in which men and women participate in the full range of survival tactics. Men have more moonlighting than do women, and that moonlighting accords special benefits of autonomy and income. Men also are more fully engaged in self-provisioning efforts and thus experience special opportunities to define themselves in traditionally masculine ways. Both of these latter activities offer occasions on which men can control the labor of their wives. Women too may engage in moonlighting and self-provisioning, but they derive fewer benefits and less autonomy. Differences between men and women also emerge from the nature of the obligations generated in interhousehold exchanges. Men develop concrete, time-limited obligations; women develop more amorphous ties of sociability and more expansive commitments to caregiving. There is also a different valuation placed on the work of men and women in these exchanges: Men's work is equated with market values even when it doesn't really function in the market at all but rather is part of a social economy; women's work is "naturalized," and its market value is slighted.[17]

All these differences have surprising consequences for household hierarchy. On one hand, men are even more constrained than are women. In addition to their "regular" jobs, they engage in a broad variety of activities over which—from time to time—they have very little control; they have a wide range of clearly stated obligations they must fulfill. On the other hand, as we will see in the next chapter, these constraints provide men with autonomy vis-à-vis the household itself.

BAD WORK HOUSEHOLDS

Gender—as both difference and hierarchy—rests on a shakier foundation in bad job households than it does in good job households. Although bad job households are less likely than good job households to assume the dual-earner form, the majority of them do so as well. Within these bad job dual-earner families, the basis for a gender hierarchy is even less sturdy than it is among the comparable dual-earner good job households. First, even though in both sets of households men are equally likely to be the primary worker, there is a significant difference in how that status is achieved. In the dual-earner *good job* households, two-thirds of men who are the primary worker in their families arrive at that designation by having better employment than their wives. Among the dual-earner *bad job* households, two-thirds of husbands are primary workers only because they are employed full time while their wives hold down but a part-time job. Second, there is a greater equality in the earnings of husbands and wives in bad job families. Among bad job families, those in which women have higher earnings are as common as those in which men do. This is in sharp contrast to the situation found in good job households, where almost no women earn wages higher than those of their husbands (Table 8, section D).

Finally, because bad jobs are not as sex segregated as good jobs— consider the workers behind the counter at any McDonald's—in households that rely on those bad jobs alone, men may be unable to find a basis for claiming difference. In fact, some men we interviewed could find work only in occupations that are highly feminized and where they worked side by side with women (e.g., electronics manufacturing[18]), and some women could find work only in occupations that were predominantly male and where they worked side by side with men (e.g., farm work[19]). Recall that Jake Dwire worked at Wilson Contract Manufacturing, where the workforce was 80 percent female, and that his sister had been employed there as well, as was his sister-in-law. Some couples even worked side by side. For example, Laura Manning and her husband had shifted jobs together:

> I had one or two other jobs and then I went to a place in Carterville. I worked there for nine years, . . . and that's where I met my husband. . . . They made ski racks, ski poles, things like that. . . . When I left [the pay] was a little over $6 an hour. My husband and I just saw that there was no room for advancement . . . so we tried to find something [else]. We did go to another place but that didn't work out too well. . . . We worked there only a few months.

Similarly, Lester and Dolly Keating both did the same production work in the same place for some time. This kind of blurring of gender is part of what makes already degraded work feel even more degraded.[20]

In short, in dual-earner bad work households, several of the structural bases for gendered relationships dissolve at a much more dramatic rate than in good job households. First, in bad job households, when husbands do have "better" work than their wives, all too often this rests on the number of hours they put in rather than on the nature of their jobs. Second, in contrast to the situation in good job households, husbands are no more likely to earn the higher wage than are their wives. Third, in their places of employment, at least some of these men work in settings where gender distinctions are erased. Finally, although in both sets of households there is often a rough equality in the work hours of men and women, in good job households the relative similarity of men and women is often an effect of both having full-time work; in bad job households, that similarity more often results from the fact that each partner can find only a part-time job (see Table 8, section C). Not only have men lost status vis-à-vis their wives in bad job households, but this also occurs in conjunction with the degradation of the quality of their own work. Moreover, what status men in bad job households retain often depends on a degradation in the quality of employment of their wives.

To understand this point more fully, let us turn to the substantial minority of bad job households that have but a single earner. (We will then return to women's employment in dual-earner families.) In most of these single-earner bad job households, that single earner is a man (see Table 8, section A). Thus, for almost one-third (28 percent) of all bad job households, gender appears to rest on a quite traditional basis: Men are breadwinners; women are housewives.[21] These single-earner bad job households, even if they bear a formal similarity to the Fordist household of the past, are actually quite different. Husbands are not earning family wages, and the single-earner strategy itself is often forced by circumstance.[22] Moreover, there is reason to believe that male privilege, rather than male "superiority" in employment opportunities, determines that the man will be the one who remains in the labor force (when only one person can keep a job).[23]

Nevertheless, no matter what the differences are *between* the two sets of households, we found no consistent difference in patterns in the attitudes expressed about women working. In both sets, some husbands minimize the importance of the work done by their wives and define themselves as the family breadwinner; in both sets, some husbands clearly acknowledge the importance of their wives' wages.[24] Although women in both sets of households sometimes reject disparagement, in both sets women occasionally collude in this degradation of their work, defining it in the same trivial terms as do their husbands. (Recall, for example, Lois Donahue, who referred to her job as "a real borderline thing.")

If the members of bad job and good job families hold a similar range of *attitudes* toward women's work, there are significant differences in the patterns of accommodation women in the two kinds of households make with respect to holding a job itself and with respect to the nature of employment when it occurs. We have noted that among bad job households, wives are likely to earn wages higher than their husbands as often as husbands earn higher wages than their wives. This equality between husbands and wives in dual-earner families might result from the selective employment of only those women who can secure relatively good wages: When their wages are relatively high, they are sent into the labor force; when their earnings are minimal, they are kept out. There is reason to believe, however, that the picture is not so simple and that women rather than men remain without gainful employment (when the family is not in the position to follow a dual-earner strategy) even when women might have better employment possibilities. That is, there is good reason to believe that how the economic value of men's versus women's employment is calculated does not always follow a straightforward logic.

Take the Huber family as an example. Three years before we interviewed her, Julie Huber was working full time. She enjoyed her job, the time away from home, and the fact that she was making what that family considered a substantial income. In fact, her earnings were twice those of her husband. But she and her husband, Randy, believed her job cost the family too much. After deducting child care expenses, her earnings appeared considerably less substantial; after subtracting the cost of gas and the time her husband spent driving Julie to and from her workplace (they only had one car, and it was considered Randy's), her earnings evaporated. Moreover, Julie said Randy felt threatened by the fact that she had better employment than he did: "He didn't like it that I was making more than him." After several months, they decided that it would be more sensible if just one remained at work. It was Randy. Other couples in bad work households said the same thing. When it was a choice between jobs, the husband's took priority.

Although the objective reality was that it was no more costly in monetary terms for Randy to give up his job instead of Julie—indeed, in this case, it would have been less costly—there were clearly other considerations. In the absence of the status conferred by good work, Randy's only source of privilege was the assertion that he rather than his wife was the breadwinner. The causal connection between work and status was reversed. Rather than work conferring gendered status, as it does in good work households, in bad job households gendered status shaped who would work. Pleck found the same pattern:

> Linking the breadwinner role to masculinity . . . means that women must not be allowed to hold paid work. For the large majority of men who accept dehumanizing jobs only because having a job validates their roles as family breadwinner, their wives' taking paid work takes away from them the major and often only ways they have of experiencing themselves as having work.[25]

Women in good job households also assess the costs of child care and transportation against the earnings from *their* employment,[26] but in good job households, the "status cost" of work can be more easily absorbed. No woman in a good job household said that she sacrificed an employment opportunity because her husband felt threatened by her working. The vast majority of wives in these families keep their jobs: 90 percent of women in good job households but only three-fourths of women in bad job households are employed. In fact, being in a good

TABLE 9. INDIVIDUAL LABOR
FORCE PARTICIPATION

	GOOD JOB HOUSEHOLDS		BAD JOB HOUSEHOLDS	
	Men	*Women*	*Men*	*Women*
A. % of men and women who work part time at principal jobs (earners only)	15% (84)+	23% (78)	27% (67)+	45% (53)
B. % of men and women who commute less than 20 minutes to work (earners only)	51% (84)	52% (78)	53% (67)	70% (53)

NOTE: Numbers in parentheses are the numbers of households on which percentages are based.

+Differences between men and women within households are significant at the .05 level or higher.

job household not only less often constrains a woman's labor force opportunities but also may even *enhance* her labor force position. The networks, support, and flexibility that come from having at least one worker with a good job in the family help the other worker establish his or her own employment history; when there is that one good worker, the second has the leeway to be selective about jobs and to make choices about when, where, and how much to work.[27] Even if wives in good job households do adjust their work lives to accommodate "breadwinning" by their husbands or other family needs, those adjustments do not invariably produce significant disadvantages in their own careers.

There are two additional pieces of evidence that suggest that women in bad job households make special accommodations that are not required of women in good job households. First, there is the well-known difference between women and men in their "willingness" to take part-time work. Both sets of women work part time more often than men (Table 9, section A), but wives in bad job households are almost twice as likely as women in good job households to hold down part-time work (45 percent versus 23 percent).[28] On the assumption that lower labor force commitment limits one's chances in the labor market, it would appear that women in bad job households either choose to make compromises or are forced to by virtue of their circumstances. This pattern then leads to a kind of gender degradation that has little to do with the quality of their husbands' jobs and a great deal to do with the quality of their own. To a much greater extent than women in good job households, those in bad job households are compromised in the labor market simply by virtue of the jobs they have.

There is a second piece of evidence that women from bad job households are more likely to make accommodations in their work lives. It is generally a safe assumption that the farther one is willing to travel to work, the greater the likelihood one will find a good job. In good job households, there was a rough equality between men and women in their commuting patterns: About half of both men and women travel more than twenty minutes to their jobs. When we get to bad job households, we find that women were much more likely than men in these households—and considerably more likely than women in good job households—to stay close to home (see Table 9, section B). Although the length of a commute may seem trivial, much like part-time work, it signals the degree to which job opportunities are circumscribed.

What can we conclude from consideration of these relative labor force patterns? Simply this: Given that by definition men in bad job households have degraded employment, whatever advantage they retain relative to their wives is a function of their wives' labor force disadvantages rather than any advantage they hold themselves. This is an uncertain foundation for gender privilege but, as we will see in what follows, it hardly keeps men in bad job households from exercising that privilege. By way of contrast, recall that most men in good work households have decent jobs and a greater relative advantage. They thus enjoy a more "secure" basis for gender privilege.

Moonlighting does little to bolster gender in bad job households. To be sure, men in bad job households moonlight more often than do women (34 percent versus 26 percent), as is the case in good job households. A larger proportion of the moonlighting done by men in bad job households occurs when they are the only worker in the household than is the case among men in good job households, and therefore moonlighting is not a new basis for status but an intensification of an already existing one. When both husband and wife are in the labor force, men in bad job households are less likely to be the only moonlighter than in similarly situated good job households. In the dual-earner good job households, more than four-fifths of men who moonlight are the only household member to do so; fewer than two-thirds of men in bad job households have this singular status. Thus, husbands in the dual-earner bad job households can less often make claims of preeminence on the simple basis that they have a second job. In fact, moonlighting among men in bad job households in general is less important as a basis on which to have more jobs than a spouse than it is among men in good job households. Two-thirds of men in good job households have more jobs than their wives because they moonlight; two-thirds of men in bad job households have that "numerical" superiority because they are the only worker. Moreover, men in dual-earner bad job households are no more likely to take on a moonlighting job when their wives have employment as good as theirs than they are when their wives have lower-quality employment. Unlike the situation in good job households, men in dual-earner bad job households more often hold down two jobs simply because conditions allow them to do so and not because they choose that practice with reference to their relative position in the household.

Other differences between men's and women's moonlighting found among good job households also disappear within bad job households. Of course, men and women do still have "gendered" skills. Even so, the difference in the content of moonlighting jobs sometimes begins to evaporate here (as it did in their principal employment). It was not at all unusual for men's and women's waged moonlighting activities to cross the usual gender divide: Don Dwire did at least part of his moonlighting in retail sales, and Sandy Kayhart did part of her moonlighting in agricultural employment. In this respect too, those in bad jobs experience a form of gender degradation easily surmounted by those in good jobs.

In bad job households, individuals sometimes reserve moonlighting income for personal use. More often, both men and women have to devote this additional money to the purchase and maintenance of necessary household goods. Moreover, because moonlighters in bad job households have extra *jobs* rather than supplemental self-employment, it makes little sense to refer to gender differences in investments and the location of work. In fact, there is little occasion to mark the importance of this work at all: These jobs come and go quite rapidly, they do not command household resources, and they do not parade as important by virtue of a separate place under the direct supervision of the "owner," who in turn can call on family members as subservient labor. Rather, they bear a striking resemblance to these moonlighters' other bad jobs. In fact, because of the similarity between the two kinds of jobs, it is often difficult to tell which job is the primary one.

Much like the function of their primary job—just having it is justification for superiority in the family circle—a second job does not so much create a superior position as assert it. Even when their wives work at second jobs, men use the existence of their *own* multiple jobs to proclaim superiority. Joan Currier was proud of the fact that, like Paul, she would soon be holding down two jobs. Dripping with sarcasm, however, Paul called her work a "position" and made fun of the money that she earned through her efforts:

PAUL: We've got three jobs. I've got two and she's got one.

JOAN: I might have another half one.

PAUL: [*sarcastically*] Position; fill in the rest of it. Answering the phone at your own house, that wouldn't be too rough a job.... [You'll earn] big bucks. I could probably quit working in that shop.

Mocking the work of a wife cannot change the nature of one's own. Given how empty these second jobs are for men in bad job households, it is not surprising that they turn to trading as a kind of ersatz on-the-side entrepreneurial activity. Like "real" entrepreneurial moonlighting, that practice has the appearance of generating (and spending) *discretionary* income, but in most cases this is much more appearance than reality. Trading actually represents a particular kind of consumption activity through which men claim scarce household resources and use them for their own ends. (Some of these ends are particularly "masculine"—cars and sporting equipment—and therefore of particular symbolic importance.) Unlike the "real" businesses they mimic, however, these ersatz entrepreneurial activities almost always exact huge costs on the household. When husbands spend in this way, they wrest status from the family's well-being rather than earn it in the workplace.

Consider the case of the Seeleys. Walt liked to buy boats and justified that expenditure on the grounds that it was like a business in which he earned discretionary income:

WALT: One time there was a good deal on a boat. I wanted the boat. It was $500. I knew it wouldn't last long. I didn't have the $500 right at the moment, called up Randy, said, hey, I found this boat. I need $500 for a couple of days. Yup, no problem.... When I finished the job I got the money, I took $500 and paid him back. That was three boats ago. I bought and sold, bought and sold boats.

INTERVIEWER: Do you make money with all this buying and selling?

DOTTIE: NO! No you do not, don't you say you do.

WALT: Some I do, and some I don't.

DOTTIE: No, never, ever.

WALT: When you buy something for $1,000 and you use it for two years and you sell it for $1,000, I consider that making money. You've used it for nothing.

DOTTIE: When you buy something you never ever get what you put into that, I don't care if you bought it for a thousand. You always put money into it. It's $1,500, and when you sell it for $1,000 you just lost $500.

Here again, a causal pattern is made to stand on its head.

Without the substantial projects of home construction and renovation, self-provisioning does not so easily become a way in which men or women in bad job households can gain a sense of self-worth or a clear basis for the differentiation of gender. In fact, because routine self-provisioning is difficult in households with only one earner, wives who are *not* employed might find that some traditional sources of gender are absent altogether: They cannot do the "womanly" things that housewives did in the past. The consequences of bad work are a kind of degendering—or at least deprivation around gender performance—that affects women as well as men.

One area of routine self-provisioning does offer these benefits for men in bad job households even more than is the case in good job households. These men constantly look for used cars to buy, and they devote long hours to car maintenance and repair. Some of this is essential work: In a rural area, adequate transportation is critical for finding and keeping employment. Moreover, because their families can rarely afford a new car, men have to tinker simply to keep what they have in running order. Some of this tinkering is clearly voluntary, chosen by men who love to exercise their skills and who find in car mechanics a significant opportunity to confirm their own masculinity. Because car repair is often a collective activity, it offers an opportunity to experience and express sociability and perhaps to reinforce traditional gender roles:[29] "We're always doing something. A lot of my buddies work on their cars, if I want something I give them a call, if they want something they call me." For those who live in housing that precludes other forms of routine self-provisioning, car repair may be not only the signal activity of gender but also one of the few that remain.

Consider Julie and Randy Huber again. They live in a trailer on a single income earned by Randy from what is clearly a bad job. They have had no room to grow a garden, no equipment with which to haul and chop wood for burning, and no plow with which to take care of their driveway. Julie does not make her own (or her children's) clothes. Zoning prohibits the possibility of keeping chickens. Quite simply, they have to rely almost exclusively on their wages, as do most working people without decent jobs. Randy, however, does an extensive amount of fiddling with the car. Julie says that he spends money on tools "whenever he has it." Sometimes this produces conflict in the family: "I've told him that he spends a lot of money on his toys." In fact, according to Julie, there have been times when the family was short of food but her husband still spent money on those "toys." As is the case in this household, some of the efforts that are made by men with bad jobs seem less a response to genuine need than a kind of pseudo–self-provisioning that consumes resources that the household requires for other purposes.

As noted above, in both kinds of households, whether characterized by good jobs or bad ones, gender almost always shapes interhousehold exchanges, and these exchanges are thus a vehicle for expressing gender differences. Among bad job households, however, barter for private uses is a less viable practice (because more self-employment occurs as one's principal job). In addition, threats are attached to a common form of exchange that limit the degree to which these families exchange in it. Some bad job households are forced—by the withdrawal of others, by their own fears of being entrapped—into drawing in their wagons and thus either absolutely reducing the size of their networks or shifting their network configuration from both family and friends to members of their extended families alone. When this reconfiguration occurs, there are fewer opportunities for men and women to re-enact customary patterns of giving and receiving to others. Women like Ellen Rivers try to avoid "owing" anything to anybody.

In lieu of informal giving, those in bad work families sometimes sought to make money from favors and odd jobs that would normally enter a more casual accounting scheme. In one bad work family, the husband provided transportation to the doctor for his relatives in return for which he expected not just a casual reciprocation of the favor or reimbursement for the cost of gas but a flat "taxi" rate. One woman, who cleaned houses for a living, collected used clothing that she then sold, rather than simply handed down, to others in her community. In these practices, both sociability and paid work have diminished value, but there is nothing to differentiate men from women here or to give men preeminence over women.

In short, a sizable proportion of bad work households look like the "traditional" nuclear family of old: Men are in the labor force and women remain at home; thus, the source of gender hierarchy seems unproblematic. As we have argued above, even here appearances are deceiving. Neither the terms of men's employment nor those of women's domesticity are the same as they were in the past. Men are no longer in jobs that confer male privilege, and they are unable to act like their more patriarchal fathers. Women who remain "at home" cannot engage in self-provisioning to reduce the pressure on the wage. In fact, being a housewife is less a permanent status than a transitory one, adopted when wives are compelled to leave the labor force and abandoned when the job situation changes once again. Sometimes these decisions are shaped by simple opportunity. More often, they are determined by gender, but there is little in the objective reality to give license to these decisions because women in these households can earn as much as their husbands. When both men and women are in the labor force, gender in the sense of difference is challenged by the degraded nature of men's work and men's preeminence is challenged by the greater similarity to their wives in the conditions of employment. In bad job households, moonlighting is more often required of both men and women. These moonlighting jobs can also blur gender lines without providing men with a basis for claiming hierarchy. In many of these households, trading substitutes for entrepreneurial moonlighting; it is an activity that gives men the illusion of control over scarce resources but also is a practice that—from time to time—becomes extraordinarily disruptive.

CHAPTER 6

Dividing the Labor

As we have seen, the paid work of wives in good job households offers a significant threat to male supremacy. To the extent that gender privilege is a product of the lack of parity in the labor force, these changes in the circumstances of wives in good job households bring a strong possibility of a new and more equitable relationship between them and their husbands. Yet, as we demonstrated in the previous chapter, the good jobs of men in these households allow them to find new outlets to regain a more favorable balance. Entrepreneurial activities that occur on the side, substantial self-provisioning, and some kinds of interhousehold exchanges are to a significant degree reserved for men in good job households, and they become occasions to re-enact traditional gendered roles. They do more than provide occasions for men to act like men, however. In good job households, the division of labor surrounding the routine tasks of family maintenance revolves around men's participation in these extraordinary kinds of work. Moreover, in these households the nature of those tasks has changed dramatically. The members of these families are busily engaged in a round of very complex activities, the sum total of which is aimed at keeping the family secure and even thriving. All this busyness can give rise to tensions, but the resources provided by decent work also allow for stability, predictability, and control over one's own life.

All this contrasts strongly with what goes on in bad job households. Wives in these households are considerably less likely to have jobs at all, and when they do, wives' work is even more similar to that of their husbands than it is among good job households. In the single-earner bad job households, it might well be expected that the division of labor would be highly conventional; in the dual-earner households, however, it might well be expected that more sharing would occur. This is especially the case because whether by choice or not, these husbands have little else that "automatically" grants them male privilege. As we will see, as with the basis for gendered relationships alone, the picture is more complicated. In bad job households as in good job households, the relative superiority of men's work is relevant to the extent to which they share in routine tasks, but, as we will see, it functions in an entirely opposite manner. Inside these bad job households, the picture of domestic activity is just as complex as it is in good job households, but here it is not about using resources cleverly to enhance one's living conditions but about constantly repairing the cracks that result from less than ideal work situations. Busyness here too can produce strains and tensions, but more often these result from the uncertainty that is a feature of the lives of bad job families.

THE CASE OF HOUSEWORK

GOOD JOB HOUSEHOLDS

Because good job families are often busy places, "housework" entails the coordination of multiple activities. The dual-earner strategy produces one obvious set of extra tasks: Arranging child care and transportation are constant struggles.[1] Other aspects of the survival strategy create additional work. For example, the entrepreneurial activity of car repair yields both interruptions of domestic life (as clients stop by or telephone for appointments) and ongoing demands (machines have to be maintained, supplies have to be ordered, shops have to be cleaned).

Self-provisioning carries yet another set of burdens, not the least of which are the housing arrangements families make in order to remodel or build their own homes. At least four of the good job families we interviewed lived in a trailer for some time to save money and to be close to the construction site. Moving out of the trailer does not always ensure the promised comfort and might even spell increased domestic labor. George Kemp described how his family lived before their construction was complete:

The first week of November we moved in. That was basic, floors were painted green and the ceilings weren't even done here, the loft wasn't even done. I did all this last Christmas vacation. [My employer gives us] two weeks off, I did all that last year. Still have a lot to do but at least now it's livable. I can peck at it and not be so stressed out.

Susan Drake likes to tell her story:

We started building a house about four years ago and we moved in three years ago when there was no insulation in the walls. We had nothing. We had one running toilet and the tub—that was it. We had a garden hose that ran from where the toilet was over to my sink, which was a utility sink— one of those big plastic utility sinks. And I had a hot plate for two years. That was my kitchen. I like to tell people that story.

Susan also acknowledges that retelling the story is more fun than living it: "Once we moved in here, the hardest part was living in construction all of the time. I had a table saw that I put dishes on and I couldn't have any things around because there was construction so much." Thus, while substantial self-provisioning—a privilege reserved for good job families—had long-term payoffs, there were short-term costs.

Extensive home remodeling projects can also alter household dynamics around housework: When men have become deeply invested in the appearance of their homes, they find reason to take a more active role in how that work is performed. They thus diminish women's autonomy in that domain. Susan Drake suggested this had happened to her:

I still don't have pictures on the wall because [Dave] still doesn't like to put nails in the walls. So we are working on that. I just bought curtains this weekend, a couple of curtains upstairs. So we are working at it slowly be- cause he doesn't want to put curtain rods up because of the finishing work on the windows. . . . I wanted him to just put little wooden dowels, those little wooden things on the inside of the window. He just doesn't like curtains. . . . I can live without curtains if he feels that strongly about it . . . but every woman that comes in here says, "You don't have curtains?" All of my friends who come in. . . . I was beginning to get paranoid because so many people have said, "Why don't you have curtains?"

Routine self-provisioning carries similar, if slighter, additional de- mands. A lush garden requires ongoing maintenance as well as an in- tensive period of canning and preserving at the end of the summer. When households rely on wood heat, everything gets dirty faster. Men who spend their free time repairing cars generate more laundry than men who spend their free time reading. In short, the busyness of good job households gives rise to a whole set of "extra" burdens for women. The consequence is a strong tendency to use gendered understandings of the household division of labor to rationalize how that work gets done.

To be sure, in good job households neither men nor women have a great deal of leisure as that concept is usually defined. Both put in long hours:

FRANK WOODWARD: We seem to always be in this situation. I have to mow the grass. It takes five hours to mow the lawn, plus weed-whacking, plus hand trimming. You are here for an interview. We take a class. I have a business meeting. I do occasional plumbing jobs. . . . The [day care] kids don't leave until six or close to it.

ELLEN WOODWARD: You have your ordinary housework to do in the evening, like washing and ironing, and vacuuming and dusting, and that sort of thing. We don't have a lot of [free] time. . . . I probably have green beans to pick in the garden now. I should have done it yesterday. Yesterday, I had to clean the day care because I hadn't done it on Friday. . . . So, yesterday we did it, and Frank mowed.

INTERVIEWER: And that is a full day?

FRANK WOODWARD: Even then, you can't do it all. You have to weed-whack, and hand mow and . . . we do things, like the fence around the day care, now we put that in. We don't hire very much done. That takes time. You've got to remember to buy everything, plan it and then do all the work. That consumes the weekend or two weekends. The mowing didn't get done, or if it rains. . . . Summer time is constantly a thing about mowing, weeding. . . . We've actually weeded everywhere and it has grown back. We had a new septic system put in and I've got to grade off all those pieces where the stones stick up. I need to buy some topsoil and spread it, just get it done. . . . [I] only sided two sides of the barn, got to put siding on the other two sides. The two I did put up need re-painting.

Busy as both husbands and wives are, the content of the work that interferes with leisure is different for each, as are the obligations attendant on that work. Good job families follow a well-known division of labor: Women have more involvement in tasks that take place "inside," and men have more involvement in tasks that take place "outside." Hence, we find a 40 percent difference *in favor of women* in women's and men's regular involvement in housework and a 21 percent difference in their participation in child care; we also find a 31 percent difference *in favor of men* in men's and women's involvement in lawn work and a 57 percent difference in their engagement in car repair (Table 10).[2]

As noted above, housework as it is normally understood—even with the addition of self-provisioning—constitutes only part of the work in these busy households because the busyness itself creates the burden of artful coordination.[3] These burdens also fall mostly on women's shoul-

TABLE 10.   HOUSEWORK IN GOOD WORK AND
BAD WORK HOUSEHOLDS
(Percentage of Men and Women who Routinely do Each Task)

	HOUSEWORK	CHILD CARE	LAWN WORK	CAR REPAIR
Good work households				
Men	59	76	93	69
Women	99	97	62	12
Difference between men and women	−40	−21	31	57
Bad work households				
Men	34	52	90	74
Women	90	98	64	5
Difference between men and women	−56	−46	26	69
Difference between good work and bad work households				
Men	25	24	3	−5
Women	9	−1	−2	7

ders (rather than leading to the promised equality in domestic labor) even though they, like their spouses, also have employment outside the home. Susan Drake, for example, suggested that this was indeed the case, although she could not quite explain why it was so:

SUSAN: But as far as coordinating our schedules for other things, that has been a little bit stressful because I do that. And I do 95 percent of the care for Jessica and I am the one that drops her off in the morning and picks her up at night.
INTERVIEWER: Why is that?
SUSAN: I don't know. It just is.

Those who stress women's agency might point out that quite possibly this is Susan's choice, that she seeks out opportunities to enact traditional womanly chores. What Marjorie DeVault, drawing on the idea of gender as a product of "social doing," says about feeding the family may thus be generalized to housework as a whole.[4] When a woman says, as did one of our respondents, "I do the housework. I like the way I do it better I guess," she may mean that these activities offer her satisfactions beyond those of a well-ordered home. One of those satisfactions is the enactment of gender. This enactment might be all the more important when the major prop of gender (i.e., being a housewife) is given

up for employment outside the home and when many traditional gendered activities (e.g., sewing) have all but disappeared.[5]

There is substantial reason to question this notion of unfettered
choice. In *The Second Shift*, Arlie Hochschild observed that when she
divided the men in her study into three groups—those who earned more
than their wives, those who earned the same amount, and those who
earned less—she found, paradoxically, no sharing of housework among
the last group and moderate sharing among the first two groups (21
percent and 30 percent, respectively). To explain this finding, she introduced the principle of "balancing," according to which "if men lose
power over women in one way, they make up for it in another way—
by avoiding the second shift, for example. In this way, they can maintain
dominance over women."[6]

Because we are specifically interested in how the range of tactics that
constitute a family's survival strategy shapes the role of husbands and
wives with respect to conventional housework, we explored whether
that work was more equitably divided when husbands and wives held
the same number of jobs than when they did not. By Hochschild's rea-
soning, we would have expected that men with more employment than
their wives would respond more generously because they did not have
to reassert balance. In fact, among good job households we found just
the opposite (Table 11). Men's responsibility for housework *increases*
slightly (by 3 percent) when their wives have either the same number of,
or more, jobs than they do, but it *decreases* more substantially (by 15
percent) when they have more jobs than their wives. This pattern
emerges even more clearly with respect to child care (an increase of 14
percent versus a decrease of 28 percent). Moreover, men do not reshape
their involvement in traditional male activities (mowing the lawn, maintaining the car) as their relative status shifts. This suggests that they are
not simply driven to reassert their masculinity when their wives' employment status challenges their primacy but that they may be making
a "rational" response to claims on their time. Nevertheless, the choice
still appears to be a male preserve. Regardless of the number of their
activities relative to that of their husbands, women maintain a relatively
constant rate of engagement in these conventional household tasks.

An engagement in entrepreneurial moonlighting (and substantial self-
provisioning is probably relevant as well, although we did not quantify
that variable in the random sample) is so constructed that it gives license
to men to absent themselves from domestic chores.[7] In these busy house-

TABLE 11. HOUSEWORK IN GOOD WORK AND BAD WORK HOUSEHOLDS:
Variations with Work Responsibilities of Husbands and Wives
(Percentage Who Routinely Do Each Task)

	MEN				WOMEN			
	House-work	Child Care	Lawn Work	Car Repair	House-work	Child Care	Lawn Work	Car Repair
A. Good work households								
All households	59	76	93	69	99	97	62	12
Households in which men have more jobs than women	50	55	94	72	100	100	64	6
Percentage shift relative to all households	−15	−28	1	4	1	3	3	−50
Households in which women and men have the same number of jobs or men have fewer jobs than women	61	87	93	68	98	96	60	14
Percentage shift relative to all households	3	14	0	−1	−1	−1	−3	17
Difference between households in which men have *more* jobs and those in which men have the same or fewer jobs than wives	−11	−32	1	4	2	4	4	−8
B. Bad job households								
All households	34	52	90	74	90	98	64	5
Households in which men have more jobs than women	48	55	86	69	95	97	68	0
Percentage shift relative to all households	41	6	−4	−7	6	−1	6	−100
Households in which women and men have the same number of jobs or men have fewer jobs than women	26	50	95	77	86	96	62	8
Percentage shift relative to all households	−24	−4	6	4	−4	−2	−3	60
Difference between households in which men have *more* jobs and those in which men have the same or fewer jobs than wives	22	5	−9	−8	9	1	6	−8

holds with the privilege of having access to one decent job, husbands are especially busy with seemingly (even if they are self-imposed) inflexible obligations. Constantly on the move, they are, quite simply, not there to engage in any significant or equitable way in the routine work that all households require as well as the extraordinary work that derives from the busyness of all this activity. Whether this lack of availability is a cause or effect of the on-the-side work these husbands take on is open to question. (Recall, however, that husbands are much more likely to take on this extra work when their wives' jobs afford them equal status in the formal labor force.) Having lost the traditional basis for claiming the privilege of not having to engage in housework, men find a new basis for avoiding those tasks. Invariably, then, women pick up the slack—and they do so not just with respect to the routine work of daily maintenance, but also with respect to the ongoing work of making sure that everything gets done. Hence, we have a traditional division of labor in untraditional circumstances.

BAD JOB HOUSEHOLDS

The situation is quite different in bad job households. Although these too are often busy places, the pieces that compose this busyness differ both in content and in basic character. In the absence of the centerpiece of good work, artful coordination frequently gives way. First of all, these pieces are less predictable. Jobs come and go, and some of these jobs are, by their very nature, episodic. This unpredictability has its consequences. Transportation arrangements that work when two people are employed near to each other and can share a car fall apart when each adult has to find transportation to a different work site, and child care arrangements that cover daytime work become inappropriate when someone finds part-time employment in the evening. Some moonlighting jobs mesh well with other household activities; others don't.

Domestic life is also complicated by the invariable breakdown of used cars and appliances. At the very least, secondhand goods require far more maintenance than would new purchases. Here is one husband in a bad job household describing the situation of his family:

> When we got married and her mother sold the house, she sold us a washer and a dryer. A pair cost us $400 which is cheap for washer and a dryer. . . . The washer we put in here and used. The dryer had to sit outside for two years. I just barely got it in that front room and got it hooked up. . . . I paid $5 for this rug when we first moved in. It was a nice rug. Now it's stained

and trashed and cut—you see how it's been altered on the top. The door that
we had on here was all broken and trashed. . . . The TV and the stereo are
the only two things we ever bought new, and we put those on layaway. It
was six or seven months before we could get them. Ten dollars one week,
whatever we could afford. We've had those for five or six years now. Everything is old.

In short, in bad work households domestic life is complicated by uncertainty, by not knowing how much income is coming in, and by the rapid
circulation of consumer goods. It is for this reason that the double burden assumed by working wives in bad job households has an especially
high cost. Not only, as we show below, must they do a good deal more
than their partners, but in assuming that responsibility these women also
assume the sense of failure when their household economy prevents that
responsibility from being adequately exercised.[8]

Budgeting represents the same kind of cost. Unlike good work households, where paying bills can follow a predictable pattern from week to
week or month to month, this work is extremely difficult in households
that lack a decent job and where not only is one's income unpredictable
but the "solution" of trading also can throw a careful budget into disarray.[9] In fact, making a woman responsible for paying the bills under
these circumstances is a way in which men protect themselves from an
ongoing confrontation with the knowledge of just how limited their
resources are.[10] Because they can claim ignorance, they preserve their
right to spend as they wish.

Other arrangements characteristic of bad job households also place
strains on the family and push at its edges. These households sometimes
have to go outside the boundaries of the nuclear family—to friends and
relatives as well as to the state—to meet their daily needs.[11] This too
requires enormous adjustments. Jeff and Martha Blair live in the house
his parents gave him, but this was in exchange for caring for his grandmother for several years. Tiffany Farrell and her fiancé are supported
by her parents, who own the land on which their trailer sits and from
whom they borrowed money to buy that trailer, but this involves them
in their parents' lives and exerts its own costs.

Finally, the scrambling in bad job households has another set of consequences for domestic life. The normal tasks that constitute family life
as we have known it begin to disappear.[12] Tiffany described how she
and her fiancé had abandoned eating together for more casual "grazing":[13] "A lot of times we eat at different times. So we just make our

own pick-me-up food." Similarly, Walt and Dottie Seeley, who argued about his spending money on a boat, suggested that in spite of the presence of a young child, they grazed as well and that they had a dwindling concern with traditional housework.

INTERVIEWER: Who does the cooking around here?

DOTTIE: I do.

WALT: Hey! Who cooked the stuff tonight?

DOTTIE: It was cooked. He just heated it up.

WALT: Let's put it this way. I'm going to be totally honest with you. About once a week we really have a sit-down meal, the rest of the time it's get what you want out and make it yourself.

DOTTIE: This has happened in the past year and a half, two years. I'm the one that usually does cook and have the meal ready. But in the past year I haven't. One day a week I cook.

WALT: The rest is, you open the door, you see something you want, and you get it.

INTERVIEWER: [to twelve-year-old-child] Who feeds you?

CHILD: Myself.

INTERVIEWER: [Who does] the cleaning [and] dishes?

WALT: I don't like dishes. I don't do windows. I don't know, you can call it old-fashioned. I believe that if I'm going to be out working all day I shouldn't have to come home and do the dusting.

INTERVIEWER: What about if Dottie's been out working all day?

WALT: Then it looks like hell through here.

There is another issue as well that has to do with the *satisfactions* attendant on these activities. A man in a good job family spoke about the solace provided by living in a house rather than a mobile home: "I think it would be different if we were still in the trailer. The house is a great source of comfort to us. The trailer, it would be harder to still be there. You know, I can come home to this, no problems." Many bad job households do still live in the trailer, and they do so with secondhand furniture and used appliances. They might boast about how adroitly they accumulate these goods ("We don't buy nothing unless we get a deal"), but there is a cost. In this context, housework carries few rewards and few satisfactions. Nancy Sharp compared her own well-being with that of her friends:

Some are a lot more financially stable than we are. . . . You don't begrudge them, you're glad they have what they have, but yes, it's not easy to entertain because a lot of our friends—I've met a lot of people at the store, and they all have beautiful homes and I know they're not looking at us for that. But it's not easy to say that for your home you have a trailer and that's it. It gives you a funny feeling.

Nancy lived in a trailer even though she and her husband Bruce both had regular jobs and Bruce was able to engage in entrepreneurial moonlighting (snowplowing) *and* hold down a waged moonlighting job (working for the same logger as Paul Currier). Or consider Pamela Seward. Pamela works part time as a church secretary, as an assistant town clerk, and (like Dottie Seeley) as a turkey processor in the fall; she is also trying to complete a two-year degree at a nearby community college. Even with these substantial accomplishments under her belt, Pamela indicated that she held herself to a standard that was built on appearances: "Some days I wonder if I amount to anything. My house is a mess and housework is not one of my top priorities." Another woman simply acknowledged that she had failed to maintain traditional standards: "A lot of housework doesn't get done. The windows, and oven and cobwebs and that type of thing."

We do not mean to suggest that these wives are not still left with *responsibility* for household labor. Quite the opposite. In bad job households (as in good job households), wives are more likely than their husbands to have responsibility for housework (difference of 56 percent) and child care (difference of 46 percent). Men are more likely than women to have responsibility for lawn work (difference of 26 percent) and car repair (difference of 69 percent).

These are not "just" relative differences with respect to husbands and wives: Men in bad work households are considerably less likely than men in good work households to assume a regular responsibility for housework (difference of 25 percent) and for the care of their young children (difference of 24 percent). There are no differences of that magnitude between women in good job and bad job households with respect to their responsibility for either traditionally female tasks or traditionally male ones. As a result, bad work households actually have an even more rigid division of labor around housework and child care than do good job households.

Moreover, men in bad job households respond quite differently from men in good job households to a "challenge" from their wives. In good job households, when men had *more* work than their wives, they reduced their level of participation in the routine tasks of child care (by 28 percent) and to some extent housework (by 15 percent). When their wives had as much—or more—work than they did, they increased their level of participation in these activities (by 3 percent for child care and 14 percent for housework). Whether this greater level of cooperation was in response to women's demands or a voluntary recognition of need and fairness, men in good job households heeded the call of equity.

Men in bad job households do just the reverse. They are *more* likely to share housework and child care when they have a more extensive labor force involvement than their wives. Under these circumstances, they increase their participation in housework by 41 percent and in child care by 6 percent. This increase is especially notable because in a larger proportion of these cases, their wives are unemployed altogether and thus might be "expected" to assume a larger role in routine domestic tasks. When they are challenged by their wives' employment, they withdraw from an equitable arrangement of domestic responsibilities, particularly with respect to housework itself. Men in bad job households are almost twice as likely to do housework when they work more jobs than their wives as when they work either the same number of jobs or fewer. Once again, the situation that gives rise to this challenge is worth noting because it differs from the basis for the challenge among good job households: In a greater portion of bad job households, this challenge is the result of women moonlighting and thus increased work obligations for both men and women.

As authors like Hochschild predict, when men's identity as the breadwinner in the family is challenged, they respond in ways that suggest a reassertion of a kind of traditional masculinity. Our comparison between the two sets of households indicates that this reassertion becomes a "psychological" necessity only when the workplace itself offers little occasion for men to feel good about themselves. Some men may have ample reason to indulge in what Hochschild calls "balancing"; these are the men with degrading work.

Moreover, the evidence suggests that men in these households do not just resort to balancing—they actually command the labor of their wives with respect to domestic work. In response to her husband's comment about the house looking "like hell," Dottie Seeley said, "And he'll bitch." And Walt continued, "When I really get aggravated and really scream and holler then things happen. That's the way it goes."

KEEPING THE HOUSEHOLD TOGETHER

In good job households, the various pieces of the household strategy demonstrate a complex combination of requirement *and* voluntary activity. In these cases, it is difficult to draw conclusions about precisely how gender patterns in housework are recreated. In some households, it is clear that men are trying to sustain privilege; in others, the situation is less clear. Similarly, the importance for women of sustaining a conventional domesticity is ambiguous: Some women speak with enthusiasm about these roles; others acknowledge if not coercion, an absence of desired sharing. Whatever the cause of recreated patterns surrounding housework in these households, the requirements of the various components of the survival strategy and pre-existing gendered expectations do not work at cross-purposes: The need to sustain a variety of tactics allows, indeed demands, customary practices.

This is not to say, however, that these households are without internal tensions. Both busyness and the lopsided division of labor within the household place strains on individuals and on their relationships. Some women complained that they did not have the time—or the resources—to develop their own independent activities. Some women complained that their husbands were "gone all the time," that they had little time to spend together. Some women also complained that men used their incomes to make household purchases that they neither wanted nor approved. Lois Donahue mentioned all of these:

> I also do stained glass, and I haven't done anything, except a few little suncatchers for Christmas presents, for about three years. I have all the equipment, and enough glass to last me forever, but I just don't get that opportunity. It's not something you can do with the children around. . . .
> One of the biggest problems with [building the] house was because Eric was always there. It caused a lot of trouble, but you deal with that stuff. . . .
> This year we have overspent, between the addition and impulse purchases—the boat out in the driveway. . . . I used to be very good about making sure we had at least three months worth of income in a savings account, but Eric's gotten to be more aware of where the money is, so we don't save as well as I used to.

In some cases, the income from good work, even when supplemented by income from extra activities, was insufficient to sustain the family at a level that allowed them to meet all their ongoing expenses. In these cases, money shortages, and sometimes the need to deny them (both to save face with friends and relatives and to support a husband's self-image), were constant sources of tension and anxiety:

> It seems that it's not very often that I can be this honest about it. It seems that I have to present this face of everything's okay and I'm just like everyone

else and that money isn't a problem. . . . It's hard for [my husband too]. He works hard at his job. He does other things as well. He's also the zoning inspector in [this town]. . . . Every permit application comes with $10 which he keeps but he also has to drive to the places to do the inspection and so forth so that's not all clear profit. And the number of applications can vary . . . so that's not any income that we can count on but yet there will be phone calls even at mealtimes. . . . He frequently schedules his inspections after work so he does that on his way home and it delays the time that he gets home. . . . We also own a trailer—perhaps I should say that my husband owns a trailer that he bought before we were married. It's very old, it must be thirty-five years old or so. And there are tenants in that who rent it. And I believe the rent is $200 a month and they provide the utilities. It's old enough that things break down there too and he has to go there and repair things. . . . So that may use up some of his weekend time. So he works very, very hard too for the money that he makes. So I don't want to be complaining to Arnie or saying that I'm dissatisfied with what we have.

Even with these kinds of constraints, many good job households seemed secure and peaceful. In a society that still values difference, the reconfirmation of gender plays a significant role in creating that sense of well-being. The same could not be said of many bad job households.

Although women in bad job households often do speak about domesticity (whether because they are out of the labor force altogether or because they hold down only part-time work) as something they have chosen for the valued opportunity to care for their children, they also recognize the precarious quality of that opportunity, and more often than not they are making a virtue out of necessity. Without decent homes and working appliances, much less adequate furniture, wives in these families frequently find it impossible to carry on traditional household responsibilities and almost as frequently give up in despair. When gendered roles become a site for failure, new and perhaps equally tormenting relationships between spouses take their place. In some bad job households—and these were the ones with the most uncertain job histories—problems were close to the surface. Women said they felt the need to conceal inadequate resources from friends and relatives, and to conceal from their husbands how they felt about that inadequacy. In many of these households, money was the major issue of struggle:

We fight about [money] all the time. It's not fair because I don't pay as much [toward the household] as he does and I don't do as much as he does. . . . That's all we've ever fought about, it's because I don't pay my share. . . . He would never say anything [but] in the middle of a fight some nights when we're both extremely tired, things will come out that we don't mean.

This is not surprising. Bad work households undergo constant change in their employment and therefore in their income. Some of them are living quite close to the edge, some have had to draw on governmental assistance, and some had special difficulties created by male consumption patterns. While Lois Donahue (in a good work household) snorted with contempt at her husband's toys, women in bad job families saw these toys as a more significant threat to their economic security. Lois Donahue was furious because her husband bought a boat when she didn't think they could afford that luxury, and her outrage was directed at a purchase that cut into her family's *savings*. The situation is quite different in bad job households, where impulse buying might affect the capacity of a household to meet more basic survival needs. Such spending generates greater discord:[14]

> He spends a lot of money on tools. It has at times [become a source of conflict]. I've told him that he spends a lot of money on his toys. . . . Most of that stuff we have is his. It's his idea to buy two VCRs, all those movies, it's all his idea. I would rather spend the money on something else. . . . Before we started getting food stamps he wouldn't spend as much on food for the whole household as he would, say, on getting himself something.

None of these findings comes as news, but they indicate that the economic struggles of these households have significant costs.

In every family we studied, husbands and wives work hard. In some, hard work pays off in a broad range of advantages. In others, it merely sustains the family. The members of both kinds of households also hold onto a kind of traditional gendered organization of rights and responsibilities, but those with good work do so at much less cost than those with bad work. This difference is largely a function of how, in bad job households, husbands especially but also wives try to reproduce gendered expectations of themselves in the face of the objective conditions that make those expectations all but impossible to meet. The result is despair. In short, what we found missing was not "family values" but the ability to rise to the standards those values imply.

CHAPTER 7

Work Matters

In this final chapter, we once more reverse our gaze. Rather than asking how good and bad jobs shape survival strategies and gendered relationships within the home, we ask how these strategies themselves, and the gendered relationships on which they rest, affect the manner in which family members construct attitudes toward work and the political economy.[1] Admittedly, these were loaded issues at the time we were conducting the interviews. As we noted in Chapter 1, some major employers were moving out of the area or going out of business altogether; others were engaged in downsizing and outsourcing. Meanwhile, a series of new jobs was created. These new jobs offered lower-quality employment in terms of the possibility for skill development, wages, and benefits.[2] Led by conservatives—but far from limited to them alone—a war on welfare was being waged and, as part of that war, there was a resounding critique of support by the government, on one hand, and of all kinds of "dependency" by citizens, on the other.[3] It is against this backdrop that workers themselves have to evaluate the meaning of the work they do and their place in the world. Not surprisingly, those in good jobs and those less well situated expressed different concerns in their discussions of these issues.

GOOD JOB WORKERS

ATTITUDES TOWARD EMPLOYMENT

Individuals in good jobs define their expectations of *themselves* in terms that include—but go beyond—fulfilling their contractual obligations. They believe in putting full effort into their employment: "I think they have to be dedicated to do an excellent job for the company and give them their undivided attention while they're there"; "They should give their 100 percent, not just be there for the paycheck. [They should] give their all." Good job workers also believe that it is important to offer *loyalty* to the firm.

This loyalty has to be earned by the firm. Four responses predominated when workers in good jobs were asked what they expected *from* their employers. The first—and the most common—response spoke directly to this issue. Most good job workers believe that the loyalty they offer should be matched by job security:[4]

> The company owes when they're in hard times, they owe something to you *to try to keep you* . . . and I don't see that happening a lot. . . . The people stand by the company when the going gets rough and *I think it should be a fair exchange* . . . I think there's a moral aspect.

> I think that if you do a good job and you are loyal to the company, then you should expect the company to be loyal to you to a certain extent. . . . What I really mean, I guess, is that they shouldn't lay you off even though I know that isn't feasible all the time.

As the second of these comments suggests, some workers have bought into the corporate view that downsizing is a forced necessity rather than a carefully selected practice.[5] Believing in the necessity of downsizing puts them in a troublesome contradiction with respect to their belief— also firmly held—that "loyal" workers should be protected.[6] Some workers resolve this contradiction by rewriting history so as to characterize recent (and relatively massive) layoffs as opportunities the firm was using to get rid of "deadwood." They thus mentally re-secure the notion of a fair exchange. As Wendell King said,

> I would say, if you do the best you can and have your goals and have a management that supports them, it may not be tomorrow, or it may not be next week, but eventually you will reap the benefits of that investment. Same way with sloughing off, it may not be tomorrow, but they will catch up with you. It's the reaping and sowing thing. I really believe it.

This attempt at reinterpretation of downsizing contains its own problems. Every person who survived the layoff at the Sterling Aeronautical Company, for example, knew someone who had not been so lucky; they had to know full well that not all of those dismissed had been "sloughing off." Yet they passionately wanted to believe that a "Fordist" contract remained in force. One man tried to justify what had happened: "One of the things that I'm sure you must, or maybe you don't, realize by now (I don't know how many people you've interviewed), this layoff for the first time in about six years did actually sort out some deadwood." At the same time, sitting next to his wife, who had just lost her job, he also had to acknowledge, at least publicly, that it was a "mixed bag" that was "let go." Another man whose wife also had been laid off sought to interpret his good fortune as evidence that his efforts had been rewarded: "But they still appreciated the work I did for them. So it was one of these things, they let me know that. I'm still there. And, I don't think some of the [other] people are still working." In protecting his own self-image, he implicitly suggested something less praiseworthy about his wife.

Older men especially also held on to the expectation of a "family wage" or, at the very least, a wage substantial enough to mean that they would not have to moonlight and that their wives would not have to work (or not have to work full time).[7] These men were disappointed that they were no longer able to carry out the role of the family breadwinner alone: "I'd like to be able to [work at a single job] and support my family. But . . . every time you turn around it's something else."[8]

Although not as common as the ideals of security and a family wage, some workers anticipated opportunities to rise within the company and encouragement for personal growth. When asked what he expected, Wendell King responded:

> A good employer has obligations to help the employee find their way through the company, not to give him a checklist and if you meet these things you can move someplace else, but supply an environment that is safe enough to work in, that has enough opportunities within and some growth to provide some motivational factors other than just financial.

Career growth proved as elusive as the other expectations. Recall the man (Chapter 1) who remembered Sterling to have been a flexible firm. When asked about the more recent situation, he responded that it had become "a lot more structured than it was before." Others articulated an acute awareness of the limits placed on their careers. Robert Hutton had recently been demoted:

> I used to work in engineering [as a] technician, I worked there for the last four years and last summer they were having a shakedown, what they were doing was getting ready to have another layoff, so they didn't want to lose me apparently, so they brought me back down into production into the tool room. They froze my pay and dropped me back two pay grades, two levels, and red circled my pay.

He did not attempt to hide his hurt:

> It was like having to go back to fifth grade. And I'm not kidding you. I mean, I don't know your education but just say I told you that you aren't capable—this is the way it felt—nobody said this to me—it's just like somebody said, "You aren't capable of teaching so you've got to go and learn all over again." And this is just the way it feels to me.

He bluntly characterized his work life as imprisonment: "I think I'm sort of caught, I'm sort of like doing time."

Finally, good job holders wanted a reasonable amount of work. They had a mental calculus of a "fair day's work" generated equally by employees and employers. They resented times when they were asked to do too *little* as much as they did times when they were asked to do too *much*; they viewed the layoffs as occasioning more of the latter.

Many workers found that their jobs did not measure up to this set of ideals. To be sure, a minority still believed their employment met these traditional expectations: They kept their jobs, they earned acceptable wages and found opportunities for advancement, and they maintained an acceptable balance between demands imposed and effort willingly made. Nevertheless, even when individual workers expressed satisfaction with their own experiences, they were quick to note with alarm evidence of major shifts happening around them.

The response to these disappointments took very individualistic forms.[9] Rather than asking what could be done for them—or even how in conjunction with other workers they could better protect all employees—they thought about what they could do to better protect *themselves*. One man said, "I used to ask that question [of what employers owe] a lot to myself, but recently, especially after this layoff, I've turned it around saying what can I do as an employee to make sure that the employer gives me what I've got coming to me." Thus, rather than viewing their situations as having a collective solution, they sought to position themselves in a way that would improve their chances down the line. Some workers positioned themselves within the company by leaving a paper trail that could be called up at the right time. Robert Hutton was one such worker. He was acutely aware of the extent to which past promotions and demotions—and therefore future chances as well—rested on "a mixture of chance and influence":[10]

> And before I left I knew I'd never get back into the engineering group because it was an uphill battle all the way to get there and . . . I asked [my supervisor] if he would write some kind of a statement about how he felt I did help the group, you know, give me a little something I could put in my file, so that any time down the road I could get another interview with somebody and say, "Look in my personnel file and see what I have done." And he wrote up that I was outstanding in my job for what I did. I was part of a support group for all the engineers. Whatever they had to do I would do it for them as far as machines and things like that. So he wrote this all down.

Others made attempts to obtain training that could secure a better position either within their present jobs or elsewhere. One man explained why he was taking classes at night:

> The only reason [I am in school] at this point is the security and my job marketability if I did get laid off or had to go elsewhere, or wanted to go elsewhere. In my present position at Sterling, as a manufacturing engineer, there are people with on-the-job training as well as degreed people. With a two-year degree I am kind of in the middle. I do have the experience so I think it will give me good security.

Many workers have been "disciplined" by their own careers. They recognize the insecurity of employment when they see it, and they know they must protect their futures, but if their work histories can account for this individual (and ultimately quiescent) response in the face of assaults on their expectations, it is not the whole picture.[11] Many of these workers, while they have one foot in the industrial door, have another foot outside it as well. Just as their incomes come only partly from their waged work, so are their identities only partly forged in the workplace.

The two survival strategies that are unique to good job households—entrepreneurial moonlighting and substantial self-provisioning—can be understood as emerging, at least in part, from the failure of waged work either to give reason for a positive self-conception or to ensure security. These other tactics, then, offer an alternative basis for individual pride. Indeed, when the members of good job households speak about *why* they engage in on-the-side entrepreneurship, they generally do not mention—or at least they do not mention first—the requirement of generating cash.[12] In fact, some men and women make enormous investments in their entrepreneurial moonlighting; others turn all their profits back into the business. Jack Curtis spent so deeply on his landscaping equipment that he would have had to work six good years before he would be in the black. George Kemp allows his on-the-side welding business to absorb all its earnings:

> I've invested quite a bit. . . . It's all paid off. I've done a little at a time. I didn't jump into it but every year I buy more stuff and try to put a little into it. The building right now needs some work and I'd like to put an overhead door in, spruce it up a little, get it insulated. It's like one step at a time, I've made the money I put into it. . . . I don't even show a profit, I just keep putting it back into it.

If those engaged in entrepreneurial moonlighting activities do not stress financial rewards, they *do* speak about the importance of other, nonmaterial ones. They talk about opportunities for autonomy, opportunities to exercise a valued skill, and opportunities to work with, and to exchange services with, other people in their social world. Even when they still hold good jobs, they explicitly link the need for these satisfactions to job-related disappointments. For example, when Barbara Lattrey was asked why her husband invested heavily in a lawn mowing business that was not reaping any profit, she simply answered, "Because he wasn't happy at [his job]." When asked what was wrong, she amplified her initial response: "Kevin loves computers. But he also likes to be tired at the end of the day, physically feel tired, not just mentally and that is what he said. He would come home and mentally be a wash." Susan Lee characterized her husband Mark's on-the-side repair work in similar terms:

> Sometimes if there's someone who wants some work done he'll do it in our own garage at night. . . . That's his own little niche that he likes to do and stuff. He doesn't do mechanical work any more; he more or less pushes a pencil now being a shop foreman. He does do some mechanical work [but] not a whole lot, so he kind of likes to keep his hands in the grease and stuff.

One woman said, quite frankly, "I don't think I could survive the nine to five job if I didn't have the other. . . . We still squeeze in stuff that we just like to do. Everything doesn't generate money."

By engaging in these activities, workers with good—but unsatisfying—jobs not only find rewards outside (and unavailable in) the workplace, but they have justification for the belief that they are *good workers* (and not just workers with good jobs).[13] Robert Hutton defines syrup production as a "hobby," as "exercise," and as a way to carry on a family tradition. But syrup production can be identified as a "leisure activity" only by someone who believes in the necessity for—and the virtue of—constant work for himself. Jack Curtis works days for the State Department of Wildlife, runs his own lawn mowing business "on the side" during summer evenings, and cuts all his own wood. He describes this latter activity as a useful way to spend what otherwise would be "leisure" time:

> I usually buy some wood from somebody or standing log tops or somebody gives me a tree in their yard [that] is dead and I cut it down and that's the way we've been heating since the 70s. . . . I guess you think you are [saving money]. But if you consider all of your time and did something on a paid basis you probably could have paid for it to come there or be delivered but . . . many times there wasn't another opportunity to do another part-time job that I'd get paid for instead of cutting wood, *so what was I going to be doing, nothing anyway, so I might as well work up my woodpile.* (emphasis added)

Or consider Molly Collins, who describes her *vacation* in terms of accomplishments even as she considered those accomplishments minor in comparison with those of other years:

> We stayed home. For the first time in a year we stayed home. I just—I painted some spots around in the house that needed painting and I took the curtains down and washed them and washed the screens and . . . I just enjoyed being around the house for the week. In the past few years we've either had a major project we were doing or we went somewhere. Last summer I put the sidewalk in out front during our summer vacation. So it seemed nice just to stick around and do things that get neglected.

There is also the additional benefit of not believing oneself to be bound to paid employment. Although on one hand (and in one breath), those with good jobs speak about their dependence on waged work as the source of a steady and secure paycheck as well as health insurance, pensions, and other benefits, on the other hand (and in the next breath), they carelessly ignore the advantages that good work ensures and assert that they could get by without a job. Robert Hutton, at one moment while speaking about his work, is a broken and disappointed man with an instrumental attitude born of resignation: "The only reason I'm really hanging on to my job [is because] I got a son that just barely got into Kansas State University and I figured I can hang in there and carry it out for at least five more years." A moment later, he declares his own independence: "I've never worried about not having a job because I figured I could always do something. I can do carpenter work. I've done masonry work. What you see here, I've done everything, right here." The tension between autonomy and dependence can be heard as well when Jack Curtis muses about how he would manage if he were laid

off: "I'm sure [the lawn mowing business] could help me. I would just
have to start scrambling more than I do now."

Some of the women had also developed an entrepreneurial activity.
On the whole, however, they were less likely to have done so, and they
were also less likely to be engaged in self-affirming construction and
repair projects. Women's self-images were thus bound more tightly to
their waged work. This assertion contradicts an accepted wisdom. Many
authors argue that employment is less important for women than it is
for men. For example, Robin Leidner asserts, simply, that "adult female
identity has not traditionally been regarded as something that is achieved
through paid work."[14] In many cases, our respondents suggested something quite different. In answer to the question of what her work outside
the home meant to her, a woman who had recently started a new job
said proudly,

> It's a real chance to prove myself. It's the most responsible position I've held
> throughout my entire career, and . . . because of the type of company that
> they are and because they are a growing company establishing themselves in
> a unique market, the sky is basically the limit. . . .

In contrast to those who would believe that women place their domestic
concerns above their occupational ones, Martha Croft continued, "Any
place I've ever worked, it's my personal philosophy you live at work
and you reside at home. You have to have a certain level of happiness."[15]

In spite of Martha's comments, it is clear that women join men in
bemoaning the loss of security in workplaces they had anticipated would
stand them in good stead. Because women were less likely to have the
resources to turn that despair into a work life outside the factory gates,
the loss of personal identity and self-esteem that accompanied the loss
of a job had a more significant impact.

There is yet another reason women invested more in their jobs than
would normally be expected. To be sure, many women *did* anticipate
that they would spend their lives working in both paid and unpaid activities, and they linked their pride to a lifetime—and a family history—
of unremitting effort. Darlene Hubbard, for example, viewed constant
work as part of her own identity: "I have worked ever since I've known
it. I grew up on a farm and I worked outside when I was in high school
all the time. I don't know, I just enjoy working." Kathy Hastings mod-
eled herself after other women in her family:

> I came from a long line of working women. My grandmother worked her
> whole life; my mother has always worked; she was a secretary [at Sterling];

she retired at sixty-two. . . . And I really never thought about it otherwise [for myself].

Yet, the women had not necessarily expected to find *meaningful* employment. Recent history, however, has meant that at least some of them have found new and unexpected opportunities to grow and to develop their skills. When these working women compare themselves to their mothers, they find themselves doing much better—they have opportunities their mothers did not. By way of contrast, men's lives have offered not only less than their fathers had, but less than they, as white males, might have believed was their due. Men see their horizons shrinking; women see theirs expanding. The same quality of employment—a job that is constantly threatened by layoffs, that does not offer a family wage, and that offers only some opportunities for personal growth—is regarded very differently by men who, given a historical perspective, are on their way down and by women who, given their historical perspective, are on their way up.[16]

EMERGENT POLITICS

In good job families, an engagement in entrepreneurial moonlighting and substantial self-provisioning has two implications that extend beyond that of leaving intact a self-identity as a good worker. First, respondents link their participation in these activities to a moral culture that finds virtue in self-sufficiency.[17] Although from time to time he would hire a friend to repair his car, Jack Curtis, for example, spoke proudly about doing "all [the] maintenance of the house that [he was] capable of doing." Note the repetition of his use of "I":

> I do my own painting, I do my own papering, I lay my own floor, I do my own interior painting and exterior, I redid my whole kitchen myself because after we rebuilt our house we decided we didn't like the kitchen so I tore one section of cupboard all down and rebuilt them all over again. Water problems I can usually take care of unless it involves pump work. Sewer problems or bathroom problems I'm capable of doing.

Don Sanford linked his engagement in home improvement activities to a valued personal history of self reliance:

DON: [We] re-did the whole living room over. Every room we touched in here. Did the whole front bedroom over. The kids' bedrooms upstairs. . . .

INTERVIEWER: Have you done most of the work yourselves?

DON: Yuh, that's the other thing. That's kind of the way we were brought up. Kind of, trying to be self-sufficient, I mean. It's not the first time I've painted this house, growing up here.

Self-provisioning thus has a special importance to men who have the material conditions necessary to engage in it. They can sustain the illusion that they are self-sufficient even in the face of their obvious dependence on waged work. As they reinvigorate a view of themselves as especially virtuous, they can justify their contempt for those who appear to make less effort on their own behalf. George Kemp, for example, resented tax money going for the support of people who were "just sitting back having a good time" when he was holding down a job and struggling to meet mortgage payments on a house he built himself:

> I think that we're overtaxed. Like when I was working construction, I'm grossing $700, I was paying $300 in taxes so that somebody on welfare can go and whatever. So that to me is not fair. I'm busting my butt from day one and everybody else is getting all the benefits but me. What's the deal? It's like this house. There's a trailer here before. I bought that, $6,000 down, I put that down [and then] built this house from scratch. I got friends that bought houses $70,000 first home, 2 percent interest, and I'm like—what have I gained. They're paying $237 a month and I'm paying $625. . . . FHA [helped them]. So it seems like the more you work the more they take.

To sustain the notion that these activities are an expression of their *essential* identity, these men seldom if ever credit their regular work for its capacity to underwrite their engagement in substantial self-provisioning. Not only would such a calculus challenge the psychological payoff of on-the-side activities, but it would also invest more dependence in paid work than these men want. For both reasons—the inflation of the idea of individual merit and the deflation of the power of their paid work—it is not surprising that men with good jobs view those who do not engage in similar self-provisioning activities as being less worthy. Those others are seen as being victims of their own failing rather than of external pressures to which anyone could be subject no matter how meritorious their aspirations and energy.

In addition, engagement in activities like self-provisioning and entrepreneurial moonlighting produces a set of satisfactions individuals become eager to protect. Wage earners with entrepreneurial side-work express attitudes of the petty bourgeoisie, insistent on keeping government out of their "extracurricular" lives, especially when that intrusion involves zoning or environmental regulations that interfere with what they believe to be natural rights:[18]

> If Don builds a building I know he's going to have to go through a lot of problems, probably like Act 250 or whatever. I don't know a lot about that stuff. I know he'll probably have to jump through hurdles and do all that

other stuff. It doesn't seem like Vermont tries to help people develop new businesses or build businesses or build houses, they really seem to make people jump through hoops. . . . I know a man up the road wanted to build a house and he went through a year of proving the water was good and this was good and that was good. A lot of money involved. Maybe they could make that easier.

Even in the face of objective evidence to the contrary, the *belief* that survival depends on individual efforts and an engagement in those efforts themselves engender a relatively conservative outlook. Both men who experience the benefits of self-provisioning or entrepreneurship directly and the women who make sacrifices to support those efforts hold this point of view. R. E. Pahl made a very similar point about the politics of those who are most engaged in self-sufficiency:

> The more work people do to meet their own needs, the more likely they are to vote Conservative. . . . Bending nature to one's will and exercising craft skill as Karl Marx or William Morris might have wished, may be more successfully and agreeably accomplished in the sphere of self-provisioning than through employment or even self-employment. . . . It may be one of the great paradoxes of our time that as workplace generated class consciousness is weakened, new forms of work-generated consciousness and forms of identity are emerging outside employment. Informal work may depend on access to employment for the basic income in order to engage in it. However, the actual *experience* of engaging in informal work outside employment may have deeper consequences for the development of social consciousness and hence new and perhaps longer enduring social divisions.[19]

BAD JOB WORKERS

ATTITUDES TOWARD EMPLOYMENT

Not unlike their more privileged counterparts, workers with bad jobs believe they have obligations to their employers. In contrast to those understood by workers with good jobs, however, this set of obligations reflects a narrower sense of responsibility. Rather than believing that they should work over and above what was expected of them, bad job workers spoke more simply about being there and doing the job: "[They owe] honest time, I guess. They should do their work as they are asked. Everybody gets along when they do." Most of them see themselves as good workers who are willing to put in that "honest time."[20]

Not surprisingly, those without decent work also have lowered expectations of employers. Forgoing security, a family wage, and career growth (which are basically unavailable in their workplaces), they focus instead on appreciation and respect, on the way they are treated at work:[21]

> [What is] owed? I don't know. I just see a lot of employers that people have been at a long time kind of taken for granted and I don't think that's right. If I owned my own company and I had somebody working for me and they were a good worker and they were dependable I think I'd show them a bit more *appreciation* than what we get.

> [What is] owed? Just good treatment. I feel that . . . because if you don't get *treated good on the job* you are not going to be happy. If you are not happy there is no sense in being there.

As important as it was, good treatment was not the sum total of expectations. Some bad job workers also say that they believe that they should be receiving benefits and that they should also be getting the perks that are part and parcel of decent work:[22]

> I think they should offer health insurance for everybody. No matter who it is, it should always be offered. A decent wage, a decent place. Good hours, decent hours. You know, where you're not asked to come in at the wrong time, you know what I'm saying, until really late or something, you know. That and insurance. Maybe retirement.

Some moderate their expectations. As did some good job workers with respect to the issue of security, some bad job workers buy into a point of view that takes into account what they believe are pressures faced by their employers:

> Depending on the job I feel the pay should fit the work, the stress. It would be nice if they could give them benefits but I realize a lot of places can't but the places that can afford it I feel should be able to give them benefits rather than never coming through.

Thus, both sets of workers—those with good jobs and those with bad ones—share a capacity for exonerating employers for the indignities employees experience. In all other ways, however, the responses of those with bad jobs stand in vivid contrast to those held by workers in good jobs who, while they also wanted good treatment, understood it to entail job security (loyalty to them), adequate wages, and meaningful (and appropriate quantities of) work.

From the responses of bad job workers—some of which hint at previous experiences with bad treatment—we know that many employees with bad jobs have been disappointed in their work lives. In fact, disappointment is structured into jobs that rarely offer either "respect" or the benefits that workers desperately want (and need). As we noted in a previous chapter, for at least some bad job workers, degraded work is also degendered work and thus especially problematic from the point of view of self-respect.[23]

One of the principal characteristics of bad jobs is that they are in firms that have a record of employment instability. Layoffs are common, as are whole factories simply closing down: "Well, they picked up and moved south." Many of those workers who find jobs in this kind of firm don't wait around to be fired; they "voluntarily" leave. One of the principal reasons for quitting a job, according to these workers, is that they do not receive the respect they believe is their due. Self-worth is not measured by these workers by the job they are doing, the opportunities that job provides, or even their wages; rather self-worth is located in a refusal to be pushed beyond some limit.

Consider the following lengthy statement by Greg Goulette, whose work experiences (in a series of bad jobs) demonstrate a curious admixture of coercion and choice. Sometimes he says that he was fired from jobs; at other times, he says it was his decision to leave. When a potential employer pointed out to him that he was a poor risk because he had been fired, he defended himself by asserting that he wasn't simply fired. Rather, he insisted, he challenged employers until they had no option but to fire him. In short, fired though he was, he was still in control. To his way of thinking, he has thereby preserved self-esteem.

> I was a stock clerk at Ralph's Mart . . . and the main reason I left is I couldn't [get] full time. I was working thirty-five hours a week part time. No benefits. They kept telling me when they put in their [new] store I'd get full time, but when I left it was another four years before they actually built that [store]. . . . I left, I said, "Look I'd be vested in the company in part time, I'd have ten years in part time." . . . I had another job at Discount Beverage. Between the two I was getting pretty run down. I was working thirty-five [hours] at one and thirty [hours] at the other, and sleeping really funny hours, because one was night crew, and one was days, and they both fired me the same week. I was bothering Ralph's [where I was a stock clerk] a lot for a raise, and I wasn't showing up on time for the other job because I didn't feel it was that important. I figured Ralph's was the more important one. So I'd show up late [at Discount Beverage]. And I told them I needed Sundays off and he said, "No you gotta work Sundays." . . . So I think Discount Beverage fired me on a Sunday, and Monday when Ralph's heard about it they said, "Good time to fire him." *Actually, I kind of asked for Ralph's [to fire me]. I was giving them a real hard time. I chewed my boss out. I don't consider it being*

fired. . . . [Then] I went to Stuart's Trucking. . . . I did that for about a year. I did get into towing at the end, but he wouldn't give me a full-time wrecker, and that was where the money was at. . . . I left there. . . . I drove truck for an office supply store. . . . That didn't pay well. I did that for two and a half years, figuring okay, I got training, they won't give me the money right away. After two and a half years I had all the out of town routes. . . . So I went in and I said, "Look, I haven't damaged the truck in two years, I'm one of your most important drivers, and I'm making less than five of the other guys. I deserve a raise." [I was making] like $5.25 an hour, and the only thing that made it worthwhile was that there was lots of overtime. I'd work twelve-hour days. I'd work sixty hours a week. So he said, "What are we talking?" I said, "I don't know—a dollar this week, a dollar next week, and a dollar the week after that. Eight and a quarter." He was like, "Oh, I thought you meant like a twenty-five cent raise. I can't get you a three dollar raise." I said, "Schedule me a day off so I can go look for a job." And three days later he fired me. *So I just kind of piss people off so they fire me.* I've never quit a job. Then I went to G.E. and applied there, and one of the receptionists said, "You've been fired?" I said, "Yeah." And she said, "I wouldn't expect to hear from us. You were fired from your last job. We don't usually hire people that have been fired." I said, "What do you mean?" She said, "Well, if you've been fired it shows the type of person that you are." I said, *"I've been fired from every job I've ever had and in my aspect that shows that you don't quit." I said that would show what type of person you are.* . . . That ruined that. I don't expect to ever hear from G.E. (emphasis added)

Admittedly, Greg is unusual in his willingness to force situations so that they become unacceptable to him (and he to them), but he is far from unique. Other respondents also indicated that, when their efforts went unacknowledged, the line between quitting and being fired became a very fine one.

At least some bad job workers, then, preserve pride through their own refusal to stand for bad treatment.[24] Because bad treatment is often built into the jobs they take, they are more likely to leave their jobs. Like good job workers who respond to disappointment by improving their personal chances within (or outside) their current jobs, the response of quitting among bad job workers is an individual action. Like the response of the good job worker, this action neither directly challenges the employer to make work better nor occasions a collective response.[25] Unlike the efforts of a good job worker, quitting is a highly problematic response: The loss of even a bad job can throw a household that relies on that income into further disarray. Of course, quitting also increases the probability that the next job will be equally bad—or worse.

To be sure, not all employers—even if they offer only bad work—treat their employees with blatant disrespect. Workers in bad jobs—

both men and women—express extreme loyalty to those who treat them well, even as they acknowledge the limits attending that employment. Listen to how Dolly Keating discussed her last two jobs in retail sales. She started with her current one:

INTERVIEWER: Tell me what you do at Bob's Market.

DOLLY KEATING: I'm cashier, stocker, you name it, I do it.

INTERVIEWER: Do you like the job?

DOLLY KEATING: I love it.

INTERVIEWER: What do you like about it?

DOLLY KEATING: At Bob's, what do I like about it? You're always seeing different people. It's just different every day. It's not the same old thing day after day. There's not very many places that you can go into where your boss works right along beside you. Bob and Karen are your friends, your bosses and sometimes, yuh, your enemies, but I think I like the idea, mostly that they work right along beside you and treat you as though you are family. You don't see that very many places.

INTERVIEWER: What do you think an employer owes the people who work in their shop?

DOLLY KEATING: To treat them like individuals.

INTERVIEWER: Which of the places that you've worked do you feel that you got what you needed from an employer?

DOLLY KEATING: Bob's Market.

INTERVIEWER: That's the only place?

DOLLY KEATING: Steve's Deli. Steve was another one who used to work right along beside us. That's about the only two places that I can really say that I felt comfortable.

INTERVIEWER: What did you earn when you first started working at Bob's?

DOLLY KEATING: $4.50.

INTERVIEWER: How much has it gone up since then? You've been there sixteen months.

DOLLY KEATING: I got my raise last week to $5.25.

INTERVIEWER: Do you get benefits?

DOLLY KEATING: No, I'm only part time.

INTERVIEWER: Why do you work part time?

DOLLY KEATING: They don't hire full-time cashiers.

While women like Dolly Keating are less likely to quit than are men even when they *do believe* they are treated badly, as we showed in Chapter 5, these women frequently accommodate their work lives to their domestic lives rather than vice versa. The fact that their work lives offer few advantages makes this accommodation relatively easy. (Recall, for example, that Barbara Badger disliked the fact that her late shift at the Prime Beef Restaurant kept her from her baby and her husband and that she quit that job even though her family needed the income. Because she did not like the job itself, that solution was readily arrived at.)

If the members of good job families—and especially the men within them—have an alternative identity provided by moonlighting that can be drawn on to compensate for indignities at work, bad job workers are in a more troublesome spot. Their moonlighting simply means more bad work. Even when they do enjoy that work, the sociability of getting out and about, or the break from their regular employment, they cannot find in these jobs the same satisfactions found in entrepreneurial moonlighting or substantial self-provisioning projects.

Consumption is a frequent substitute—at least for men. They describe boats, guns, fishing gear, big-screen televisions, and a host of other consumer goods in a way that makes it clear that these objects have become the material representation of their self-worth. But consumption also has its downside. It is not only foolhardy from the perspective of survival, but also a chancy practice when next week's layoff can require that those goods be given up entirely.

EMERGENT POLITICS

When discussing politics, in many respects those in bad job households sound much like their better-off peers. They too value self-reliance and self-sufficiency. Like more fortunate workers, those with bad jobs also express strong anti-state sentiments. They talk about the problems of government regulations and often about government handouts, and they draw sharp lines between those "handouts" and "getting by with a little help from my friends." Unlike their better-off peers, who may, in fact, have at least the hope of engaging in some kind of entrepreneurial activity (even if it is only substantial self-provisioning), it is questionable just what these anti-state sentiments are all about. For these men, to hold down a job at all must substitute for any pride one might ordinarily gain from the job itself. For example, Harvey Gagne said:

> I'm working, believe me, fifty, sixty, seventy hours. I'm not afraid to work.
> . . . But to work that much and not be able to get the things you need—not
> the things you want but the things you need, the necessities. Insurance on
> the trailer, that's a priority; health insurance, things like that. When you can't
> afford those things, what's the sense. Jeez. How much will welfare pay for?
> I've got more pride than that. I was brought up the old-fashioned way that

my parents were brought up. I mean I can count on myself. Do what you have to do. A lot of help from family. A lot of help from friends. That's how we're making it.

Nancy Sharp, who, along with her husband, made extraordinary efforts to sustain the family, had contempt for those who did not appear to make equal efforts to help themselves:

I had to pay for my son to have drum lessons when he was in grade school for a few years. Now people on welfare, their kids are playing instruments. Do you know how much we had to scrape and pinch? We were making about $9,000 just a few years ago . . . and then these kids on welfare are going in and they're playing instruments for free. We're paying for that too. I don't want to see them deprived, but it's not because they're deprived. It's because the parents are not out working and they are so capable of working. They're being paid so much and getting so much benefits from welfare. And all that's around here are minimum wage jobs, they can't make it. Look, tough. We're in the same boat.

Members of bad job families occasionally found themselves in situations where they could no longer avoid drawing on a means-tested form of social support. When this happens, they reinterpret their dependence so that it meshes with a basic stance of self-sufficiency. They believe they differ from others who rely on assistance as a way of life; they just need a little help to get over a particularly rough patch:

There was just three months once one winter, my husband I were both out of work and I was due for the baby, my first one. And I went and I just asked for something. We needed fuel. We could not keep up the fuel payments. And I just asked if there was something I could get maybe to help with that and they gave me what they call General Assistance, food stamps and they paid a certain percentage of your fuel bill. They did that for three months and then that was all. It was just enough to get us over that hump.

Men not only engage in this reinterpretation but also deny their dependence on the support they do receive. When asked whether his family had ever relied on a government program, one man openly acknowledged the receipt of Medicaid and fuel assistance. But, he added, "I am supporting the family. They are just helping us with heat and medical insurance." Similarly, Jake Dwire referred to W.I.C. as something that his wife received rather than the source of commodities the whole family enjoyed. Through their mental gymnastics, men preserve for themselves a sense of their own independence and autonomy—albeit one that they suspect is a bit tarnished.[26]

The struggles of workers with decent jobs and of those less fortunate are different in many ways. With considerable effort, the former group can easily find a basis for self-esteem outside the workplace, and they can preserve a moral stance on which to claim a special virtue. For the latter, self-esteem becomes elusive. Not surprisingly, the efforts the members of bad job families make to sustain that self-esteem in the face of daily challenges sometimes take problematic forms. Both the privileges of good job workers and the predicaments of bad job workers are rooted in the entire gamut of survival strategies each has at its command. In turn, these very different strategies are a consequence of the kind of employment each holds. Work matters. It shapes the means families have available to sustain themselves, and it shapes the expectations and attitudes that emerge from embodying those means.

Conclusion

Throughout this book, we have emphasized the difference that the quality of employment makes, not just for individual satisfaction with a job but also for the capacity of the household to sustain itself through both good and bad times.

The early chapters argued that although the notion of a household obscures the differences and tensions that exist within that unit, it still makes sense to speak about households as entities in which certain collective ends are met. Contrary to the contemporary claim that households have lost their economic rationale, the way people sustain themselves goes far beyond the individual wage and requires a set of strategies based on familial relationships. The survival strategies of households emerge from and are grounded in the connections they have with waged labor. Both households with a hold on good jobs and those without such an advantage serve as examples of these points, but there are dramatic differences between the two sets of households that stem from this link.

Elaborate busyness was a defining characteristic of good job families. It existed in spite of their members' differences in ages, earnings, education, backgrounds, and "personalities." This characteristic derived from the character of employment in those households through both direct and indirect links. These direct links include the ways in which good work supported a dual-earner strategy by ensuring protected leaves during family crises and by underwriting the costs of holding down a job, thus eroding traditional barriers to a second earner entering the labor force. These links also include the ways in which good work provided resources such as predictable time and predictable incomes that secured opportunities to engage in entrepreneurial moonlighting and substantial self-provisioning. Indirectly—through the relationships between the dual-earner strategy and moonlighting—good work underwrote a variety of interhousehold exchanges: Household members use their resources (e.g., time, tools, skills, and money) as the basis for making a contribution toward others in their social networks.

These links went in the other direction as well. Because the members of good work households were enmeshed in broad networks of social support, they were well positioned to locate good jobs (should they find themselves "downsized") and to carry out self-provisioning and entrepreneurial moonlighting projects. With the significant exception of those good job households in which one person had recently been laid off from a good job (we interviewed the members of a number of such households on purpose), good job households were often quite stable year to year, at least at the level of their primary employment and often at the level of their other activities as well. Moreover, through enormous personal effort, the members of good job households could coordinate their various activities to form a coherent whole.

The references to the Donahues throughout these chapters illustrate well the full panoply of economic activities in which good work families engage. Eric Donahue has good waged work, and Lois Donahue works part time at a job she enjoys even though it does not pay much. Eric also has a shop at home where he repairs cars. Lois would enjoy making crafts but, with primary responsibility for two young children, she can rarely find the time to do so. Lois and Eric heat their house with wood that they have delivered in blocks, which they then cut and stack themselves; they constructed their own house, and they extensively renovated another they rent out. Even this relatively detailed accounting underreports the extent to which Lois and Eric exchange with, and help support the economic activities of, others in their networks. Eric exchanges help and advice about car repair with his friends: "A lot of my buddies work on their cars; if I want something I give them a call, if they want something they call me." When Lois and Eric could not handle a task when they were constructing their home, they called in resources: "We needed sheetrock moved one day. It was a four-man job. We would just call people and they would come." They barter with others to keep the driveway plowed:

LOIS: We have some friends who plow out the duplex that we have on the other side.

ERIC: I put his plow on his truck.

LOIS: Right, you put the plow on the truck, and you tend to servicing the truck when it needs to be, so that's a given. They always keep the house plowed out for us and he never charges us any money.

Finally, we might note that when the Donahues' friends were getting ready to build their home, they relied on the knowledge about that process that they had acquired helping the Donahues on theirs.

In short, households use good waged work as a jumping-off place for engagement in a vast array of activities which, although they depend ultimately on that employment, allow for the creation of a life that gives the appearance of being free from reliance on employment itself. But how important is that good work itself? We may seem to have made a paradoxical argument about the precise relevance of good work for the complex survival strategy. On one hand, *any* waged work can undermine, in direct ways, important nonwaged activities. Formal employment can require geographical mobility that disrupts networks, it can take time that might be devoted to activities like self-provisioning, and it frequently means deskilling and thus the disappearance of capacities one can sell independently.[1] On the other hand, some waged work—more particularly, what is called throughout this book "good work"—serves as the *centerpiece* for these other economic activities. Hence, the paradox dissolves, but only with respect to households that are still lucky enough to have access to at least one good job. Although much of that described here may be peculiar to a particular region in its *content*, there is every reason to believe that similarly situated families in other regions engage in comparable forms of economic activity.

One also might ask, how vital are these "other" economic activities? Once again, we seem to have made a paradoxical argument about the economic rationale of various elements of the survival strategy of good work households. On one hand, we call many of these activities components of a survival strategy, and we have demonstrated that they reap earnings and secure savings. On the other hand, when we spoke of good job households, we denied the exclusive economic rationale of some of these elements—or at least some of them at some time. For example, we suggest that the second earner sometimes does not earn enough to cover the cost of employment, that some entrepreneurial moonlighting activities are simply investments in "toys," and that some self-provisioning costs more than it saves. This paradox cannot be dissolved entirely by looking at the household as a unit. The full resolution depended on showing that these pursuits serve individual *as well as* collective ends and that these individual ends have implications for the internal structure of the household and for how people make judgments about themselves and the world in which they live.

Several other pieces of the resolution were implicit in looking at the households as units. Taken as a whole, good work households are economically secure, and they bolster that security by taking care of at least some of their own needs. If not all pieces pay for themselves, they enhance the lives of these families without threatening economic security; good job families move beyond "getting by" to a deep enrichment of their daily lives. Taken as a whole, these activities allow households to gather a measure of independence from the formal economy—even as they rest squarely on it.[2]

Although the firms that moved to Coolidge County two or three decades ago did not invariably offer high wages for their workers, they did offer full-time, year-round, stable employment and reasonable benefit packages. A combination of resources, built on the centerpiece of this good work, secured the construction of predictable and relatively secure lives. The centrality of good work shows up most clearly by its absence. This "absence" is the result of three dynamics characteristic of the contemporary economy. Older firms (e.g., Sterling Aeronautical Company; Master Forms, Inc.; Ajax Corporation) shed responsibility for their employees by moving out altogether and by downsizing, relying on temps, and outsourcing. The vast growth of the service economy creates jobs, but the majority are bad jobs. Finally, the newer small manufacturing firms (e.g., Wilson Contract Manufacturing, Green Mountain Cuddly Toys) that emerged fail to assume the responsibility for *their* workers that was normally associated with the firms they replaced.

Households attached to this new employment—the bad work households—develop a complex set of economic activities, like their good work counterparts. Without the centerpiece of good work, these "extra" activities confront different barriers. They thus both take on a different form and have a different meaning to the individuals engaged in them. This is precisely why we have argued that it is not enough to note the impact of lower wages on these families. In addition, we must examine what bad jobs imply for how families actually survive.

In some ways, bad job households differed little from good job households. Like their counterparts, bad job households could also be extremely busy places, actively tied into both the formal and the informal economy. In a substantial number of bad job households, both husband and wife were in the labor force, and in even a slightly larger proportion than found among good job households, at least one worker had a moonlighting job. Members of these households were even more likely to be actively engaged in routine self-provisioning, and they too made nonmonetary exchanges with those in their social network. A closer examination of bad job households, however, revealed fundamental differences from good job households. The household activities of bad job households were tied to the kind of employment that characterized the household, but because bad work stood at the center of the household economy, both the direct and indirect links had different consequences.

Perhaps most significantly, bad work undermined the capacity of the household to maintain the dual-earner strategy as an ongoing achievement, especially when there were young children within the household. This was so because the instability of bad jobs constantly disrupted employment patterns, because the lack of paid time off meant that families could not respond to crises without jeopardizing employment, and because the wages paid were insufficient to cover the costs of employment. Without two labor force participants, families found it difficult to sustain the other pieces of the survival strategy.

In the absence of substantial resources and predictable schedules, members of bad job households take on *waged* moonlighting jobs (or engage in ersatz entrepreneurial activities such as trading) rather than developing on-the-side businesses. As a consequence, members of bad work households have little control over what happens to them outside their "regular" employment (or, for that matter, inside it). When the burden of holding down poorly coordinated jobs becomes too great or when the work itself is too degrading, individuals may well abandon one job or another. Some of them then become bad workers and not just workers holding bad jobs.

In spite of living in a rural environment that seemed to support traditional self-provisioning and exchange activities, bad job households cannot easily get by on lower wages.[3] Even routine self-provisioning depends on the strategy of two earners. Although, like their good job counterparts, individuals in bad job households rely on social networks to assist with daily living and extraordinary crises, there are drawbacks to these behaviors. Some households experience the withdrawal of offers from those on whom they have depended too greatly in the past. Some individuals fear becoming trapped in networks of obligations, and *they* choose to withdraw. As a consequence, those bad job households with low incomes often find themselves quite isolated. The reverberations of economic restructuring tend to disrupt even the most reliable of these arrangements, such as those that exist between parents and their adult children.

The busiest good job households in terms of employment (those with two earners and at least one individual engaged in moonlighting) are the *same* households that engage in self-provisioning and make frequent exchanges with others. All these arrangements are stable and predictable, but the bad job households with two earners, though more likely to have a moonlighter and high rates of self-provisioning, are not necessarily the same households that rely on social exchanges. In fact, those who do self-provisioning are also the ones who find themselves most isolated—whether by choice or not.[4]

These interconnections among the various elements of the survival strategy produced a kind of cumulative disadvantage: As one piece unraveled, so too did other pieces. Even when they *could* be maintained, activities fit together less coherently. Moreover, bad job families as a group exhibited greater variety. Thus, no single family is as emblematic of the experience of bad job households as the Donahues are of their more privileged counterparts. Several families, however, vividly illustrated the struggles of those without access to good work. The Seeleys relied on Walt's self-employment and Dottie's various part-time jobs. Their uncertain income patterns (compounded by Walt's trading practices) precluded long-range investments that could improve their lives at the same time that the recent hospitalization of their young son resulted in long-range medical debts because of the absence of employer-guaranteed health insurance. Two sisters—Barbara Badger and Patricia Slater—each waited to see if their husbands' temporary work would reap a permanent improvement in their lives. This waiting was made all the more anxious as they watched their father's world—and thus their fallback security—crumble when he was laid off by Sterling. The Riverses, while formerly a good job family themselves, scrambled to keep from losing all they had acquired during their more prosperous years.

In both sets of households, gendered relationships persist in spite of the fact that some of their "traditional" preconditions are gone, but that persistence has different features in the good job and bad job families. Among some good job households, gender is sustained because men have better and different work from their wives. Even when these sources of difference and privilege are absent, as they are beginning to be, gender is reconstituted on the basis of the multiple activities that make up the family's varied survival strategy—a survival strategy that, although it uses good waged work as its centerpiece, proclaims its independence from that work. These survival strategies rest on assumptions that are encoded in traditional gender behavior and thus, whether it is intended or not, breathe new life into gendered roles.

In fact, some elements of this survival strategy are maintained, at least in part, because they allow—indeed demand—the recreation of gender. By engaging in entrepreneurial moonlighting and substantial self-provisioning, men in good job households can reenact a stereotypical male role; by joining into the cooperative ventures that accompany these activities, they create a set of significant social networks that act back to reinforce masculinity. They have access to a discretionary income and are in a position to command the labor of their wives. They reassert their difference from women and their relative privilege. All of this has consequences for who normally takes responsibility for what we usually consider housework. When men have more jobs than their wives, they can claim that their activities keep them busy: They have a "legitimate" reason for not sharing routine household tasks. Bound to their own income-producing activities and their moral obligations to others, they shed responsibility for the ongoing routines of daily life even as they increase the burdens placed on those routines. In households where the responsibility for bringing in income is more evenly shared by husbands and wives (as measured by the number of jobs they hold), so too are the tasks involved in everyday maintenance. Equity is not an entirely elusive goal, and whether there is sharing or not, the survival strategy of good job households requires complex coordination. The flexibility of each component of the survival strategy allows for its completion; the fact that these components rest squarely on the centerpiece of good waged work ensures that households have at least the minimal resources necessary to get by.

The bad job households tell a very different story about the intersections of gender, the household division of labor, and the causes of tension. Their survival strategies offer fewer occasions for men and women to feel good about themselves. Neither the principal income activities of men nor the additional jobs they take on offer a secure base for the establishment of self-esteem. When their wives are employed, the work they do is often of a quality equal to the men's, even if it is done on a part-time basis, and in the absence of sufficient resources, men are unable to acquire the material underpinnings for the accomplishment of major self-provisioning activities. Even so, men in these households assert a certain autonomy—especially when they might be expected to do just the reverse: When they have fewer jobs than their wives, they do less housework. Some men buy and sell luxury items at a rapid clip. Trading, like other practices in these families, compounds the unpredictability of the lives of their members. Some women have a basis for believing themselves equal partners with their husbands in supporting the family, but many women find that their work lives have to be sacrificed to other concerns. As a rule, women retain more of the responsibility for housework and child care, but there are fewer rewards in enacting that traditional role. Without flexibility in the component pieces of the survival strategy, coordination gives way to a diminishing satisfaction with domestic life and frequently to understandable tension.

In spite of evidence that U.S. workers have experienced losses in real wages, growing insecurity in the workplace, and a decline in the quality of employment,[5] one hears little from workers themselves. This quiescence is increasingly attributed to a particular set of attitudes that exonerates public policies and corporate practices.

Some argue that a strong streak of individualism not only stands in the way of a collective response to threats to job security but also leads Americans to blame themselves rather than those who have a hand in determining their fate.[6] Thurow, for example, in comparing French and American reactions to corporate downsizing and threats to the viability of unions, suggests that "the French believe that much of the success or failure of life is caused by social organization," that "if something goes wrong in their lives they are not necessarily to blame." By way of contrast, he argues, "Americans take individualism seriously. They are personally responsible for their own failures."[7] From this viewpoint, it is not necessary to blame the victims for what has happened to them: They already blame themselves.

An alternative popular interpretation for worker quiescence is even more pernicious in suggesting that American employees are willing to trade meaningful work, good wages, and job security for reduced working hours and increased leisure.[8] Juliet Schor, for example, in a discussion of a 1994 Gallup Poll showing that about "one-third of respondents were amenable to reducing their household income by 20% in exchange for reducing working hours," coined the phrase "downshifting or personal downsizing" to describe a rising perspective "wherein people choose to live more simply on smaller incomes in order to have more free time and less stress."[9] In spite of studies showing (as we have here) that Americans are putting more hours into paid work than ever before, holding down more jobs, and requiring employment of a larger number of family members, the American Enterprise Institute proclaims that "people's free time has actually been increasing."[10] Rather than blaming the victim for his or her misfortunes, this viewpoint eliminates both victim and blame; workers and corporations jointly embrace the end of work. Nobody liked it much anyway.

The evidence in this book suggests a more complex interpretation—both with respect to good job workers and with respect to those who are less privileged—even though both sets of workers did, as the scholarship suggests, exonerate employers from responsibility. Among good job workers, side by side with that exoneration is substantial disappointment stemming from the fact that the historical Fordist contract has been broken. Men especially seem to believe that their careers do not represent what they had been led to expect might be their due as white males. They see their privileges declining. Still, some of these workers, with persistent optimism, do view their relationship with their employers in very individualistic terms; they believe that remediation will come from their own efforts. Hence, they position themselves—by leaving a good paper trail, by acquiring further training—to make the most of what they have. This particular individualistic effort does not represent the whole picture of their response. Many of these workers turn to entrepreneurial moonlighting and self-provisioning, not only as a way to increase their household income or as a means of gaining access to discretionary income or even as a means to evade household responsibilities, but also as a direct response to disappointment. Having done so—that is, having created a viable on-the-side business or engaged in home construction—they have an alternative source of satisfaction and meaning in their lives. Thus, they almost willingly embrace limited career expectations and reduced demands on their employers.

Many of these members of good job households clearly recognize their dependence on employment (for a regular salary and for benefits), yet, given the efforts that they put into "work outside employment," they also simultaneously discount that dependence and proclaim their own independence.[11] Drawing on the knowledge of their own skills and their own achievements, they conceive of themselves with considerable pride as individuals who could get by without the job that now underlies their on-the-side activities. Many of them dream of a life of freedom from employment and toy with the idea of going into business for themselves.[12]

Obviously, these responses have repercussions in the workplace. Individuals who believe they have their own personal careers outside their "regular" jobs are less likely to think collectively. The link between these regular jobs and these outside careers is less important than people's conception of themselves as nearly entrepreneurs capitalizing on their own skills. In fact, ironically, their outside work makes their regular employment appear incidental and unimportant.

There is another irony here. Men with good jobs engage in a variety of activities that give them experiences that help sustain an illusion of self-sufficiency. Their wives, even if they are not as directly involved in those activities, benefit from them as well. Both men and women work extremely long hours on a daily basis, but their daily lives—the comforts of a well-constructed home, the harvest from a well-tended garden— confirm the virtues and rewards of this hard work and what seems to be a kind of modern-day self-reliance. It is small wonder, then, that many of those with good jobs—both men and women—when asked what contributions the government could make to their own well-being, answer that the state should allow them to continue to reap the benefits of their efforts and make things easier for them as working people through day care, lower taxes, and assistance with educational expenses. The government should not take from them, however, to support those who appear less willing than they are to make similar efforts to support themselves. Hence, self-provisioning and on-the-side entrepreneurial activities directly engender an individualism rooted in apparent self-reliance. These attitudes directly feed into a set of political attitudes that resonate well with the current attack on an activist government.

Greenberg makes a very similar point about politics in the 1990s. He points out that valuing their own responsibility and hard work, working-class people are critical of those who, they believe, live by a different set of values.

> They see the world through this prism: those who support their personal efforts and those that undermine them; those who respect their virtue and those who disregard or take advantage of it; those who live by the same values and those who do not. It is the tension between virtue and grievance— rather than between labor and capital—that animates the working- and lower-middle-class electorate and that creates political energy. Political and

economic messages will have to be rooted in this discourse about virtue if they are to capture the attention of downscale America.

The "bad guys" are those who do not respect the struggle and the virtues of working- and middle-class America. Government is a big part of the story, though not all of it. . . . The "good guys," on the other hand, are the working- and middle-class people, the people who work, who are self-reliant, and who take responsibility; they include the small business people who put everything on the line.[13]

To the extent that we can generalize, bad work employees, although they also often exonerate employers, express a different set of attitudes, born of a different set of experiences. First of all, they have already lowered their expectations. Few expect the Fordist promises of security, a family wage, and career opportunity, but they do want to be treated well.[14] Sometimes, this orientation gives bad job workers a way out, a reason for abandoning their current jobs. Unlike good job workers, who have at stake plant-specific skills and employment benefits, those with bad jobs can often—albeit occasionally after some struggle—find another work site with more or less equal opportunities, even if these opportunities are minimal.

Few of these sites offer the occasion to develop a positive self-image, a sense of one's own worth. The result is that many bad job workers locate their sense of worth in their refusal to stand for bad treatment and in their willingness to look for another job when they are no longer willing to put up with their current ones. Hence, they too proclaim— on a basis that is quite different from that of good job workers—an individualism rooted in autonomy and independence. Many of them share with their good job counterparts the dream of self-employment.

Like their good job counterparts, bad job workers also proclaim the values of self-sufficiency and self-reliance. Self-sufficiency here often takes the form of making deals. In a keen eye for trading and in the ability to "make do," some find a rough-and-ready self-esteem: They recognize a good bargain when they see one, they don't let anyone cheat them, and they know how to get hold of what they need. Individuals in bad job households, like those in good job households, thus also proclaim an ability to get by without the government; however, this getting by not only has greater costs (to the household members) but also is less reliable. Some bad job households have to seek governmental support. Women in these households struggle to balance family needs and a husband's pride. Men in these households can sometimes protect themselves from acknowledgment of dependence and thus preserve an individual stance that trusts themselves to provide for their families.

Although this book has stressed the differences between good and bad job households (because that indeed has been the goal), there are commonalities that should not be overlooked. Neither good job workers nor bad job workers readily speak in a collective voice about possibilities for improving their workplace or about possibilities for improving the conditions of their lives. Both are basically distrustful of the state, even if they believe it can provide specific kinds of help in their own lives and even if those in bad job households have had to rely on assistance more often than have those in good job households.[15] They openly express attitudes of resentment toward the way they believe the government acts—too intrusive, too much self-interest on the part of politicians, too many broken promises, and too much waste and misspending. Both see virtue in their hard work and self-sufficiency. Both strive to distinguish themselves from others who appear to work less hard and be less self-sufficient. Both take pride in their accomplishments, and their accomplishments are often the same. Women in both sets of households are especially likely to point to their families. When asked what she was proudest of, one woman answered simply, "My daughters"; another, when asked the same question, said "My family"; yet another, when her husband pointed to other achievements, reminded him "The kids are pretty good kids." Men also sometimes put family first:

INTERVIEWER: What in your life do you feel proudest of?
RESPONDENT: I guess first, my family. Secondly, what I have achieved personally. I guess I'm most proud of my family. (Bad job man)

A good job man replied

I'm proud of my family and the fact that we can have a life where we can enjoy things and not be too worried about it. I've grappled with that question a lot lately, because of the [changes at work]. But, I'd say family I'd be most proud of, the most I can show for life.

Quite a few respondents, including both men and women in both sets of households, located pride in their simple capacity to get by, to make it on their own:

I guess I am proud of coming through life as well as I have. Taking things that could be bad and making them better, getting something out of them instead of just letting them get you. That's the best thing I could think of. (Bad job woman)

[I'm proudest of] the fact that I am out on my own and that I'm not getting any help from anyone. I'm making ends meet by myself. Not having to rely on anybody to lean on all the time. (Good job man)

[I'm proudest of] having a home that is mortgage free, knowing that you did it all yourself. (Good job man)

Most fulfilling I think is that I can take and make it on my own. I know now, because I put myself through college and everything, that I am a self-sufficient person. I don't need my husband. If I had to do without my husband. I wouldn't like it much with the kids, because it would make things very hard. But I'm determined enough that I could do that. And he knows that, too. We've had that talk a few times. (Bad job woman)

We're very proud of what we've done. We've come a long ways. We got married, I think we had $300 combined, he had a car payment, we had my bed from home, and a used kitchen table and four chairs and that's all we had. (Good job woman)

I would say our independence. The fact that we've done everything we've done so far without any help, from either family. . . . Whatever we've accomplished we've done pretty much ourselves. . . . There are problems that we have had that we have ourselves to thank for, too. (Good job man)

When the popular (and academic) press restates these sources of pride and this sense of "virtue" as a kind of ungrounded and simply recalcitrant "individualism" or even worse, as "personal downsizing," it both confirms conservatism and further isolates those who believe themselves to be misunderstood. This restatement also allows business (and politics) to carry on "as usual."

The policy implications of *this* study are not so readily aligned with the status quo. As individuals and as members of households, men and women alike need access to stable employment that carries paid time off, health insurance, and the opportunity to engage in meaningful work. This is not meant to slight the importance of wages, but the evidence presented suggests that in the absence of those other benefits, even households that are relatively well off financially may be unable to secure a way of life that can sustain them through hard times. The poverty of bad jobs is deeper and more devastating than that created by low wages alone, and self-employment—even if it carries with it obvious personal satisfactions—cannot do the trick.

As a nation, we seem headed in precisely the wrong direction. At all levels of employment—from managers who have been downsized and are now being hired back as temporary contract workers to those who are cast off welfare rolls and then required to accept the first job that comes along—an increasing number of lives are marked by bad work.

Meanwhile, the continued political emphasis on family values insistently asserts that problems lie within the household itself, even though the economy (as a consequence of political decisions) fails to offer the support that families need if they are going to embody their commitment to those values.

There is room here for political mobilization, and there are signs of that possibility as well: Union membership is on the rise, and when people are asked about specific social policies—paying for health care for the poor, for example—they give generous responses. Overall, however, the 1996 presidential election, which moved politics to the center (or, more accurately, the right) and disenfranchised the working poor as well as those with even fewer resources, leaves little room for optimism. To shift to a new direction, progressive politicians must develop a political message that recognizes that working people have primarily turned inward—to their own virtues and self-reliance—because the economy has failed them and because in the face of that failure they believe the government is "more an obstacle than an ally."[16] On the surface, that inward turning resonates more with political conservatism than the traditional progressive line, with a perspective that blames people for their own failures and tells the government to let people alone. If progressive forces are going to capture the interest, and respond to the concerns, of people like the Donahues and the Riverses, the Hubbards and the Badgers, they will have to offer a program that "allows people, short of heroism, to achieve a better life for their families."[17] They will have to offer as well a justification for that program that helps people understand that they need not make that better life entirely on their own. Finally, they must demonstrate the ways in which working families have common interests and concerns with those who are even less fortunate than themselves. This is no small task.

Methodology

We provide here a more detailed discussion of our research methods than is found in the Introduction. We include a discussion of our data collection procedures and of our variable measurements.

DATA COLLECTION

Between 1991 and 1992 (with the assistance of several research assistants), in-depth interviews were conducted with a sample of 117 individuals in 81 households in Coolidge County.[1] With very few exceptions, each interview subject was interviewed but one time.[2] Most of these interviews were conducted in the respondent's home.[3] All were tape recorded, and the tapes were fully transcribed.

The interviews covered a wide range of topics, beginning generally with the background of the family members (e.g., parents' education and occupations, jobs held as a teenager) and moving on to their current situation (e.g., employment, self-provisioning activities, exchange relationships with other households, and the household composition). Throughout the interview, we paid particular attention to the household's location in the broader economy, asking not just about the income derived from a member's principal employment but also about income derived from on-the-side activities. We also paid particular attention to the sources of a wide range of goods and services the household relied on for its daily survival. For example, we asked whether the family heated its home with wood and, if so, how the household obtained that fuel; how many cars it had, where they were purchased, how they were financed, and who repaired them; and whether it made or grew any of its food and clothing and where it obtained those items it did not supply itself. These questions served to identify additional people we could interview (and thus enlarged our sample); more important, they helped us ascertain the extent to which the household relied on different aspects of the economy of the region in which it was located. Each interview ended with the more sensitive set of issues about hopes, disappointments, political affiliation, and sources of household stress.

The households for the in-depth interviews were located through a snowball sampling technique, starting with individuals who currently had or had just lost employment in a major firm in Coolidge County and extending out from these households to other households and individuals with whom they were connected either as family members, workplace colleagues, or providers of goods and services. There are three consequences of this strategy.

First, we obtained a sample more heavily weighted toward manufacturing than would have been the case otherwise. We consider this to be an advantage: Because we are particularly interested in the restructuring of work in the manufacturing sector, the fact that 39 percent of the household members held as their principal occupation a job in that sector (in contrast to 17 percent of Coolidge County labor force and 15 percent of those in the random survey discussed below) means that we were able to gather more information about both what good workers in this sector had experienced and the consequences for those less fortunately situated in the same sector.

Second, because we started with a manufacturing firm that had recently had a major layoff, we could explore attitudes during this period of crisis and how individuals responded to the loss of employment. In fact, although 52 percent of the households we interviewed had been good work households in the recent past, nine of those households had recently become bad work households and another ten, although they had lost one individual's good work, remained good work households. Interviewing families in transition lent insight into the processes through which individuals made sense of the role of a particular kind of employment for the household's survival strategy and understood their place in the world.

Third, through this strategy of snowball sampling that focused on the links among households, we were able to understand how networks guide activities in both the formal and the informal economy. For example, in one relatively simple grouping, we interviewed the three Dwire brothers (and the wife of one and the live-in girlfriend of another) as well as coworkers of one of the brothers (a group that happened to include the wife of one of the other brothers) and a man (and, separately, the wife of this man) with whom one of the brothers jointly raised pigs (Chart 8). By interviewing one of the coworkers (of the youngest brother and his sister-in-law), we gained access to a whole different, albeit interconnected, network of individuals bound by similar ties of exchange and affiliation, such as the babysitter of one of the coworkers, her husband, and his co-owner of a small-engine repair shop (Chart 9). This led us to two sets of part-time employees of a logger, individuals who purchased wood from that same logger, and, of course, the networks of each of their households as well (Chart 10). In following networks in this way, we gained a deeper understanding not only of routes of social interaction and economic transactions (broadly defined) but also of the mutuality and reciprocity that were associated with these connections. Hence, we could "observe" both the extent to which individuals

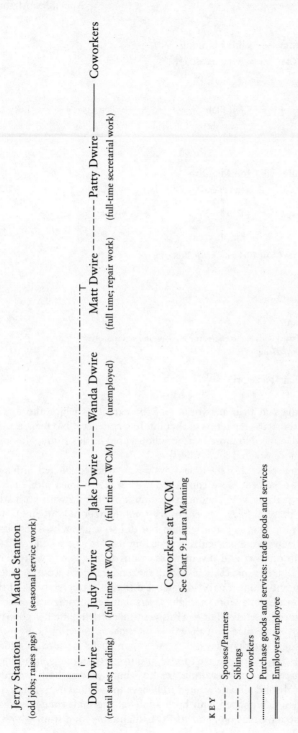

Jerry Stanton ----- Maude Stanton
(odd jobs; raises pigs) (seasonal service work)

Don Dwire ----- Judy Dwire ----- Jake Dwire ----- Wanda Dwire ------- Matt Dwire -------- Patty Dwire ------- Coworkers
(retail sales; trading) (full time at WCM) (full time at WCM) (unemployed) (full time; repair work) (full-time secretarial work)

Coworkers at WCM
See Chart 9: Laura Manning

KEY

----- Spouses/Partners

--- Siblings

—— Coworkers

············· Purchase goods and services: trade goods and services

═══ Employers/employee

Chart 8. Dwire Network

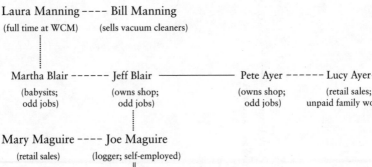

Laura Manning ---- Bill Manning
(full time at WCM)   (sells vacuum cleaners)

Martha Blair ------ Jeff Blair   Pete Ayer ------ Lucy Ayer
   (babysits;   (owns shop;   (owns shop;   (retail sales;
   odd jobs)   odd jobs)   odd jobs)   unpaid family worker)

Mary Maguire ---- Joe Maguire
   (retail sales)   (logger; self-employed)

Employees

See Chart 10: Paul Currier, Bruce Sharp

KEY
- - - - -   Spouses/Partners
—·—·—   Siblings
————   Coworkers
············   Purchase goods and services: trade goods and services
=======   Employers/employee

Chart 9.   Blair Network

relied on others in their networks *and* the extent to which those others accepted—or resisted—the terms of that interdependence. "No man is an island,"
wrote John Donne. No more so is any household in this study, although some
are indeed more isolated than others.

Thirty-three percent of the interviews we use were conducted with adult men
alone, and 46 percent were conducted with adult women alone (Table 12).
Twenty-one percent were conducted within a household with both adult men
and women present. In 20 percent of the total number of households, we interviewed both the man and the woman but did so separately. These latter two
sets of interviews were particularly revealing insofar as they allowed access to
differences in opinion and divergent reactions to the same events and issues.
Needless to say, in some cases, especially when interviews were conducted separately, men and women gave somewhat different interpretations of the same
events. For example, a woman might assert that her income was critical to the
survival of the household, but her husband might denigrate her contributions.
Alternatively, some men said that they fully participated in housework while
their wives suggested that they did no more than "help" on rare occasions where
we found discrepancies, we are careful in our interpretations, believing neither
version as necessarily representing "reality" but believing both as understandings of what the individuals wanted to believe (or wanted us to believe) was the
case. Interviews conducted with both adults at the same time revealed households' interactions, tensions, and efforts to maintain—or disrupt—both individ-

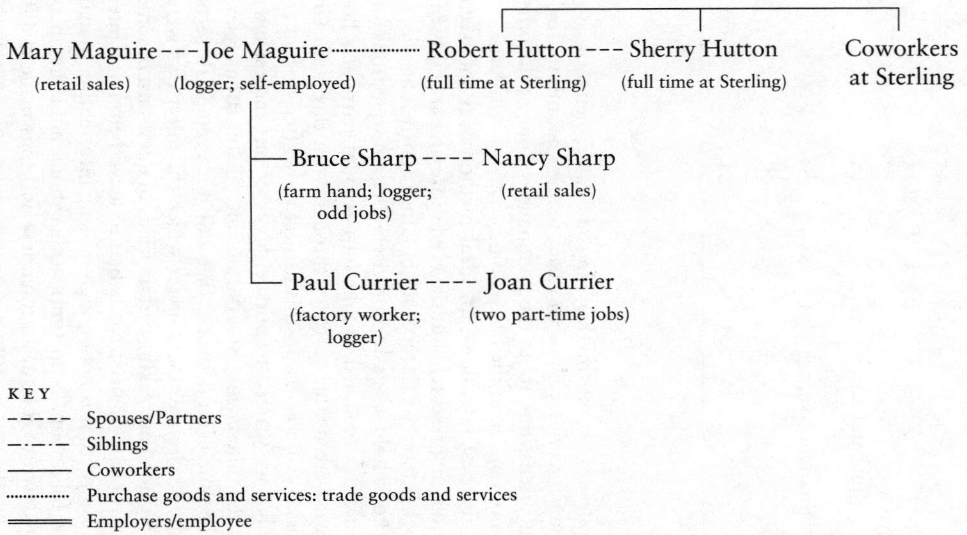

Mary Maguire --- Joe Maguire ·················· Robert Hutton --- Sherry Hutton   Coworkers
(retail sales)   (logger; self-employed)   (full time at Sterling)   (full time at Sterling)   at Sterling

                        Bruce Sharp ---- Nancy Sharp
                        (farm hand; logger;   (retail sales)
                         odd jobs)

                        Paul Currier ---- Joan Currier
                        (factory worker;   (two part-time jobs)
                         logger)

K E Y

- - - -   Spouses/Partners

- · - · -   Siblings

············   Coworkers

············   Purchase goods and services: trade goods and services

========   Employers/employee

Chart 10. Maguire Network

TABLE 12.   NONRANDOM SURVEY INTERVIEWS

	TOTAL NUMBER OF PEOPLE OR HOUSEHOLDS INTERVIEWED	% OF INDIVIDUAL OR HOUSEHOLD INTERVIEWS
Individual interviews		
Men	52	44
Women	65	56
Total	117	100
Household interviews		
Joint interviews (husband and wife together)	16	20
Separate interviews (each separately)	20	25
Husband only	16	20
Wife only	29	36
Total	81	100

ual constructions and "family myths."[4] In some cases, men took over what were meant to be joint interviews. In other cases, women became more dominant. In some cases, the discussions about the dominance of one or the other revealed a particular kind of tension in the household.

In spite of the best intentions, an ideal methodology intersected with the realities of conducting research and the even more urgent reality of conducting research through interviews. Hence, although we aimed at a series of interviews in which each household was asked precisely the same questions (or at least the same set of questions modified to take into account particular household circumstances), we were unable to carry through with this goal. First, we fully identified the issues of concern to this project only after we had enough interviews to see what we wanted to pursue. Some of our earliest interviews were exploratory in the fullest sense and did not include questions relevant to what subsequently became central issues. (We did not exclude these partial interviews.) Second, the circumstances under which the interviews were conducted occasionally precluded our asking certain kinds of questions. In some cases, time alone was the problem: Some subjects had to leave before the interview could be completed, but there was not enough missing information to make it worthwhile to do a follow-up. Sometimes, other household members wandered through or sat down to join in an interview and thus made it difficult, if not impossible, to pursue certain topics. On some occasions, we quite simply had to let people tell their stories in the way that they wanted them told and, in so doing, we used up more than our allocated time with them without asking about all that we wanted to know.

Finally, sometimes individuals were under such extreme stress that we felt that we could not push them to cover material that might have been difficult or distressing. Two particular occasions come to mind. One of the authors interviewed a man the night before his firm announced massive layoffs. Although he had agreed to be interviewed on that night—and did not want to put it off until a more suitable time—he was almost mute with anxiety. One of our research assistants conducted an interview with a woman who sat holding her very ill child; the child died three weeks later. Even the more typical interview situations could be distressing. One of our interviews was conducted with a man who had just lost his job. Our research assistant wrote these notes at the end:

> I didn't think he was going to start crying or anything, but he's definitely very discouraged. It's interesting to see how this has really changed his view of people who are unemployed, and who aren't bothering to look for jobs because he's getting very discouraged. Very, very nice guy. He took a lot of time with me and thanked me for coming over and that sort of thing. Very nice.[5]

The "unevenness" of our interviews, combined with the absence of a random sample, justifies our preexisting bias against quantifying these qualitative data. From time to time, we do precisely that (for example, we talk about substantial self-provisioning occurring only among good job households). By and large, we can avoid quantifying these data, which purposefully sacrificed exactitude for depth, because we have another source of data that we describe below.

As a second data collection technique, we conducted a telephone survey of households in Coolidge County. For the telephone survey, we used a random sample drawing 3 percent of the population of each town.[6] The response rate for this survey was 54 percent. The total number of respondents was 358. The profile of these households resembles closely that obtained in the 1990 census with respect to age, education, household income, industry sector, and occupations. Using the criteria defined in the Introduction, we selected 158 of these interviews for the analysis in this book. This subset of households closely resembles married-couple families in the county with respect to income (with the exception that we have fewer of the very richest families included). The individuals in this subset also closely resemble the population in the county with respect to occupations, the sector in which those occupations are found, and the class of worker. (Unless otherwise indicated, the numerical data are drawn from this survey.)

This survey asked questions about the household configuration, the labor force involvement of the different members of the household, self-provisioning efforts, exchange relationships, and responsibility of household members for housework. These questions were developed after we had done extensive interviewing, and therefore they focused more precisely on the issues with which we were concerned.

Even so, we made errors. For example, although we were highly aware of just how hard the struggle for survival was among some of those we interviewed, we underestimated just how intense this struggle could be. Having left room for four economic activities for each adult, in several cases we found individuals with more activities than we had room to record. We also had one major disaster, which, fortunately occurred after we had completed the bulk of our interviewing.[7]

Recent critiques of sociology point a finger at both of these methodologies, not only because they are coercive, are objectifying, and fail to locate the researcher in the research process (and thus assume a kind of objectivity in interpretation), but also particularly because they rely on individual narratives and they *trust* those narratives. We appreciate the impulse behind these critiques and we have made some of them, at other times and in other places, ourselves. We acknowledge the coercion involved in these practices: In fact, we found out just how coercive they were when one respondent asked, in a telephone interview, if she really had to answer all the questions.

We also acknowledge the difficulties we have in objectifying subjects, particularly when that involves classifying them by criteria that are not their own. Dividing a set of households into two separate groups presents no problem for the researcher dealing with anonymous units identified only by some randomly assigned number (as we do when we draw on the data from the random survey). Why would we care about any given household and how it got assigned to one group or another? Once assigned, as any researcher knows full well, the divisions develop their own meaning, as we, perhaps necessarily, reify the classifications we have developed and the conceptual apparatus that surrounds them. We can also ignore, with aplomb, deviant cases. This rending is far more problematic when the individual households that constitute the original whole are "known" in their complexity and subtlety by the researcher (as is the case when we draw on our in-depth interviews). We can then see the ways in which a household placed through "objective" criteria into one group has characteristics of, and maybe even the "feel" of, the other group. The resistance we feel to classification—although classification is a key element of this entire venture—should be heeded. That resistance, and the "deviant" cases that occasion it, are constant reminders that although we have to simplify to explain, in fact the world is never as simple as the explanations we offer.

Not only does the research process turn people in all their individuality into simplified objects of analysis, but much sociological analysis also intensifies this objectification. Individuals known to the researcher in at least partial complexity become known to the reader only as represented in phrases such as "one man who did welding" or lumped together as "some women without employment outside the home." In an effort to resist or at least inhibit the extent of this objectification, in the body of this book we do refer to some individuals by name (or rather, by pseudonym).

Although we have noted that we were affected by, and deeply engaged in, the research, we do not believe it is about us, although who we are (white women in professional careers) and our political orientations clearly determine the analytic framework that we chose and the particular issues that we address. Finally, we openly acknowledge the possibility for misrepresentation by the subjects of both sets of interviews. At the same time, we believe the stories—if not in every concrete detail—because of their repetition (that is, sets of "stories" followed similar lines) and because they make intuitive sense to us. We hope that we can persuade the reader as well.

In addition to the interviews conducted with "respondents," we conducted interviews with representatives of four firms in which respondents were employed (Wilson Contract Manufacturing; Green Mountain Cuddly Toys; Master Forms, Inc.; and Ajax Plastics), one firm that supplied temporary workers to the labor force in the area (Temporary Employment Agency), and a firm that sold tools to both individuals and small businesses (Handy Tools).*

VARIABLE DEFINITIONS

As noted in the Introduction, we examine four aspects of a household's survival strategy. Each of these tactics is briefly defined there. The following further discusses our terminology and introduces some additional terms.

Among households that employ a dual-earner strategy, we distinguish between the "primary worker" (the worker with the "better" or only job) and the "second" worker (the worker who either has a job of lower quality or is absent from the labor force altogether). Because the vast majority of households in the United States now have at least two earners at work at any given time, it is questionable to resurrect the notion of a "second" worker. In fact, a "statistical" designation as a "second worker" did not invariably correspond to the family's definition: In our in-depth interviews, we often found that the person we might have designated the "second" worker was in fact the mainstay of the family's economy and was regarded as such by the other family members. (Not surprisingly, gender plays a role in family designations of "first" and "second" workers independently of the actual contributions husbands and wives make to the family's well-being. We consider the role of gender at length in Chapters 5 and 6.) Overall, however, the person who held down the job of lesser quality was, from the point of view of the family, the "second" worker, by which was meant that their job was the first to go or to be rearranged to make room for the employment situation of the "first" worker.

Within our sample of households, both the second worker's employment and the second "job" of either moonlighting worker might well occur within the informal economy; we did not limit our definition of income-producing activities to those that would be reported on taxes. We did, however, "require" that *at least one* worker within the household held a formally organized waged job.

"Moonlighting" is often referred to as multiple job holding.[8] A more common reference than moonlighting or even multiple job holding might be to someone's second or even third job. We wanted to preserve the term "second" to refer to the worker within the household who held the job that was less significant to the household survival strategy.

In recent years, scholars have drawn attention to the fact that families do not survive on wages or earnings alone (whether from a principal job or from moonlighting) even in the midst of highly developed regions of the world, but indeed rely on many different activities to get by. This awareness has led to considerable discussion of how to categorize these "other" activities.[9] There are any number of different terms—domestic economy, complementary economy, social economy, interhousehold labor, and intrahousehold self-provisioning, to name a few. The complexity of the various typologies that give rise to these terms reflects the

* As with names of individuals, names of firms in Coolidge County are pseudonyms.

difficulty of defining and capturing activities that by their very nature defy easy categorization.

Most typologies make two central distinctions. The first is between activities done by household members for themselves and activities that are exchanged with members of other households. As noted, we too make this distinction below: We differentiate between *self-provisioning* and nonmonetary *interhousehold exchanges*.

The former was assessed in the random telephone survey by presenting respondents with a list of five different goods and services and asking which they provided *for themselves*. The list was composed of those items mentioned most frequently in the in-depth interviews. It included growing vegetables, snow-plowing, raising livestock, gathering wood for fuel, and changing the oil in the car. (Although it is difficult to separate self-provisioning from what is commonly referred to as housework, we believe that our measures are relatively clear insofar as they do not refer to "the chores of daily maintenance" that characterize all households.[10] Hence, there is an obvious distinction between, say, washing the dishes and gathering wood. Other scholars make a similar distinction.[11])

While the routine self-provisioning scale measures the range of self-provisioning activities, the indicator of substantial self-provisioning—whether or not family members had built their own house or substantially renovated an existing one—is a measure of intensity.[12] It also captures an activity that has the potential for enhancing living conditions and for reaping more significant savings. Individuals who change the oil in their cars *sustain* their daily practices and calculate their savings in the hundreds of dollars (at best). Individuals who construct their own homes improve their environment and calculate savings in the tens of hundreds (and even tens of thousands) of dollars.

The second common distinction, referring to exchanges with members of other households, is between those in which money exchanges hands and those in which it does not.[13] We do *not* make this same strict division. Following the work of Levitan and Feldman, when analyzing interhousehold exchanges, we examine a variety of different kinds of practices.

Informal assistance to other households (one component of interhousehold exchanges) was assessed in the random telephone survey by presenting respondents with the same list of goods and services as used for the self-provisioning measure and asking which other households had provided *to the household* within the past year. As noted, we also examined barter, reduced rates, and moving in with other households. Even if money sometimes changes hands in these transactions, they can be differentiated from other economic transactions, as Levitan and Feldman argue, because they partake simultaneously of an economic and a social logic: If they are paid for with money, it is not with money alone but also "in currencies where value may be measured by gratitude, bonding, or the development of a sense of mutual obligation."[14] Moreover, what is important here is not whether money changes hands in these transactions but how they can be understood to fit into the household's complex survival strategy. As we showed in the Introduction with the example of Bruce Sharp, our respondents could easily make fine distinctions.

Notes

INTRODUCTION

1. For an example of the kind of activities we anticipated finding among the "second" group, see Rhoda Halperin, *The Livelihood of Kin: Making Ends Meet "The Kentucky Way"* (Austin: University of Texas Press, 1990). Smith and Wallerstein argue that among the lowest paid workers, novel sources of income act as a defense against low wages; that is, that multiple forms of income are employed as a way of subsidizing the wage (Joan Smith and Immanuel Wallerstein, *Creating and Transforming Households* [Cambridge, UK: Cambridge University Press,1992]).

2. In the nineteenth century, there had been considerable industrialization in the area, especially in textiles and extraction. Some of those industries lasted well into the 1950s.

3. There are many definitions of Fordism, but the common aspects agreed on by most authors are (1) an internal transformation of the industrial production processes and (2) the expansion of the internal market by increasing the purchasing power of workers. See, for example, Mike Davis, *Prisoners of the American Dream* (London: Verso, 1986); Alain Lipietz, *Mirages and Miracles: The Crises of Global Fordism* (London: Verso, 1987); Linda M. Labao and Michael D. Schulman, "Farming Patterns, Rural Restructuring, and Poverty: A Comparative Regional Analysis," *Rural Sociology* 56, no. 4 (Winter 1991): 565–602.

4. Robert Benincasa, "Vermont Income Down $2,700," *Burlington Free Press* (September 30, 1997): 1A, 9A.

5. Alejandro Portes, Manuel Castells, and Lauren A. Benton, eds., *The Informal Economy: Studies in Advanced and Less Developed Countries* (Baltimore: Johns Hopkins University Press, 1989); Smith and Wallerstein, *Creating and Transforming Households*.

6. Barry Bluestone and Bennett Harrison, *The Deindustrialization of America* (New York: Basic Books, 1982); Barry Bluestone, "Is Deindustrialization a Myth? Capital Mobility Versus Absorptive Capacity in the U.S. Economy," *Annals of the American Academy of Political and Social Science* 475 (1984): 39–51; Michael J. Piore and Charles F. Sabel, *The Second Industrial Divide: The Possibilities for Prosperity* (New York: Basic Books, 1984); Marta Tienda, "Industrial Restructuring in Metropolitan and Nonmetropolitan Labor Markets: Implications for Equity and Efficiency," in *Symposium on Rural Labor Markets: Research Issues,* ed. Molly S. Killian et al. (Washington, DC: U.S. Department of Agriculture, September, 1986); Bennett Harrison and Barry Bluestone, *The Great U-Turn: Corporate Restructuring and the Polarizing of America* (New York: Basic Books, 1988); Shirley Porterfield, "Service Sector Offers More Jobs, Lower Pay," *Rural Development Perspectives* (June-September 1990): 2–7; Cathy Kassab, A. E. Luloff, and Fred Schmidt, "The Changing Impact of Industry, Household Structure, and Residence on Household Well-Being," *Rural Sociology* 60, no. 1 (Spring 1995): 67–90.

7. For general overviews, see Porterfield, "Service Sector Offers More Jobs, Lower Pay"; Charles M. Tolbert and Thomas A. Lyson, "Earnings Inequality in the Nonmetropolitan United States: 1967–1990," *Rural Sociology* 57, no. 4 (Winter 1992): 494–511; Lucy Gorham, "Changing Employment, Earnings, and Skill Requirements in Manufacturing: The Implications for Rural Workers," in *Rural America and the Changing Structure of Manufacturing,* ed. G. Andrew Bernat Jr. and Martha Frederick (Washington, DC: U.S. Department of Agriculture, Economic Research Service, Agriculture and Rural Economy Division, 1993): 142–47; Daniel T. Lichter, Gail M. Johnston, and Diane K. McLaughlin, "Changing Linkages Between Work and Poverty in Rural America," *Rural Sociology* 59, no. 3 (1994): 395–415; Kassab, Luloff, and Schmidt, "The Changing Impact of Industry, Household Structure, and Residence on Household Well-Being." For a discussion that links restructuring in rural areas to issues of poverty, see William P. O'Hare, *The Rise of Poverty in Rural America* (Washington, DC: Population Reference Bureau, 1988); Ann R. Tickamyer and Cynthia M. Duncan, "Poverty and Opportunity Structure in Rural America," *Annual Review of Sociology* 16 (1990): 67–86. For a discussion of the impact on rural communities in Canada, see Belinda Leach and Anthony Winson, "Bringing 'Globalization' Down to Earth: Restructuring and Labour in Rural Communities," *The Canadian Review of Sociology and Anthropology* 32, no. 3 (1995): 341–64. For a discussion of the significance of looking separately at rural areas, see Joachim Singelmann, "Will Rural Areas Still Matter in the 21st Century? (or) Can Rural Sociology Remain Relevant?," *Rural Sociology* 61, no. 1 (Spring 1996): 143–58. For specific case studies of rural areas, see Janet M. Fitchen, "Rural Poverty in the Northeast: The Case of Upstate New York," in *Rural Poverty in America,* ed. Cynthia M. Duncan (New York: Auburn House, 1992): 177–200; Nancy A. Naples, "Contradictions in Agrarian Ideology: Restructuring Gender, Race, Ethnicity, and Class," *Rural Sociology* 59, no. 1 (Spring 1994): 110–35; Tim Knapp, "Rust in the Wheatbelt: The Social Impacts of Industrial Decline in a Rural Kansas Community," *Sociological Inquiry* 65, no. 1 (February 1995): 47–66.

8. Because the population under investigation is predominantly white, we have not considered how these practices affect people of color. Studies that are more concerned with women note that although women have been moving rapidly into the labor force, much of the new employment occurs in low-paying occupations (e.g., services and retail trade). Research on men focuses on the loss of manufacturing jobs and the corresponding decline of wages of less-skilled male workers leading to increased wage inequality. For comparative overviews of the effects of economic restructuring on the labor force activities of men and women, see Gerda R. Wekerle and Brent Rutherford, "The Mobility of Capital and the Immobility of Female Labor: Responses to Economic Restructuring," in *The Power of Geography: How Territory Shapes Social Life*, ed. Jennifer Wolch and Michael Dear (Boston: Unwin Hyman, 1989): 130–72; Monica Boyd, Mary Ann Mulvihill, and John Myles, "Gender, Power and Postindustrialism," *Canadian Review of Sociology and Anthropology* 28, no. 4 (1991): 407–36; David D. Dabelko and Robert J. Sheak, "Employment, Subemployment and the Feminization of Poverty," *Sociological Viewpoints* 8 (Fall 1992): 31–66; Teresa Amott, *Caught in the Crisis: Women and the U.S. Economy Today* (New York: Monthly Review Press, 1993); Françoise Core, "Women and the Restructuring of Employment," *The OECD Observer*, no. 186 (February/March 1994): 4–11.

Women in rural areas might confront special problems with these changes. In Vermont, where this research is located, for example, recent job growth has occurred in low-wage industries which pay significantly less to women than to men (and which perform worse in this regard than many other Vermont industries). See Joy Livingston and Elaine McCrate, *Women and Economic Development in Vermont: A Study for the Governor's Commission on Women* (Montpelier, VT: Governor's Commission on the Status of Women, 1993): 14. See also Tienda, "Industrial Restructuring in Metropolitan and Nonmetropolitan Labor Markets: Implications for Equity and Efficiency"; Daniel T. Lichter, "The Underemployment of American Rural Women: Prevalence, Trends and Spatial Inequality," *Journal of Rural Studies* 5, no. 2 (1989): 199–208.

9. For a good review of the former issue, see Frank Levy and Richard C. Michel, *The Economic Future of American Families: Income and Wealth Trends* (Washington, DC: The Urban Institute Press, 1991); for a good review of the latter, see Edward N. Wolff, *Top Heavy: A Study of the Increasing Inequality of Wealth in America* (New York: The Twentieth Century Fund Press, 1995).

10. Michael Storper and Richard Walker, *The Capitalist Imperative: Territory, Technology, and Industrial Growth* (London: Basil Blackwell, 1989): 176.

11. For a discussion that argues that rural areas have become more vulnerable to macroeconomic trends in recent decades, see Jill Findeis, "Utilization of Rural Labor Resources," in *Economic Adaptation*, ed. David Barkley (Boulder, CO: Westview Press, 1993): 50–68. For discussions of the more general point, see Doreen Massey, *Spatial Divisions of Labor: Social Structures and the Geography of Production* (New York: Methuen, 1984) and R. E. Pahl and Claire Wallace, "Household Work Strategies in Economic Recession," in *Beyond Employment: Household, Gender and Subsistence*, ed. Nanneke Redclift and Enzo Mingione (New York: Basil Blackwell, 1985): 189–228.

12. Pahl argues that he finds the terms "urban" and "rural" "sociologically unhelpful in themselves" because, in fact, many urban areas provide opportunities that are thought to be more common within rural areas, such as growing or gathering food. R. E. Pahl, "Employment, Work and the Domestic Division of Labour," *International Journal of Urban and Regional Research* 4, no. 1 (1994): 14.

13. U.S. Department of Commerce, *County and City Data Book* (Washington, DC: U.S. Department of Commerce, Economics and Statistics Administration, Bureau of the Census, 1994).

14. Families with a heavy reliance on either farming or other forms of self-employment are thus included *only* if at least one member of the family is employed in waged work as his or her principal occupation.

15. Roberts, with reference to urban population, writes

> the mix of strategies . . . can be reduced to combinations of four main types: (a) reducing household expenditures by cutting consumption or ejecting nonproductive members; (b) intensifying the exploitation of internal household resources through self-provisioning and reciprocity with kin and friends; (c) adopting market-oriented strategies, which in the urban context are usually labor market strategies, but not exclusively so as the flourishing of an informal economy indicates; and (d) seeking aid from powerful external agents, such as the state, as of right or in return for political support. (Bryan R. Roberts, "Household Coping Strategies and Urban Poverty in Comparative Perspective," in *Urban Life in Transition*, Urban Affairs Annual Reviews 9, ed. Marc Gottdiener and C. C. Pickvance [Newbury Park, CA: Sage], 140–41)

Our emphasis is on Roberts's second and third points. We chose not to explore the issue of reducing household expenditures because we were more interested in how households obtained goods and services than in how they spent their resources; we chose to explore state support only in a limited way because we were focusing on households with waged employment. Only 12 percent of the households in our study had received any means-tested state support during the previous year.

16. R. E. Pahl, "The Restructuring of Capital, the Local Political Economy and Household Work Strategies," in *Social Relations and Spatial Structures*, ed. D. Gregory and J. Urry (Basingstoke, UK: Macmillan, 1985): 251.

17. Pahl, "The Restructuring of Capital, the Local Political Economy and Household Work Strategies": 20 n. 7.

18. Pierre Bourdieu, "Marriage Strategies as Strategies of Social Reproduction," in *Family and Society: Selections from Annales* (Baltimore: Johns Hopkins University Press, 1976); Louise A. Tilly and Joan W. Scott, *Women, Work and Family* (New York: Holt, Rinehart, and Winston, 1978); Tamara Hareven, *Family Time and Industrial Time: The Relationship Between the Family and Work in a New England Industrial Community* (New York: Cambridge University Press, 1982); A. V. Chayanov, *The Theory of Peasant Economy* (Madison: University of Wisconsin Press, 1986).

19. See, for example, the discussion in the session devoted to this term at the 1986 Social Science History Association meetings (Leslie Page Moch et al., "Family Strategy: A Dialogue," *Historical Methods* 20, no. 3 [Summer 1987]: 113–25) or the more recent collection of essays in Daniel C. Clay and Harry K.

Schwarzweller, eds., *Household Strategies*, Research in Rural Sociology and Development, vol. 5 (Greenwich, CT: JAI, 1991).

20. For discussions of these issues, see Moch et al., "Family Strategy: A Dialogue": 113–25; Graham Crow, "The Use of the Concept of 'Strategy' in Recent Sociological Literature," *Sociology* 23, no. 1 (February 1989): 1–24; David H. J. Morgan, "Strategies and Sociologists: A Comment on Crow," *Sociology* 23, no. 1 (February 1989): 25–29.

21. Of course, each of these rules is subject to variation: the numbers of those within a single household, the linkages between households, the boundaries that mark off one from the other, and the rules to which one adheres in order to maintain standing in the household—these are all products of historical change as well as of contemporary, and quite specific, cultures. (For discussions of this general point—for example, that the contemporary family came into existence in some places where it had not existed before and failed to materialize in other places—see Immanuel Wallerstein and Joan Smith, "Households as an Institution of the World Economy," in *Creating and Transforming Households*, ed. Joan Smith and Immanuel Wallerstein [Cambridge, UK: Cambridge University Press, 1992]: 3–23.)

Obviously, as well as being economic units, households are sites of enormous social investment, psychological stress and strains, and deeply subjective understandings of where one fits into the general scheme of things. Furthermore, there is a relationship between these two aspects of household function. It is precisely because they are sites of this kind of emotional investment that families are both (and often simultaneously) ports in a storm and emotional prisons. That they have both a material base and a deeply psychological one gives them the power they exercise over their membership. To reduce families to one or the other is to miss exactly what distinguishes them from other forms of social and economic life.

22. Judith Lorber, *Paradoxes of Gender* (New Haven, CT: Yale University Press, 1994): 3.

23. Joan Wallach Scott, *Gender and the Politics of History* (New York: Columbia University Press, 1988): 42.

24. For a discussion of the challenge to traditional methodologies presented by "idiosyncratic forms of livelihood," see Gavin Smith, "Towards an Ethnography of Idiosyncratic Forms of Livelihood," *International Journal of Urban and Regional Research* 18, no. 1 (1994): 71–87.

25. In addition to taking place in a somewhat unusual location, the research was conducted during a somewhat unusual time period. In retrospect, the years 1990 and 1991 have been dubbed a recessionary period, one with unique features that distinguish it from earlier recessions (Randy E. Ilg, "Long-Term Unemployment in Recent Recessions," *Monthly Labor Review* 117, no. 6 [June 1994]: 12–15). However, if the recession intensified certain economic problems, it did not recreate, in and of itself, the economic picture. Coolidge County's troubles were rooted in processes that had begun before—and would continue after—that particular downturn.

26. We mean here to distinguish those who are employed *by* a company from those who work *for* a company as some kind of "temporary" workers.

27. In what follows, we concentrate on the quality of the job independent of the absolute value of wages. We were concerned with how the structure of employment affects a family's ability to utilize its labor resources. We did take note, however, of the relationship between wages and utilization patterns. What we found, in part, was only a modest correlation (0.4) between wages and job quality, with wages measured in relationship to the minimum wage.

28. The eigenvalues show that three common factors are present. There are three relatively large positive eigenvalues that together account for 61 percent of the common variance. Both benefits (vacation, health) have positive loadings on the first factor. Both frequency of layoffs and need to bring one's own equipment load negatively on the second factor. Number of employees had a positive loading on the third factor, and relationship to employer (that is, if one is related to one's employer) had a negative loading.

29. Negative answers to the following questions were scored as "1": Does the workplace lay off people frequently? Does the workplace have fewer than fifty employees? Does the worker need to bring his/her own equipment? Is the employee related to the employer? Affirmative answers to the following questions were scored as "1": Does the workplace provide health insurance? Does the workplace provide a paid vacation?

30. In many ways, our distinction between good jobs and bad jobs corresponds to what labor economists define as primary and secondary labor markets. However, we include among bad job workers those who, though employed in a primary sector type of firm, have a current job experience (e.g., as a temporary worker) more like that found in the secondary sector. In general, primary sector workers have better-paying jobs that are secure. Their skills are valuable to the employer and relatively scarce. In contrast, secondary sector workers have few skills valuable to the employers, earn low wages, and enjoy few benefits. What is important to note is that these differing characteristics are features of labor markets and not of specific industries. There has been much criticism of this dichotomy; nevertheless, it sheds considerable light on the fortunes of the two kinds of households we studied. For fuller discussions, see Duncan Gallie, *In Search of the New Working Class* (Cambridge, UK: Cambridge University Press, 1978) and Suzanne Berger and Michael J. Piore, *Dualism and Discontinuity in Industrial Societies* (Cambridge, UK: Cambridge University Press, 1980).

31. See Pahl's discussion of the distinction between self-provisioning and do-it-yourself activities in "The Restructuring of Capital, the Local Political Economy and Household Work Strategies."

32. Lois Levitan and Shelley Feldman, "For Love or Money: Nonmonetary Economic Arrangements among Rural Households in Central New York," in *Household Strategies*, Research in Rural Sociology and Development 5, ed. Daniel C. Clay and Harry K. Schwarzweller (Greenwich, CT: JAI, 1991): 156.

CHAPTER 1

1. Michel Aglietta, *A Theory of Capitalist Regulation: The U.S. Experience* (London: Calmann-Levy, 1976); Michael J. Piore and Charles F. Sabel, *The*

Second Industrial Divide: The Possibilities for Prosperity (New York: Basic Books, 1984). The increase in the sheer amount of production in the United States slowed precipitously. During the 1960s, the gross national product had expanded by an impressive 50 percent as the result of an annual increase of 4.1 percent in real economic growth, but by the 1970s, this rate of expansion had been cut by almost a third (Kevin Phillips, *The Politics of Rich and Poor: Wealth and the American Electorate in the Reagan Aftermath* [New York: Harper Perennial, 1990]). The 1980s and early 1990s witnessed little improvement. More recently, while the gross domestic product per capita continues to grow, this is not particularly surprising, because it always grows when the nation is not in a recession. Nevertheless, the growth is sluggish; since 1973, average growth has been slower than at any time in the previous one hundred years (Jeff Madrick, "In the Shadows of Prosperity," *New York Review of Books* [August 14, 1997]: 40).

2. Peter Gottschalk, "Inequality, Income Growth and Mobility: The Basic Facts," *Journal of Economic Perspectives* 11, no. 2 (Spring 1997): 21–40; Peter Passell, "Benefits Dwindle along with Wages for the Unskilled," *New York Times* (June 14, 1998): A1, 28.

3. Chris Tilly, *Short Hours, Short Shrift, Cause and Consequence of Part-Time Work* (Washington, DC: Economic Policy Institute, 1990).

4. Chris Tilly, *Half a Job* (Philadelphia: Temple University Press, 1996).

5. Peter T. Kilborn, "In New Work World, Employers Call All the Shots," *New York Times* (July 3, 1995): A1. Millions more pass through these agencies on their way to permanent employment. "Temps" average just under thirty-one hours of work per week, and although they fare better than other part-time workers in hourly earnings, they still earn lower hourly wages than all wage and salary workers ($7.73 versus $10.03 in 1990).

6. Kenneth A. Swinnerton and Howard Wial, "Is Job Stability Declining in the U.S. Economy?," *Industrial and Labor Relations Review* 48, no. 2 (1995): 293–98.

7. Stephen J. Rose, *Declining Job Security and the Professionalization of Opportunity*, Research Report 94-04 (Washington, DC: National Commission for Employment Policy, 1995).

8. Swinnerton and Wial, "Is Job Stability Declining in the U.S. Economy?"

9. Rose, *Declining Job Security and the Professionalization of Opportunity*.

10. Peter Gottschalk and Robert Moffitt, "The Growth of Earnings Instability in the U.S. Labor Market," *Brookings Papers on Economic Activity* 2 (1994): 217–72.

11. For historical studies of the "family wage," see Martha May, "Bread Before Roses: American Workingmen, Labor Unions and the Family Wage," in *Women, Work and Protest: A Century of U.S. Women's Labor History*, ed. Ruth Milkman (Boston: Routledge and Kegan Paul, 1985): 1–21; Martha May, "The Historical Problem of the Family Wage: The Ford Motor Company and the Five Dollar Day," *Feminist Studies* 8, no. 2 (Summer 1982): 399–424.

12. Nicole M. Fortin and Thomas Lemieux, "Institutional Changes and Rising Wage Inequality: Is There a Linkage?," *Journal of Economic Perspectives* 11, no. 2 (Spring 1997): 75–96; Bruce Western, *Between Class and Market:*

Postwar Unionization in the Capitalist Democracies (Princeton, NJ: Princeton University Press, 1997).

13. It is no news that the service economy boomed not only absolutely but, as important, relative to other industrial sectors. When McDonald's began to employ more workers than the entire U.S. steel industry, it was clear that something striking had happened (Joan Smith, "The Paradox of Women's Poverty: Wage-Earning Women and Economic Transformation," in *Women and Poverty*, ed. Barbara C. Gelpi et al. [Chicago: University of Chicago Press, 1986]: 121–40; Jane Humphries, "Women's Employment in Restructuring America: The Changing Experience of Women in Three Recessions," in *Women and Recession*, ed. Jill Rubery [London: Routledge & Kegan Paul, 1988]: 15–47).

14. Fortin and Lemieux, "Institutional Changes and Rising Wage Inequality: Is There a Linkage?"

15. Tilly, *Half a Job.*

16. Bennett Harrison, *Lean and Mean: The Changing Landscape of Corporate Power in the Age of Flexibility* (New York: Basic Books, 1994).

17. William Julius Wilson, *When Work Disappears: The World of the New Urban Poor* (New York: Random House, 1996).

18. Louis Uchitelle and N. R. Kleinfield, "On the Battlefields of Business, Millions of Casualties," *New York Times* (March 3, 1996): A1, 26–28.

19. Lobao and Schulman distinguish between two different approaches to rural regional analyses: those that focus on agrarian political economy and concern themselves with the shape and structure of farming under late capitalism, and those that offer a critical analysis of the decline of Fordist industrial hegemony. Linda M. Labao and Michael D. Schulman, "Farming Patterns, Rural Restructuring, and Poverty: A Comparative Regional Analysis," *Rural Sociology* 56, no. 4 (Winter 1991): 565–602. Our analysis falls much more within the latter perspective.

20. For a discussion of female labor force participation rates in rural areas, see Linda L. Swanson and Margaret A. Butler, "Human Resource Base of Rural Economies," in *Rural Economic Development in the 1980's: Prospects for the Future*, ed. David Brown (Washington, DC: USDA Economic Research Service, 1988): 159–79; Daniel T. Lichter, "The Underemployment of American Rural Women: Prevalence, Trends and Spatial Inequality," *Journal of Rural Studies* 5, no. 2 (1989): 199–208.

21. The low labor force participation of men in Coolidge County was not the result of the absence of young, working age men. In 1960, Coolidge County and the rest of the country had similar age distributions among the male population.

22. The 18.7 percent of the nonagricultural labor force that enjoyed union membership was but 63 percent of the level found in the United States taken as a whole. The proportion of the nonagricultural labor force in unions dropped steadily following 1964, but it did so at a slower rate than in the rest of the country. By 1978, the proportion of Vermont workers in unions was almost three-quarters of that found in the rest of the country. During the next decade and a half, Vermont lost union members more rapidly than the rest of the country, and by 1994 only 9.4 percent of nonagricultural workers in the state were

in unions, in comparison with 15.5 percent in the United States as a whole. *Statistical Abstract of the United States* (Washington, DC: Government Printing Office, various years).

23. Wayne D. Rasmussen and Douglas F. Bowers, "Rural America in the Twentieth Century," in *Rural America in Transition*, ed. Mark Drabenstott and Lynn Gibson (Kansas City, MO: Federal Reserve Bank of Kansas City, Research Division, 1988): 1–14.

24. This surge in the rate of industrialization was the result of the convergence of a variety of factors: prices for farm products rose, and the OPEC oil embargo spurred growth in domestic energy industries. As manufacturing moved into rural areas, the infrastructure of transportation and communication improved to keep pace with the new demands placed on it. These changes, in turn, made rural areas increasingly attractive to retired people. In short, employment opportunities in rural areas underwent both expansion and diversification, resulting in an increase in earnings and family income of rural residents both absolutely and relative to workers in cities. Even the century-old migration from the countryside to urban areas was halted for a time as new labor force entrants saw opportunities in their own hometowns and others followed these opportunities to settle in rural areas. Cynthia M. Duncan, "Persistent Poverty in Appalachia: Scarce Work and Rigid Stratification," in *Rural Poverty in America*, ed. Cynthia M. Duncan (New York: Auburn House, 1992): 111–33; David A. McGranahan, "Rural America in the Global Economy: Socioeconomic Trends," *Journal of Research in Rural Education* 10, no. 3 (Winter 1994): 139–48.

25. Twenty-seven percent of the 117 individuals we interviewed worked in one of these three firms either at the time we spoke with them or at some time in the recent past. The vast majority of these interviewees had worked at Sterling Aeronautical Company.

26. Ajax wages actually were low in comparison with nationwide manufacturing wages: In 1990, production workers in the United States were earning on average $10.83/hour, or $1.13/hour more than the highest-paid production worker at Ajax (because Ajax only employed men in production work, this is the logical comparison; *Statistical Abstract of the United States*, 1994). Even in comparison with local wage levels, Ajax wages were low: Hourly wages at Ajax translated into yearly wages between $13,312 and $20,176, which at that time was well below the median earnings of men in Coolidge County who worked year round, full time ($25,883). Vacation policy at Ajax was one week a year of vacation up to the third year, three weeks a year up to eight years, four weeks a year up to eighteen years, and five weeks after that. It also offered thirty-two hours of personal time a year (personal interview with Ajax manager).

27. Personal interview with Master Forms manager.

28. In rural areas, traditional industries—some of which had experienced expansion in the 1970s—also started to contract; having introduced changes in management and technology, they also began to reduce the size of their labor force. William W. Falk and Thomas A. Lyson, "Rural America in the Industrial Policy Debate," in *Rural Policies for the 1990's*, ed. C. Flora and J. Christenson (Boulder, CO: Westview, 1991): 8–21; T. Lyson and W. Falk, eds., *Forgotten*

Places: Uneven Development in Rural America (Lawrence: University Press of Kansas, 1993). For an analysis that also suggests that the rural prosperity of the 1970s did not build a sufficient infrastructure, see Mark Drabenstott, Mark Henry, and Lynn Gibson, "The Rural Economic Policy Choice," in *Rural America in Transition*, ed. Mark Drabenstott and Lynn Gibson (Kansas City, MO: Federal Reserve Bank of Kansas City, Research Division, 1988): 59–84; Alan MacPherson, "Service-to-Manufacturing Linkages among Small-and Medium-Sized Firms: Prospects for Rural Industrialization," in *Rural America and the Changing Structure of Manufacturing: Spatial Implications of New Technology and Organization. A Conference Proceedings*, ed. Andrew G. Bernat, Jr., and Martha Frederick (Washington, DC: U.S. Department of Agriculture, Economic Research Service, Agriculture and Rural Economy Division, 1993): 55–68.

29. "Job Loss of 30 Workers When Goodyear Plant in Windsor Closes Down," *Rutland Herald Daily* (November 7, 1986): A7; "Digital Strands 350 Workers by Closing South Burlington Plant," *Burlington Free Press* (October 30, 1992): 1A; "G. E. Lays Off 122 at Rutland Plants," *Burlington Free Press* (February 28, 1993): 5B; "Basket Maker Lays Off Workers," *Rutland Herald Daily* (May 23, 1996): 18.

For evidence that, in general, as international competition in goods-producing industries hit even rural areas in the 1980s, manufacturing industries laid off workers, closed up shop, or moved overseas, see Duncan, "Persistent Poverty in Appalachia: Scarce Work and Rigid Stratification"; Lucy Gorham, "The Growing Problem of Low Earnings in Rural Areas," in *Rural Poverty in America*, ed. Cynthia M. Duncan (New York: Auburn House, 1992): 21–39.

30. Vermont Department of Employment and Training, *Vermont Labor Market Bulletin. Statewide and Labor Market Area; 3rd Quarter 1995* (Montpelier: March 1996).

31. A 1996 article in *Maclean's* reported that Chrysler led the way in contract work with 71 percent of vehicle content manufactured by outside suppliers, followed closely by Ford (68 percent) and GM (54 percent). The article also reported on a survey of more than three hundred multinational companies in North America and Europe. The survey found that 85 percent contracted out one or more functions and 93 percent predicted that they were likely to do so within three years. Jennifer Wells, "This Thing Called 'Outsourcing' Has Your Job," *Maclean's* (September 30, 1996): 46–49.

32. Personal interview with Ajax manager. As it turned out, Ajax was also being squeezed by a growing labor movement. In 1994, Ajax workers voted to join the Amalgamated Clothing and Textile Workers Union. In 1995, Ajax was sold; the new owners immediately laid off thirty-four workers—23 percent of the workforce.

33. Subcontracted services included machine tool needs and upkeep to the outside of the building. The manager with whom we spoke reported that one of the workers in the factory submitted a bid to do the lawn upkeep but that it was not a low bid. "Thank God," he said, "it would have caused me a lot of grief." As we will demonstrate in Chapter 3, it is, in fact, workers like those at Ajax—workers with quite good jobs—who are able to develop small entrepreneurial businesses that can respond to Ajax's search for subcontracted services.

34. Personal interview with Master Forms manager.

35. This disintegration of the processes associated with larger firms and mass marketing is not a phenomenon reserved for Coolidge County—quite the contrary. Regions throughout the industrial world are witnessing the replacement of one form of production aimed at a mass market with another, distinguished by a more flexible approach. Piore and Sabel, *The Second Industrial Divide: The Possibilities for Prosperity.*

36. *County Business Patterns, Vermont* (Washington, DC: U.S. Department of Commerce, Bureau of the Census, various years).

37. For a discussion of the significance of local versus national ownership of firms, see Curran and Tomaskovic-Devey, who argue that "outside firms provide higher quality jobs." Sara Curran and Donald Tomaskovic-Devey, "Uneven Development in North Carolina? Job Quality Differences Between Local and Nonlocal Firms," *Rural Sociology* 56, no. 4 (Winter 1991): 681.

38. Personal interview with Wilson manager.

39. Shortly after we conducted our research, Wilson Contract Manufacturing moved entirely to an area in Vermont with even lower wages and considerably higher unemployment rates than were found in Coolidge County.

40. Robert McMath, "Niche Marketing Is the Buzzword as Manufacturers Polish Their Pitch," *Brandweek* (January 17, 1994): 36–37.

41. For a discussion linking the growth of industrial homework to economic restructuring in rural areas in the United States, see Christina E. Gringeri, *Getting By: Women Homeworkers and Rural Economic Development* (Lawrence: University Press of Kansas, 1994); Christina E. Gringeri, "Inscribing Gender in Rural Development: Industrial Homework in Two Midwestern Communities," *Rural Sociology* 58, no. 1 (Spring 1993): 30–52. For discussions of homework abroad, see Lourdes Beneria and Martha Roldan, *Crossroads of Class and Gender: Industrial Homework, Subcontracting, and Household Dynamics in Mexico City* (Chicago: University of Chicago Press, 1987). For broader discussions of homework, see Sheila Allen and Carol Wolkowitz, *Homeworking: Myths and Realities* (Basingstoke, UK: Macmillan Education, 1987); Kathleen Christensen, *Women and Home-Based Work: The Unspoken Contract* (New York: Henry Holt and Company, 1987); Sheila Allen, "Production and Reproduction: The Lives of Women Homeworkers," *The Sociological Review* 31, no. 4 (November 1983): 649–65; Eileen Boris, "Regulating Industrial Homework: The Triumph of 'Sacred Motherhood,' " *Journal of American History* 71, no. 4 (March 1985): 745–63; Eileen Boris and Cynthia Daniels, eds., *Homework: Historical and Contemporary Perspectives on Paid Labor at Home* (Urbana: University of Illinois Press, 1989); Eileen Boris, "Homework and Women's Rights: The Case of the Vermont Knitters, 1980–1985," *Signs* 13, no. 1 (1987): 98–120; Eileen Boris, *Home to Work: Motherhood and the Politics of Industrial Homework in the United States* (New York: Cambridge University Press, 1994).

42. Personal interview with GMCT manager. The manager told us that the rate of pay was set by using an average sewer and average assembler and seeing how many stuffed animals they could do in an hour and then calculating the rate per stuffed animal to arrive at the minimum wage. That calculation then became the standard rate. If a sewer or assembler did not work at a rate that

yielded the minimum wage, they were "spoken to" by someone at the factory. When the manager we interviewed was asked what the worker would do then, he suggested that they "probably go home and fudge their hours."

43. One of the financial assistance programs referred to in the quotation is help in buying sewing machines workers need to complete their production tasks. Recently, even the homeworkers hired by GMCT have not seemed to be cheap enough; GMCT is increasingly relying on work done overseas for "clothing" its stuffed animals.

44. McGranahan comments on this pattern in rural areas in general:

> The rural industrial job mixes include far more routine types of production jobs and far fewer high skill managerial and research jobs than is found in urban areas. In 1993, 9.8 percent of rural manufacturing jobs were in management and research compared to 24 percent in urban areas. About three in every four rural manufacturing workers has a production job, compared to slightly over one in every two urban manufacturing workers. This division of labor, with rural workers tending to do routine production work and urban workers more often the high skill management and professional jobs, is also found in agriculture and related services and mining. (McGranahan, "Rural America in the Global Economy: Socioeconomic Trends": 140)

45. McGranahan notes that urban areas "specializing in high-end producer services and high-tech industries, gained in these types of jobs as they continued to shed the low-skill routine manufacturing jobs" (McGranahan, "Rural America in the Global Economy: Socioeconomic Trends": 141).

46. For an overview of industry shifts during the 1980s, see Lois M. Plunkert, "The 1980's: A Decade of Job Growth and Industry Shifts," *Monthly Labor Review* 113, no. 9 (September 1990): 3–16. For a discussion of the type of job and income growth that manufacturing industries will provide for rural economies in the next decade, see G. Andrew Bernat, Jr., and Martha Frederick, *Rural America and the Changing Structure of Manufacturing: Spatial Implications of New Technology and Organization. A Conference Proceedings* (Washington, DC: U.S. Department of Agriculture, 1993).

47. David A. McGranahan, "Rural Workers in the National Economy," in *Rural Economic Development in the 1980's: Prospects for the Future,* ed. David Brown (Washington, DC: USDA Economic Research Service, 1988): 29–75; David Barkley, *Economic Adaptation: Alternatives for Nonmetropolitan Areas* (Boulder, CO: Westview, 1993); McGranahan, "Rural America in the Global Economy: Socioeconomic Trends."

Findeis argues that, in general, rural economies have become more vulnerable to fluctuations in general macroeconomic conditions than in previous decades. Jill Findeis, "Utilization of Rural Labor Resources," in *Economic Adaptation,* ed. David Barkley (Boulder, CO: Westview, 1993): 50–68. For a good discussion of the social impact of industrial decline in a rural community in the United States, see Tim Knapp, "Rust in the Wheatbelt: The Social Impacts of Industrial Decline in a Rural Kansas Community," *Sociological Inquiry* 65, no. 1 (February 1995): 47–66. For a discussion of the impact of industrial decline in a Canadian rural community, see Belinda Leach and Anthony Winson, "Bringing 'Globalization' Down to Earth: Restructuring and Labour in Rural Communities," *The Canadian Review of Sociology and Anthropology* 32, no. 3 (1995): 341–64.

48. These changes appear to have as much to do with declines in the position of men (or stagnation) as they do in improvements in the position of women. Indeed, some features of women's employment to which one might point as evidence of women's increasing relative status (e.g., labor force participation rates) are themselves possibly the consequence of men's failure to retain their position as the breadwinner in the family, and they are certain to be felt by at least some men precisely as indicators of that failure.

49. Personal interview with Wilson manager.

50. Niche market firms include one that markets certified organic milk, cheeses, and butters; a second that grows organic produce; and a third that specializes in "high-end" bow ties. One production plant assembles electrome-chanical equipment, a second designs and manufactures medical instruments and groundwater monitoring devices, and the third is the printing shop which was the spinoff from Sterling. Services include a restaurant and an agency that sells assistance and advice on financial matters to area businesses.

51. For an article that links corporate downsizing (at places like IBM) with the growth of the small business sector (at places like WCM), see J. H. Foegen, "A Sad but Needed Change," *Business and Society Review*, no. 87 (Fall 1993): 14–15.

52. One of these firms that has taken over one of the Sterling plants we call "Prestige Knits." It is a company that produces upscale (and very expensive) sweaters, and it relies on homeworkers for much of the production process. Promotional literature (found in a specialty shop in Santa Monica, California, by one of the authors) tells the Prestige Knit story:

> Eleven years ago, I designed and knit a sweater for myself. Quite unexpectedly, this sweater was bought off my back. I designed another and this, too, was sold. Dottie Laframboise and Henrietta Peach, both of whom live and work on 400 acre dairy farms in northern Vermont, began to work with me, as did others. Sweaters were shipped in spare veterinarian boxes and the headquarters was centered around the kitchen table. The cottage industry, Prestige Knits was born.
>
> Each limited edition sweater is made of 100% cotton in the home of a Vermont family. I continue to find great joy and satisfaction in creating unusual knitted designs. My husband and I work together with the wonderful staff pictured above.

Individual sweaters are described. Like many of the sweaters, "Green's Farm" takes its motif from the rural area in which it is produced: "A green tractor sits on the front of the sweater surrounded by a field of tasseled corn. On the shoulder are red and white checkers as found on a feed sack. The buttons represent a cow, pony, sheep, chicken, apple tree and two goslings." The Green's Farm sweater could hardly be afforded by most of the residents of that rural area. In 1992, Green's Farm sold for $280. One homeworker we interviewed was earning not much above minimum wage for her work on these sweaters. In 1994, the company reported sales amounting to $1 million; it had six part-time employees and eleven full-time employees in 1996.

53. For a discussion of small and mid-size enterprise development (SMEs) in nonmetropolitan areas specifically, see Miller, who argues that although SMEs "under local ownership are more innovative than large enterprises and develop stronger economic ties to the community," in nonmetropolitan areas SMEs "are less likely to innovate and generally employ relatively fewer professionals and

skilled workers than in metropolitan areas." Miller concludes that on balance "recent studies are not optimistic that the increase in SMEs through industrial restructuring will benefit rural areas." James P. Miller, "Small and Midsize Enterprise Development: Prospects for Nonmetropolitan Areas," in *Economic Adaptation: Alternatives for Nonmetropolitan Areas*, ed. David L. Barkley (Boulder, CO: Westview, 1993): 101.

54. Peace and Justice Center, *The Job Gap Study: Phase 2* (Burlington, VT: 1997).

55. Seventy-five percent of Coolidge County residents work within the county itself.

56. Peace and Justice Center, *The Job Gap Study: Phase 2: Livable Wage Jobs: The Job Gap* (Burlington, VT: May 1987): 6. In Coolidge County in 1990, 85.9 percent of men but only 64.7 percent of women worked thirty-five hours a week or more. Analyses by the Bureau of Labor Statistics for Vermont as a whole suggest that although in 1991 women were 47 percent of all workers, they constituted 57 percent of the *involuntary* part-time workers in Vermont, defined as "those working 1–34 hours per week due to slack work, material shortage, or inability to find full-time work." Joy Livingston and Elaine McCrate, *Women and Economic Development in Vermont: A Study for the Governor's Commission on Women* (Montpelier, VT: Governor's Commission on the Status of Women, 1993): 10. Lichter suggests that rural women are especially likely to be underemployed ("The Underemployment of American Rural Women: Prevalence, Trends and Spatial Inequality").

57. Between 1993 and 1994, 4,133 jobs were added in manufacturing alone (a gross change of 9.2 percent), but 3,591 jobs were also lost (a gross change of 8.2 percent). Manufacturing employment has continued to rise, but, as the Vermont Department of Employment and Training notes, "As good as growth has been in manufacturing it is probably understated and growth in services overstated. The use of subcontractors and temporary help services continues to expand. Some jobs in the past that would have been on the manufacturer's payroll are now on a service firm's payroll" (Department of Employment and Training, *Vermont UI Covered Employment and Wages*, July 1997). In short, as we have argued throughout this chapter, there have been radical changes in the *kind* of jobs available to Vermont workers.

By May of 1997, the unemployment rate in the state had dropped to an impressive 3.8 percent. In the preceding year, close to six thousand jobs had been added to the labor force—a 2 percent rate of growth. Impressive as this may seem, much of the growth occurred in low-wage work, in retail trade and services. Department of Employment and Training, *Vermont Labor Market* (June 1997).

58. Vermont Department of Employment and Training, *1994 Employment and Wages* (Montpelier, VT: Department of Employment and Training, Labor Market Information Sector, October 1995): 13.

59. In general, these shifts have occurred in other rural areas as well—declining fertility and a decline in the "traditional" family structure (McGranahan, "Rural America in the Global Economy: Socioeconomic Trends"). In 1990, Coolidge County residents were *more* likely than were families in the United

States as a whole to live in units headed by women. Families headed by women are highly likely to be poor in both urban and rural areas. Daniel T. Lichter and David J. Eggebeen, "Child Poverty and the Changing Rural Family," *Rural Sociology* 57, no. 2 (Summer 1992): 151–72; Daniel T. Lichter and Diane K. McLaughlin, "Changing Economic Opportunities, Family Structure, and Poverty in Rural Areas," *Rural Sociology* 60, no. 4 (Winter 1995): 688–706.

60. For arguments about how an informal economy is especially likely to thrive in rural areas, see S. M. Miller, "The Pursuit of Informal Economies," *Annals of the American Academy of Political and Social Science* 493 (September 1987): 26–35; Rhoda Halperin, *The Livelihood of Kin: Making Ends Meet "The Kentucky Way"* (Austin: University of Texas Press, 1990); Lois Levitan and Shelley Feldman, "For Love or Money: Nonmonetary Economic Arrangements among Rural Households in Central New York," in *Research in Rural Sociology and Development* (Greenwich, CT: JAI, 1991): 149–72; Janet M. Fitchen, "Rural Poverty in the Northeast: The Case of Upstate New York," in *Rural Poverty in America*, ed. Cynthia M. Duncan (New York: Auburn House, 1992): 177–200; Fitchen, "On the Edge of Homelessness: Rural Poverty and Housing Insecurity," *Rural Sociology* 57, no. 2 (Summer 1992): 175–93; Leif Jensen, Gretchen T. Cornwell, and Jill L. Findeis, "Informal Work in Nonmetropolitan Pennsylvania," *Rural Sociology* 60, no. 1 (Spring 1995): 91–107. See also Jessen et al., who note that the relationship between rurality and informal economic activity is not a simple one:

> When using variations in living conditions as a central explanation for the considerable differences in informal work done, do we point to more than the trivial difference between the spatial and legal possibilities of flat tenants and house owners? Pointing to house and garden as the points of crystallization of a specific *rural way of living*, however, implies more than this triviality. Owning a house is not just the material prerequisite for this way of living but its most frequent and conspicuous *result*. (J. Jessen et al., "The Informal Work of Industrial Workers: Present Situation, Trend Prognosis and Policy Implications," in *The Unofficial Economy: Consequences and Perspectives in Different Economic Systems*, ed. Sergio Alessandrini and Bruno Dallago [Aldershot, UK: Gower, 1987]: 273).

61. Miller, "The Pursuit of Informal Economies"; William Cole and Bichaka Fayissa, "The Urban Subsistence Labor Force: Toward a Policy-Oriented and Empirically Accessible Taxonomy," *World Development* 19, no. 7 (July 1991): 779–89; Philip Harding and Richard Jenkins, *The Myth of the Hidden Economy: Towards a New Understanding of Economic Activity* (Philadelphia: Open University Press, 1989); Jensen et al., "Informal Work in Nonmetropolitan Pennsylvania."

62. For an interesting attempt to measure informal economic activity at the level of the household, see Jensen et al., "Informal Work in Nonmetropolitan Pennsylvania." As Jensen et al. note, because sociologists and anthropologists have an interest in the role of the informal economy as "a household economic strategy or as a source of community cohesion," they often include as an element nonmonetary exchanges "between and within households" (p. 92). For similar examples, see Raymond E. Pahl, "Does Jobless Mean Workless?: Unemployment and Informal Work," *Annals of the American Academy of Political and Social Science* 493 (September 1987): 36–46; Pahl, "Some Remarks on Informal

Work, Social Polarization and the Social Structure," *International Journal of Urban and Regional Research* 12, no. 2 (1988): 247–67; Levitan and Feldman, "For Love or Money: Nonmonetary Economic Arrangements among Rural Households in Central New York." Jensen et al. define the informal economy as consisting only of "work activities other than regular formal employment that are remunerated either in cash or in-kind" (p. 92). They exclude "such things as outright barter, production for home consumption, or doing neighborly favors whose only reward may be some measure of social capital." As we discuss in the Appendix, it is our conviction that this distinction—between activities that are *remunerated* in cash or in kind versus doing neighborly favors—is an artificial one.

63. There are a few indirect but highly illuminating indications of a thriving informal economy at a national level. Let us describe two.

First, in a recent five-year span in the United States, the total wholesale value of building materials in inflation-adjusted dollars increased by almost 30 percent. During the same period, the number of construction workers increased by just 16 percent. In other words, building materials were being sold at a rate considerably greater than the growth in the number of workers necessary to utilize them. One explanation for the disparity could be that construction workers were becoming increasingly productive. Aside from the fact that we are dealing with a mere five-year period and that construction work is notorious for small productivity increases, if this differential is explained by productivity increases, then the construction industry puts the most technologically advanced industries to absolute shame. The much more likely explanation is that a considerable amount of these materials was being purchased not for commercially produced construction but for the informal market, to be utilized by informally organized labor—for income, for social exchange, and as self-provisioning.

Second, in the decade between 1980 and 1990, the total number of private vehicles more than twelve years old more than doubled, indeed a sign of the economic times and much to the distress of automobile companies. During that same period, the total number of officially enumerated employed automobile mechanics in formally organized repair shops increased by less than 50 percent. Much like construction, a very strong argument could be made that these older cars in 1990 needed as much repair work as their 1980 counterparts but that work was increasingly being provided in backyards and driveways.

64. Economists are particularly interested in measurement so as to adjust indicators such as the gross national product (GNP). Recent attempts to estimate the worth of informal economic activities place it at $600 billion—equivalent to 10 percent of the GNP. Economists and sociologists agree it could be considerably larger, especially when taking into account illegal activity. Schiff and Labate, "Labor Force Mysteries: The Working Poor and the Underground Economy," *Fortune* (August 24, 1992): 22. For discussions trying to estimate the cost of the informal economy for taxes—estimated at $27 billion—see Karen Pennar and Christopher Farrell, "Notes from the Underground Economy," *Business Week* (February 15, 1993): 98–101.

65. For example, the junk cars spread across backyards in Coolidge County waiting their turn to be transformed into cash are no different from those cars

urban dwellers bring to driveway mechanics who perform that service on their days off. (It may be a stretch, but it is worth noting that stripping cars in rural areas for spare parts is not much different from stripping them in the city for the same purpose, with the exception that the former is a legal activity and the latter not.)

66. Saskia Sassen-Koob, "New York City's Informal Economy," in *The Informal Economy: Studies in Advanced and Less Developed Countries*, ed. Alejandro Portes, Manuel Castells, and Lauren A. Benton (Baltimore: Johns Hopkins University Press, 1989): 60–78; Manuel Castells and Alejandro Portes, "World Underneath: The Origins, Dynamics, and Effects of the Informal Economy," in *The Informal Economy: Studies in Advanced and Less Developed Countries*, ed. Alejandro Portes, Manuel Castells, and Lauren A. Benton (Baltimore: Johns Hopkins University Press, 1989):11–40.

67. Sassen-Koob, "New York City's Informal Economy": 73.

68. Bryan R. Roberts, "Household Coping Strategies and Urban Poverty in Comparative Perspective," in *Urban Life in Transition*, Urban Affairs Annual Reviews 9, ed. Marc Gottdiener and C. C. Pickvance (Newbury Park, CA: Sage): 135–68.

69. Jessen et al. argue similarly about the link between the market and informal work. For example, they note that some market strategies reduce the possibility of informal work. They refer, for example, to the "growing technical complexity, black boxes, built-in wear and tear" (p. 280) that in combination mean that people can no longer do their own electrical work. They note as well that although there are more tools available to do informal work, they require money for purchase and they also "force certain work processes and certain ways of using them upon those who employ them. Thus informal work, too, is pushed into pockets intended for this purpose by the market, meaning that informal work is more and more integrated into the market." Jessen et al., "The Informal Work of Industrial Workers: Present Situation, Trend Prognosis and Policy Implications": 280. Roberts, writing about urban areas, also notes that "even the activities furthered by self provisioning and reciprocity often depend heavily on goods and services that originate externally" ("Household Coping Strategies and Urban Poverty in Comparative Perspective": 143). See also Joan Smith, "All Crises Are Not the Same: Households in the United States During Two Crises," in *Work Without Wages: Comparative Studies of Domestic Labor and Self-Employment*, ed. Jane L. Collins and Martha Giminez (Albany: State University of New York Press, 1990): 128–41.

70. For example, the houses and furniture of women who do day care in their own homes during the day actually become capital equipment for that period of time. Private automobiles become the input in the jitney cab business in New York City as well as providing an opportunity for the "squeegee men" found on busy corners near the business districts. One of the most recent examples of the use of commercially produced goods as an opportunity for an informal business enterprise can be found on busy corners where peddlers with large coffee containers equipped with a hose and strapped to their backs sell cups of coffee to drivers stuck in traffic jams. Plumbers and carpenters take home "leftovers" from the job to complete their own homes and work on those of

friends and relatives. In the spring of 1995, the *Boston Globe* ran a lengthy story describing police officers who use not only their skills but also their uniforms and equipment in guarding construction sites during their off hours for extra money. "Families Now Run Faster to Catch Up with Dreams," *Boston Globe* (April 30, 1995): A1.

71. Some believe that those of low socioeconomic status constitute the labor force for informal work and that this kind of employment acts as a safety net for the poor and especially for immigrant populations. Louis A. Ferman, Stuart Henry, and Michele Hoyman, "Issues and Prospects for the Study of Informal Economies: Concepts, Research Strategies and Policy," *Annals of the American Academy of Political and Social Science* 493 (1987): 154–72; Bryan Roberts, "Informal Economy and Family Strategies," *International Journal of Urban and Regional Research* 18, no. 1 (March 1994): 6–21. (Of course, Coolidge County does not have the kind of immigrant population that would have informal work as its only recourse; it is not Los Angeles or New York City.) The negative relationship between socioeconomic status and informal activity has been questioned by those who point out (much as we will below) that informal activities depend on precisely the kinds of physical and human capital that are in short supply among those who constitute the very poor. Michele Hoyman, "Female Participation in the Informal Economy: A Neglected Issue," *Annals of the American Academy of Political and Social Science* 493 (September 1987): 64–82; Alejandro Portes and Saskia Sassen-Koob, "Making It Underground: Comparative Material on the Informal Sector in Western Market Economies," *American Journal of Sociology* 93 (1987): 30–61; Jessen et al, "The Informal Work of Industrial Workers: Present Situation, Trend Prognosis and Policy Implications."

Another issue under contention is the relationship between the labor supply available to formal and informal markets. Some argue that the two act as substitutes—that loss in one leads to participation in the other. P. Guttmann, "Are the Unemployed, Unemployed?," *Financial Analysts Journal* 34, no. 1 (1978): 26–29; Duncan, "Persistent Poverty in Appalachia: Scarce Work and Rigid Stratification"; Roberts, "Informal Economy and Family Strategies." Others believe it is a mistake to see the two as alternatives. In fact, much research suggests that those with one form of employment are more likely to engage in the other. (It is from these observations that Pahl and Wallace develop their social polarization argument that is not unlike our own. R. E. Pahl and Claire Wallace, "Household Work Strategies in Economic Recession," in *Beyond Employment: Household, Gender and Subsistence*, ed. Nanneke Redclift and Enzo Mingione [London: Basil Blackwell, 1985]: 189–228.) For additional references, see Lorna McKee, "Households During Unemployment: The Resourcefulness of the Unemployed," in *Give and Take in Families: Studies in Resource Distribution*, ed. Julia Brannen and Gail Wilson (London: Allen & Unwin, 1987): 96–116.

CHAPTER 2

1. While it is true that only one-third of white women (36.5 percent) were employed outside the home in 1960, almost half (48.2 percent) of African Amer-

ican women had paid employment. See Dorothy Smith, "Women's Inequality and the Family," in *Families and Work*, ed. Naomi Gerstel and Harriet Engel Gross (Philadelphia: Temple University Press, 1987): 423. Much of the "second wave" feminist scholarship built its understanding of women's subordination on their role as housewives. Among the early "classics" that take this perspective, see, for example, Ann Oakley, *The Sociology of Housework* (New York: Pantheon Books, 1974); Heidi Hartmann, "Capitalism, Patriarchy, and Job Segregation by Sex," *Signs* 1, no. 3, pt. 2 (1976): 137–67. For an interesting critique of the assumption of the female housewife, see Geraldine Pratt and Susan Hanson, "On the Links Between Home and Work: Family-Household Strategies in a Buoyant Labor Market," *International Journal of Urban and Regional Research* 15, no. 1 (March 1991): 55–74.

2. The difference between our sample and that of the county average might be explained by the fact that respondents in the random telephone survey were more likely to report to our interviewers work done "under the table" than they would be to a census taker.

3. *Statistical Abstract of the United States* (Washington, DC: Government Printing Office, 1992): tables 619 and 620. In 1950, dual-worker families constituted less than 10 percent of all families. See also Howard V. Hayghe, "Family Members in the Work Force," *Monthly Labor Review* 113, no. 3 (March 1990): 14–19.

4. Frank Levy, *Dollars and Dreams* (New York: Russell Sage Foundation for the National Committee for Research on the 1980 Census, 1987); David M. Kotz, "Household Labor, Wage Labor, and the Transformation of the Family," *Review of Radical Political Economics* 26, no. 2 (June 1994): 24–56; Rose M. Rubin and Bobye J. Riney, *Working Wives and Dual-Earner Families* (New York: Praeger, 1995).

5. Howard V. Hayghe and Suzanne Bianchi, "Married Mothers' Work Patterns: The Job-Family Compromise," *Monthly Labor Review* 117, no. 6 (June 1994): 24–30. In the United States, on average, households with two earners had incomes 74.4 percent above those with but a single earner; households with both a husband and wife in the labor force had incomes 81.6 percent above single-earner married-couple households. In Coolidge County, a second earner appears to be even more important: The comparable figures are 83.6 percent and 95.8 percent, respectively. See also Jennifer M. Gardner and Diane E. Herz, "Working and Poor in 1990," *Monthly Labor Review* 115, no. 12 (December 1992): 20–28. There are other benefits as well. Families with two earners increase the likelihood that they will receive health insurance, and some new research suggests that the dual-earner household is altogether a happier and healthier place than the household that relies on a single income. See Nan L. Maxwell, "Changing Female Labor Force Participation: Influences on Income Inequality and Distribution," *Social Forces* 68, no. 4 (June 1990): 1251–66; Colin C. Williams and Jan Windebank, "Social Polarization of Households in Contemporary Britain: A 'Whole Economy' Perspective," *Regional Studies* 29, no. 8 (December 1995): 723–28; Cathy Kassab, A. E. Luloff, and Fred Schmidt, "The Changing Impact of Industry, Household Structure, and Residence on Household Well-Being," *Rural Sociology* 60, no. 1 (Spring 1995): 67–90;

Rosalind C. Barnett and Caryl Rivers, *She Works/He Works: How Two-Income Families Are Happier, Healthier, and Better-Off* (San Francisco: HarperSanFrancisco, 1996).

6. These kinds of instability are related, but they also measure different aspects of an underlying phenomenon. The number of layoffs measures only involuntary job loss in an individual's principal employment; it does not directly provide evidence about whether that job was replaced. The income discontinuity score measures the unreplaced loss of *any* household income activity (that is, both principal jobs and moonlighting) regardless of whether that loss was the result of an involuntary layoff or a voluntary action on the part of the household member. For example, if at some time during the year preceding the survey two members of a given household held three different jobs between them and one person gave up moonlighting (so that at the time of the survey they only had two jobs between them), they would be considered to have income discontinuity. So too would a household in which two individuals had been employed earlier, but at the time of the survey only one remained in the labor force. The latter measure, thus, is more inclusive than the measure of layoffs alone; it also extends to the full range of income activities within the household. It makes no distinctions, however, either among those various activities or among the reasons for job reductions. The 27 percent of households that had experienced income discontinuity is far in excess of the average rate of unemployment for the state at that time. An average rate of unemployment conceals the experiences of those who have lost a job during the year; it also ignores those who have lost unrecorded income sources.

7. Kenneth Cooke, "The Withdrawal from Paid Work of the Wives of Unemployed Men: A Review of Research," *Journal of Social Policy* 16 (1987): 371–82. Pahl also reports that unemployed male heads of households are less likely than employed ones to have wives who are employed. Like Cooke, he notes the influence of state support in creating this pattern. R. E. Pahl, "Some Remarks on Informal Work, Social Polarization and the Social Structure," *International Journal of Urban and Regional Research* 12, no. 2 (1988): 247–67. On this point, see also Williams and Windebank, "Social Polarization of Households in Contemporary Britain: A 'Whole Economy' Perspective"; Lydia Morris, "Domestic Labour and Employment Status among Married Couples: A Case Study in Hartlepool," *Capital and Class* 49 (Spring 1993): 37–52. We are making a somewhat different argument here insofar as we are focusing on the full range of benefits that attend *employment* rather than the state (cash) benefits that accompany *unemployment*.

8. Patricia Braus, "Dual Incomes Cushion Job Seekers," *American Demographics* 21 (October 1991): 2. See also Martha Farnsworth Riche, "Fiscal Attraction," *American Demographics* 10 no. 7 (July 1988): 19; Diane Crispell, "Dual Disparity," *American Demographics* 11, no. 9 (September 1989): 16–17.

9. *Statistical Abstract of the United States* (Washington, DC: Government Printing Office): 633; Michelotti, Kopp, "Multiple Jobholders in May 1975," *Monthly Labor Review* 98, no. 11 (November 1975): 56–61; John F. Stinson, Jr., "Multiple Jobholding up Sharply in the 1980's," *Monthly Labor Review* 113, no. 7 (July 1990): 3–10.

10. Stinson, "Multiple Jobholding up Sharply in the 1980's": 3.

11. In the United States as a whole, 6.1 percent of married men with a spouse present moonlight, in contrast to 5 percent of married women with a spouse present. Stinson, "Multiple Jobholding up Sharply in the 1980's." Among those in our sample, we found more pronounced gender differences: 17 percent of women and 27 percent of men moonlight.

There are gender differences as well in the intensity of moonlighting. In the United States, the most common moonlighting pattern is to supplement one full-time job with a second that is part time. Men who have more than one job are especially likely to follow this pattern, with 63.9 percent doing so. Fifty percent of women with more than one job also follow this pattern, but women are more likely than men to work two different part-time jobs. Within our sample, we found similar differences. Sixty-six percent of men and 59 percent of women worked a full-time job and also a part-time moonlighting job, 17 percent of men and 5 percent of women worked two full-time jobs, and the remainder (17 percent of men and 36 percent of women) worked two or more part-time jobs. Moreover, men are more likely than women to be engaged in moonlighting for long periods of time. Whereas 40.8 percent of female moonlighters had held second jobs for less than a year, more than two-thirds of men had held their jobs for more than a year. Stinson, "Multiple Jobholding up Sharply in the 1980's."

12. For example, in 1995 the *Los Angeles Times* reported, "From the factory line to gleaming office towers, many people in California and elsewhere say they are working more hours, more jobs and more intensely than ever" and that "wage stagnation, corporate cuts, changing technology and the decline in labor unions have all contributed to increased work" (Don Lee, "Employees Get Real Workout," *Los Angeles Times* [September 4, 1995]: A1). A Canadian newspaper reported that almost 5 percent of the workforce held a second job in 1994 (Bruce Cheadle, "More Canadians Moonlighting," *Halifax Daily News* [June 2, 1994]: 28). One unpublished doctoral dissertation even went so far as to suggest that the growth in the Naval Reserve is a function of moonlighting for financial reasons (Mark Regets, "Labor Supply in the Naval Reserve," Ph.D. diss. [State University of New York at Binghamton, 1989]). Interestingly, among those we interviewed, we also found several individuals who engaged in moonlighting by virtue of the fact that they served in the National Guard or did some other kind of military reserve duty on weekends.

13. In 1994, 6.1 percent of Whites reported holding down more than one job, in contrast with 4.9 percent of Blacks and 3.7 percent of those of Hispanic origin. *Statistical Abstract of the United States* (Washington, DC: Government Printing Office, 1995): 409, table 646.

Consider as well the following observation drawn from a number of studies of second job holding in Britain: "Although the holding of second jobs has always been proportionately lower among blacks than among whites, the gap widened considerably during the 1970s. On the one hand, between 1969 and 1979 there was a greater decrease in the percentage of black multiple job holders. . . . On the other, the proportion of black female multiple jobholders dropped slightly . . . while that of white female workers increased considerably"

(Bruno Dallago, *The Irregular Economy* [Aldershot, UK: Dartmouth, 1990]: 66–67).

14. Stinson, "Multiple Jobholding up Sharply in the 1980's":5.

15. Juliet Schor, *The Overworked American* (New York: Basic Books, 1991).

16. For example, because of the absence of a public transportation system, considerable self-provisioning in Coolidge County has to do with cars. The mean number of vehicles per household is greater in Coolidge County than elsewhere in Vermont or indeed in the United States as a whole; 45.4 percent of all households had two cars, and 19.2 percent had three or more. Because public transportation is so scarce as to hardly exist at all, most people need to keep their cars in good running order as a means of getting to and from work. In 1993, 0.3 percent of the population in Coolidge County used public transportation to get to work, in comparison with 5.3 percent in the United States as a whole. U.S. Department of Commerce, *County and City Data Book* (Washington, DC: U.S. Department of Commerce, Economics and Statistics Administration, Bureau of the Census, 1994).

We should also be clear that urban areas also offer rich opportunities for self-provisioning, but considerably different from those in more rural regions. Homes are not necessarily built from the ground up: There is relatively less space for new housing, and what there is comes at premium prices. Rather, they are extensively remodeled. Gardens are few and far between, but in many urban neighborhoods, families band together to shop at larger markets. This kind of shopping saves money—as do gardens—and requires additional labor—again, as do gardens.

To the extent that self-provisioning activities have been eroded in urban areas, it is largely a function of public policies that prohibit them. Licenses, insurance regulations, and strict zoning are more prevalent there and more strictly enforced. Thus, it can be argued that the erosion of self-provisioning in urban areas is less the result of the inclinations of those who would profit from these activities than it is of those who profit from their prohibition.

17. Eleven percent of Coolidge County housing stock is trailers; 17 percent of the housing stock is composed of two or more units. Seventy-seven percent of the housing stock consists of separate units, which presumably allow some room to grow a couple of tomato plants (or more) or, zoning permitting, even to raise some livestock. Twenty-three percent of Coolidge County households rely on wood heat; trailers, however, are usually heated with kerosene because wood heat is too dangerous.

18. J. I. Gershuny and R. E. Pahl, "Work Outside Employment: Some Preliminary Speculations," *New University Quarterly* 34 (1979): 120–35. This perspective also prevails among those who look at newly industrialized regions and argue that a rural area can reabsorb those who are currently unemployed. See Pugliese, who also notes that in the case of those thrust out of employment in more "developed" areas, subsistence activities have probably already disappeared (Enrico Pugliese, "The Three Forms of Unemployment," *Social Research* 54, no. 2 [Summer 1987]: 311).

19. This view has been expressed most fully by Pahl, who made the surpris-

ing observation that the benefits of self-provisioning fall mainly to those households with a greater involvement in the labor force: "These findings are un-
equivocal: employment and self-provisioning go together, rather than one being
a substitute for another. . . . Those most committed to the labour market are
also the most committed to using their own labour in their own time for their
own purposes" (R. E. Pahl, *Divisions of Labour* (Oxford, UK: Basil Blackwell,
1984): 236. See also Morris, "Domestic Labour and Employment Status among
Married Couples: A Case Study in Hartlepool"; Joan Smith, "Transforming
Households: Working Class Women and Economic Crisis," *Social Problems* 35
(1987): 416–36; J. Jessen et al., "The Informal Work of Industrial Workers:
Present Situation, Trend Prognosis and Policy Implications," in *The Unofficial
Economy: Consequences and Perspectives in Different Economic Systems*,
ed. Sergio Alessandrini and Bruno Dallago (Aldershot, UK: Gower, 1987): 271–
82.

   20. Smith, "Transforming Households: Working Class Women and Economic Crisis." For a historical overview of the disappearance of household production for the market, see Joan M. Jensen, "Cloth, Butter and Boarders:
Women's Household Production for the Market," *The Review of Radical Political Economics* 12, no. 2 (Summer 1980): 14–23.

   21. We might note that Stack's book has often been (mis)read (and, we might
add, with problematic consequences) as an indication that the African American
population Stack described was not totally without resources but was instead
quite capable of meeting its own needs. Carol Stack, *All Our Kin* (New York:
Harper & Row, 1975). Lowenthal argues much as that reading would: "It has
become clear that low-wage working-class populations are particularly depend-
ent upon non-monetized, non-market systems of production and exchange. The
operations of these systems permit working-class families to survive and to reproduce, and in this sense they have also played a crucial historical role in the
development of industrial capitalist societies" (Martin D. Lowenthal, "The Social Economy in Urban Working-Class Communities," in *The Social Economy
of Cities*, ed. G. Gappert and H. Rose [Beverly Hills, CA: Sage, 1975]: 460). See
also Mirra Komarovsky, *Blue-Collar Marriage* (New York: Random House,
1967) on lower-income working-class communities, as well as Michael Young
and P. Willmott, *Family and Kinship in East London* (London: Penguin, 1957).
See also, for single mothers, Kathryn Edin and Laura Lein, *Making Ends Meet:
How Single Mothers Survive Welfare and Low-Wage Work* (New York: Russell
Sage Foundation, 1997).

   22. These data contradict the frequent belief that exchange relationships are
especially important among the poor. See, for example, Stack, *All Our Kin*;
Lowenthal, "The Social Economy in Urban Working-Class Communities": 460.

   23. Lois Levitan and Shelley Feldman, "For Love or Money: Nonmonetary
Economic Arrangements among Rural Households in Central New York," in
Household Strategies, Research in Rural Sociology and Development 5, ed. Daniel C. Clay and Harry K. Schwarzweller (Greenwich, CT: JAI, 1991): 167. Thus,
we find little support for the common assumption that rural areas automatically
produce opportunities for these kinds of exchanges. See also Michael Merrill,
"Cash Is Good to Eat: Self-Sufficiency and Exchange in the Rural Economy of

the United States," *Radical History Review* 4 (Winter 1977): 58; S. M. Miller, "The Pursuit of Informal Economies," *Annals of the American Academy of Political and Social Science* 493 (September 1987): 26–35; Rhoda Halperin, *The Livelihood of Kin: Making Ends Meet "The Kentucky Way"* (Austin: University of Texas Press, 1990); Janet M. Fitchen, "Rural Poverty in the Northeast: The Case of Upstate New York," in *Rural Poverty in America*, ed. Cynthia M. Duncan (New York: Auburn House, 1992): 177–200, Janet M. Fitchen, "On the Edge of Homelessness: Rural Poverty and Housing Insecurity," *Rural Sociology* 57, no. 2 (Summer 1992): 175–93; Leif Jensen, Gretchen T. Cornwell, and Jill L. Findeis, "Informal Work in Nonmetropolitan Pennsylvania," *Rural Sociology* 60, no. 1 (Spring 1995): 91–107.

24. Nancy A. Naples, "Contradictions in Agrarian Ideology: Restructuring Gender, Race, Ethnicity, and Class," *Rural Sociology* 59, no. 1 (Spring 1994): 118. Similarly, writing about rural areas of New York State, Fitchen, for example, reports that the "destabilization of marriage and family is occurring in a social context that itself is less secure," and she suggests that at least some groups—single adults—may no longer "be as enmeshed in and protected by a network of relatives who, no matter how poor or 'down and out,' were always available in the past" (Fitchen, "Rural Poverty in the Northeast: The Case of Upstate New York": 194). Contemporary literature on urban areas suggests that in situations of acute poverty and disruption, the traditional bonds of neighborhood and community support may be absent altogether. See William Julius Wilson, *The Truly Disadvantaged: The Inner City, the Underclass, and Public Policy* (Chicago: University of Chicago Press, 1987). Finally, Hogan, Eggebeen, and Clogg, in a broader investigation of social support, found that the majority of Americans were uninvolved in social exchanges and that "only about one in ten were extensively involved in [both] giving and receiving support." D. Hogan, David J. Eggebeen, and Clifford C. Clogg, "The Structure of Intergenerational Exchange in American Families," *American Journal of Sociology* 98, no. 6 (May 1993): 1453. In another article, these authors conclude that their findings can offer "little comfort to those policy makers who would abandon public policies or formally organized private-sector initiatives in favor of family resolutions to the variety of social and economic pressures facing American families in the 1990s." David J. Eggebeen and Dennis P. Hogan, "Giving Between Generations in American Families," *Human Nature* 1, no. 3 (1990): 231.

25. This finding of a gender difference emerged quite vividly in respondents' replies to a straightforward question about whether anybody within the family engaged in this practice: Men often answered by providing examples of their own efforts; women usually answered that barter was something their husbands did. Interestingly, Levitan and Feldman ("For Love or Money: Nonmonetary Economic Arrangements Among Rural Households in Central New York") do not make the same observation. Other studies of informal work in rural areas also rarely distinguish among the types of informal activities individuals engage in or discuss the gendered components of these types of activities. See Jensen, Cornwell, and Findeis, "Informal Work in Nonmetropolitan Pennsylvania." The one exception to this generalization is the extensive work that has been done on women's work as caregivers. See Emily K. Abel and Margaret K. Nel-

son, *Circles of Care: Work and Identity in Women's Lives* (Albany: State University of New York Press, 1990).

26. R. E. Pahl and Claire Wallace, "Household Work Strategies in Economic Recession," in *Beyond Employment: Household, Gender and Subsistence*, ed. Nanneke Redclift and Enzo Mingione (New York: Basil Blackwell, 1985): 209. See also Emily K. Abel, *Who Cares for the Elderly?* (Philadelphia: Temple University Press, 1990); N. F. Marks and S. S. McLanahan, "Gender, Family Structure, and Social Support among Parents," *Journal of Marriage and the Family* 55 (May 1993): 481–93; Barry Wellman, "Domestic Work, Paid Work and Net Work," in *Understanding Personal Relationships: An Interdisciplinary Approach*, ed. Steve Duck (Beverly Hills, CA: Sage, 1985): 159–91. In fact, there is a similarity between the manner in which men give informal assistance and the manner in which they engage in housework. In both informal assistance and housework, they are more likely to engage in time-limited tasks rather than more diffuse, ongoing responsibilities. See Sarah F. Berk, *The Gender Factory: The Apportionment of Work in American Households* (New York: Plenum, 1985).

27. Louis Uchitelle and N. R. Kleinfeld, "On the Battlefields of Business, Millions of Casualties," *New York Times* (March 3, 1996): A26. In our in-depth sample as well, a substantial proportion of those who had lost a good job in the past four years had at least some education beyond a high school degree.

28. An additional group of individuals we interviewed had themselves shifted from good to bad work within the months before we spoke with them, not because they had quit or gotten tired of their employment, but because they were laid off. Although these individuals remained located in good job families, it was now by virtue of the fact that a spouse was still employed in good work.

29. Louis Uchitelle and N. R. Kleinfeld, "On the Battlefields of Business, Millions of Casualties," *New York Times* (March 3, 1996): A1, 26–29. Much of the research on displaced workers is associated with job loss as a result of recessions rather than downsizing alone. In general, nationwide, there is evidence that the 1990–91 recession was different from the recession a decade earlier. See also Jennifer M. Gardner, "Worker Displacement: A Decade of Change," *Monthly Labor Review* 118, no. 4 (April 1995): 45–57. For a discussion of what happened to displaced workers between 1979 and 1983, see Paul O. Flaim and Ellen Sehgal, "Displaced Workers of 1979–83: How Well Have They Fared?" *Monthly Labor Review* 108, no. 6 (June 1985): 3–18. Although the 1990–91 recession was not as deep as that in 1980–82, the total number of workers displaced was greater than it had been during the previous recession, with manufacturing workers among those most likely to be displaced, as they had been in the earlier one. Indeed, in New England the displacement rate rose from 4.3 percent in 1981–82 to 5.9 percent in 1991–92. Moreover, in the more recent recession, manufacturing workers were also hit hard in yet another way—they were especially unlikely to find new work. In 1994, 72 percent of displaced manufacturing workers had found a new job, compared with 77 percent of nonmanufacturing workers. Moreover, those affected by the more recent recession were more likely to be older workers (over thirty-five), and the long-term consequences were more likely to be devastating for this group.

It is common to note that unemployment rates conceal the full harm to workers because some workers become discouraged and stop looking for work; these "discouraged workers" are not counted as unemployed. Unemployment rates also conceal the experience of those who disappear from unemployment rolls because they have subsequently found new work. The 1991–92 recession had a profound impact on precisely that group—the displaced but reemployed worker. Although about three-quarters of those displaced from full-time jobs in 1991 and 1992 had found new jobs by the time they were surveyed in 1994, among this group, only 31.8 percent had found wage and salary jobs with earnings the same as or higher than those of the lost job. A closer look at wages reveals that manufacturing workers were especially likely to find employment at wages *below* those in their previous jobs and that they experienced a greater percentage change from their lost job to their current job. Displacement affected more than wages: During the 1991–92 recession, about 72 percent of persons who lost their jobs had health insurance coverage under their former employers' plans. At the time of the 1994 survey, only about three-quarters of these were again covered by a group health insurance plan, excluding Medicare or Medicaid. (Of course, those who were reemployed were more likely to have insurance than those who had failed to find employment: 82 percent of those who had previously held insurance found a new job with an insurance plan, whereas only 62 percent of those out of the labor force altogether and but 41 percent of those unemployed had health coverage at the time of the survey.) See Gardner, "Worker Displacement: A Decade of Change." For an article documenting the struggles of a family in Vermont, see Aki Soga, "Beating the Bad-Job Trap: Family Struggles to Regain a Dream," *Burlington Free Press* (October 9, 1995): 1A.

CHAPTER 3

1. Of course, it might be suggested that we have reversed causality here: Because good job families have two workers more often than do bad job families, the former have increased chances of getting a good job. There is ample reason to believe, however, that the disadvantage experienced by bad job families is not the result of a simple statistical probability but rather the result of being trapped in different cycles.

2. Only 29 percent of good job households have at least one worker employed part time; among bad job households, that proportion goes up to 39 percent. To a certain extent, this difference between the two sets of households depends on the definitions we use: Only those employed year round and *full time* could be included among those with good work, and therefore no "good work" household could have *two* part-time workers. Our definition alone does not account for the difference in this use of second workers because those second workers do not enter into the basic classification of households.

3. The quality of the employment was measured using the same factors as those describing good work and bad work. In good job households, the average quality of employment of the second worker is 4.2 ($n = 57$) in comparison with an average of 3.5 ($n = 29$) for second workers in bad job households. This difference is statistically significant at the .05 level.

4. Much of the social polarization literature examines families at this frozen moment; that literature thus misses the important element of variability among households that are "less fortunate." See, for example, Lydia Morris, "Domestic Labour and Employment Status among Married Couples: A Case Study in Hartlepool," *Capital and Class* 49 (Spring 1993): 37–52; Lydia Morris, "Informal Aspects of Social Divisions," *International Journal of Urban and Regional Research* 18, no. 1 (March 1994): 112–26; Jane Wheelock, "Capital Restructuring and the Domestic Economy: Family Self Respect and the Irrelevance of 'Rational Economic Man,' " *Capital and Class*, no. 41 (Summer 1990): 103–41; R. E. Pahl, *Divisions of Labour* (Oxford, UK: Basil Blackwell, 1984); R. E. Pahl, "Some Remarks on Informal Work, Social Polarization and the Social Structure," *International Journal of Urban and Regional Research* 12, no. 2 (1988): 247–67; R. E. Pahl and Claire Wallace, "Household Work Strategies in Economic Recession," in *Beyond Employment: Household, Gender and Subsistence*, ed. Nanneke Redclift and Enzo Mingione (New York: Basil Blackwell, 1985): 189–228; Colin C. Williams and Jan Windebank, "Social Polarization of Households in Contemporary Britain: A 'Whole Economy' Perspective," *Regional Studies* 29, no. 8 (December 1995): 723–28.

5. Ann M. Oberhauser, "Gender and Household Economic Strategies in Rural Appalachia," *Gender, Place and Culture* 2, no. 1 (1995): 51–70; Harriet B. Presser, "Shift Work and Child Care among Young Dual-Earner American Parents," *Journal of Marriage and the Family* 50, no. 1 (February 1988): 133–48; Sandra Hofferth, "Employer Benefits and Parental Leave Policies in the U.S.," paper presented at the annual meeting of the American Sociological Association (Washington, DC, August 1990); Peter Cattan, "Childcare Problems: An Obstacle to Work," *Monthly Labor Review* 114, no. 10 (October 1991): 3–9.
For specific Vermont data showing that single women with preschool children have virtually the same labor force participation rates as married women with young children but *much* lower employment rates, see Elaine McCrate and Joan Smith, "When Work Doesn't Work: The Failure of Current Welfare Reform" (Economics Department, University of Vermont, 1996).

6. Ellen Israel Rosen, *Bitter Choices: Blue-Collar Women in and out of Work* (Chicago: University of Chicago Press, 1987).

7. Sandra L. Hofferth et al., *National Child Care Survey, 1990: A National Association for the Education of Young Children Study* (Washington, DC: Urban Institute Press, 1991); Cattan, "Childcare Problems: An Obstacle to Work"; Jonathan R. Veum and Philip M. Gleason, "Child Care: Arrangements and Costs," *Monthly Labor Review* 114, no. 10 (October 1991): 10–17. For specific data on Vermont concerning the costs of child care measured against women's wages, see McCrate and Smith, "When Work Doesn't Work: The Failure of Current Welfare Reform."

8. Because low-waged work can rarely provide an effective route out of reliance on the state, *single* women with young children frequently cycle between welfare and work. We studied only married-couple families with at least one earner. In these families, the second worker need not turn to the state when she (or he) finds it impossible to sustain employment: She has a spouse instead. That

spouse, however, does not produce the marvel of enhancing the second worker's wages. Like single women, second workers in bad work households still have to cover the expenses of holding down a job. In going to work, they do not actually lose benefits (as is the case for women who move from welfare to work) but they do not do not receive any special privileges (such as child care subsidies and training) either. See Kathryn Edin and Laura Lein, *Making Ends Meet: How Single Mothers Survive Welfare and Low-Wage Work* (New York: Russell Sage Foundation, 1997).

9. The recently implemented Family and Medical Leave Act [FMLA] cannot solve either Jake's or his sister's problems. The FMLA applies only to establishments with fifty or more employees. (In Coolidge County in 1993, the average firm had fewer than ten employees; *County Business Patterns* [Washington, DC: U.S. Department of Commerce, Bureau of the Census, 1990].) Although Wilson Contract Manufacturing is large enough to be covered, it costs money to take advantage of that protection even if it is offered, because it does not replace lost wages. Families relying on a single income cannot forgo those wages. According to one study, fewer than 40 percent of working women have benefits or income protection that would allow them to take a six-week unpaid leave. Ellen Bravo, *Wage Replacement and Family Leave: Is It Necessary? Is It Feasible?* (Cleveland: 9 to 5 Working Women Education Fund, 1992). For estimates of the costs that existed before the FMLA was implemented, see Roberta M. Spalter-Roth and Heidi I. Hartmann, *Unnecessary Losses: Costs to Americans of the Lack of Family and Medical Leave* (Washington, DC: Institute for Women's Policy Research, 1990); Hofferth, "Employer Benefits and Parental Leave Policies in the U.S."

Of course, in much of Western Europe, government policies ensure protections that are available only privately in the United States. When we presented our findings at a conference in the Netherlands, a number of people noted that many of the issues under discussion were particularly "American" because they would not arise in a situation where workers had better protections. For discussions of European policies, see Sheila B. Kamerman and Alfred J. Kahn, *Family Policy: Government and Families in Fourteen Countries* (New York: Columbia University Press, 1978); Sheila B. Kamerman and Alfred J. Kahn, *Child Care, Family Benefits and Working Parents: A Study of Comparative Policy* (New York: Columbia University Press, 1981); Barbara R. Bergmann, *Saving Our Children from Poverty: What the United States Can Learn from France* (New York: Russell Sage Foundation, 1996).

10. We return to this point in Chapter 7, where we discuss the individual attitudes toward employment and identify other reasons why bad job workers might act in ways that are disruptive to maintaining their employment.

11. Geraldine Pratt and Susan Hanson, "On the Links Between Home and Work: Family-Household Strategies in a Buoyant Labor Market," *International Journal of Urban and Regional Research* 15, no. 1 (March 1991): 55–74.

12. Among the nonrandom sample, in 16 percent of good job households both husband and wife were employed in the same firm; others reported being employed in the same firm as a close friend or relative. Managers at two good work firms indicated that informal channels played a role in their recruitment

policies. Prior to its more extensive reliance on a "temp" agency, Ajax Plastics Manufacturing had as its principal source of employees those who had heard about job openings from other workers, and Master Forms Incorporated also used informal referrals, although it also required all applicants to register with the Vermont Job Service.

Employers offering bad jobs, like those offering good ones, also rely on informal recruiting channels. The Wilson Contract Manufacturing manager reported that his firm mostly found employees through word of mouth, and the manager we spoke with at Green Mountain Cuddly Toys said that although the company carried ads in a local newspaper, about half of its current workforce had been recruited through word of mouth and there were a considerable number of family members within that workforce.

In fact, some have argued that more informal employers and those offering less good jobs are *more* likely to use informal networks as a way to find employees than are those who offer better employment opportunities (Lydia Morris, "Informal Aspects of Social Divisions": 120). Harris argues "the characteristics of a particular worker's social world will influence both the means of access to employment and also the nature of the employment that results. Informal channels may increase the likelihood of finding work but also seem to increase the probability that the work will be short-term and held under poor terms and conditions of employment" (C. C. Harris, *Redundancy and Recession in South Wales* [Oxford, UK: Blackwell, 1987]: 134).

A substantial body of scholarship suggests that social networks play an important role in employment possibilities. See Oberhauser, "Gender and Household Economic Strategies in Rural Appalachia"; Morris, "Informal Aspects of Social Divisions"; Susan Hanson and Geraldine Pratt, "Dynamic Dependencies: A Geographic Investigation of Local Labor Markets," *Economic Geography* 68, no. 4 (October 1992): 373–405; Cornelia Butler Flora and Jan L. Flora, "Entrepreneurial Social Infrastructure: A Necessary Ingredient," *Annals of the American Academy of Political and Social Science* 529 (September 1993): 48–58. Within this scholarship, there is considerable debate as to how reliance on networks affects the quality of work individuals obtain. Granovetter argues, for example, that 60 to 90 percent of blue-collar jobs "were found informally, principally through friends and relatives but also by direct application" (Mark S. Granovetter, *Getting a Job: A Study of Contacts and Careers* [Cambridge, MA: Harvard University Press, 1974]: 5). For studies of white-collar workers, see Margaret Grieco, *Keeping It in the Family: Social Networks and Employment Chance* (London: Tavistock, 1987). There is a dispute in the literature about whether jobs obtained in this fashion reap higher or lower wages. Granovetter found that men who heard about jobs through a personal contact earned higher salaries than those who relied on formal channels. By way of contrast, others suggest that personal contacts did not produce a long-term advantage. M. Corcoran, L. Datcher, and G. J. Duncan, "Most Workers Find Jobs Through Word of Mouth," *Monthly Labor Review* 103, no. 8 (August 1980): 33–36; Grieco, *Keeping It in the Family: Social Networks and Employment Chance*. There is also a dispute about whether men or women are more likely to rely on these informal contacts and whether this makes a difference in their earnings. Some research suggests that men are more likely than women to rely on personal contacts to obtain jobs. (Given alternative reasons for wage discrepancies between men and women, the extent to which they rely on social networks is hardly likely to be the critical variable. See Barbara Reskin and Irene Padavic, *Women and Men at Work* (Thousand Oaks, CA: Pine Forge, 1994). Although the evidence we collected cannot resolve these debates, it does lend support to widespread use of informal contacts—as a recruiting tool by employers in good and bad job firms, and as a tool for finding jobs among both good and bad job employees.

13. The quality of self-employment was measured by asking about the nature of one's tools and equipment, clients, and the predictability of work. The average score of self-employment in good job households was 2.9 ($n = 16$) in comparison with 2.3 ($n = 18$) among bad job households.

14. Financial stability was not the full measure of the support from her husband's good work. Ellen also received free materials (for use in educational activities with the day care children) from the canteen at her husband, Frank's, workplace ("I have the canteen at Sterling save bread tags for me"). Moreover, most of her original clients were the children of Frank's colleagues:

> I started out with three kids. Then, a month later, I got a fourth. These were all kids from Sterling which is where Frank works. From then on, it has, pretty much, been word of mouth, that I have a day care and it is a fairly good one.

15. Vermont requires registration of family day care providers who take care of children from more than two different families. Registered providers can care for six children of preschool age full time (no more than two of these children can be infants) and can care for an additional four school-age children on a part-time basis. Care of more children requires a license. For regulations, see Vermont Department of Social and Rehabilitation Services, *Journal for Family Day Care Homes* (Montpelier, VT: Division of Licensing and Registration, 1989). For a discussion of the differences between various kinds of family day care providers in Vermont, see Margaret K. Nelson, *Negotiating Care: The Experience of Family Day Care Providers* (Philadelphia: Temple University Press, 1990).

16. Self-employment is on the rise in Coolidge County, as it is elsewhere in the United States.

17. Controlling for income does not affect this pattern at all. Whether the primary earner's wages are high or low, bad job households with but one earner are less likely than those with two earners to include a family member who moonlights.

18. For a discussion of how this kind of arrangement affects "grandmothers," see Presser, "Shift Work and Child Care among Young Dual-Earner American Parents." For a discussion of the number of people who rely on this kind of child care arrangement, see Hofferth et al., *National Child Care Survey, 1990: A National Association for the Education of Young Children Study*.

19. Williams and Windebank similarly argue that the paid informal work in what they call "resource-rich households" is likely to be "more highly paid and autonomous" than that found in resource-deprived households, where informal

work is more usually "low-paid and exploitative" (Williams and Windebank, "Social Polarization of Households in Contemporary Britain: A 'Whole Economy' Perspective": 75). In a parallel argument, Wallace and Pahl report on the research of others that demonstrates that the unemployed are deprived of the tools, transportation, and social networks that they had developed in employment and were thus further disadvantaged when it came to work in the informal or 'black' economy (Claire Wallace and Ray Pahl, "Polarisation, Unemployment and All Forms of Work," in *The Experience of Unemployment*, ed. Sheila Allen (Basingstoke, UK: Macmillan, 1986): 116–44.

20. We do not mean to imply that workers with bad jobs are without skills: That is not the point of our comparison. Rather, we are suggesting that a skilled good job worker can use his/her skills outside employment because his/her good job has already underwritten the development of side-work. We might note, however, that bad work is unlikely—even if it draws on an employee's skills—to pay for further training. By way of contrast, a number of workers with good jobs we spoke with were reimbursed for the expenses of courses even when the content of those courses was only tangentially related to their waged jobs and even when they considered using those newly acquired skills as a stepping-stone out of their current employment situation.

21. For a similar point, see J. Jessen et al., "The Informal Work of Industrial Workers: Present Situation, Trend Prognosis and Policy Implications," in *The Unofficial Economy: Consequences and Perspectives in Different Economic Systems*, ed. Sergio Alessandrini and Bruno Dallago (Aldershot, UK: Gower, 1987): 278.

22. Although bad work could also provide contacts for an entrepreneurial business or sales activities, good work provides contacts with others who—as the holders of good jobs—make *ideal* clients because they can afford to pay their bills. Because they are colleagues, they are easily tracked if they renege.

23. For an interesting article that suggests that commission sales programs are appealing to more highly educated women, see Tom Dunkel, "The Tupperware Lady Is an MBA," *Working Woman* 20, no. 4 (April 1995): 44–52. Recently, and in response to the changing reality of women's lives, the Tupperware Company has encouraged the practice of selling out of offices in addition to the traditional party (Pam Weisz, "Times Sure Have Changed When Tupperware Is Cool," *Brandweek* [July 11, 1994]: 28).

24. In fact, in some cases an overlap between the two sets of clients might raise an eyebrow about whether or not an employee is "stealing" customers. Mark Lee both works for a car dealer and does mechanical work on the side. Some of the dealer's customers use Mark to transport their vehicles to the shop; Mark then saves on gas and mileage. Other customers call him at home; whether he refers them back to the dealer or suggests they use him privately remains unclear.

25. Conversely, the stability and predictable hours of good work mesh well with entrepreneurial activities to create the possibility of reliable behavior there as well. One can make—and keep—promises about when the lawn will be mowed or the sweater knitted.

26. We might note here that Jack Curtis is engaged in work for regular

businesses—the town and its schools. He is available to fill the demand of "outsourcing." The town is thus also saving money in this way.

27. Wallace and Pahl ("Polarisation, Unemployment and All Forms of Work") describe a similar kind of work that they call scavenging: "Work outside the household to obtain food or materials without involving anyone else, or without it necessarily being illegal. Such activity would include fishing, ferreting, 'totting' and scavenging-type activities" (129). They too find that it is primarily men who engage in this kind of work. In our study, there are two exceptions to the rule of male predominance in trading. First, in contrast to the occasional garage sale that accompanies spring cleaning or a move among good job households, both men and women in bad job households purposefully accumulate items they can resell from their yards or porches on summer weekends. Second, women who clean houses regularly ask for hand-me-downs that they then redistribute (for a price or for favors) in their communities. These house cleaners thus have a kind of "redistributive" function within their communities. See, for example, Marshall D. Sahlins, *Stone-Age Economics* (Chicago: Aldine-Atherton, 1972).

28. Note that Don and Matt's practice of buying and selling cars differs decidedly from Doug Hill's practice of doing so. Doug makes careful and predictable arrangements; Don and Matt depend on chance opportunities.

29. Visitors to Vermont frequently comment on the number of items—boats, snowmobiles, tractors—sitting in yards with "for sale" signs.

30. Jessen et al. argue differently. They suggest that industrial workers do not see in their informal work an alternative to their current employment. In either case, it is ironic that it is good work that best provides this possibility of a protection against its demise (Jessen et al., "The Informal Work of Industrial Workers: Present Situation, Trend Prognosis and Policy Implications").

CHAPTER 4

1. This difference in substantial self-provisioning does not depend on a difference between the two sets of households in home ownership: In each group of households (in the random survey), three-quarters (76 percent) of families either owned their own home outright or were paying a mortgage on that home.

2. R. E. Pahl, "The Restructuring of Capital, the Local Political Economy and Household Work Strategies," in *Social Relations and Spatial Structures*, ed. D. Gregory and J. Urry (Basingstoke, UK: Macmillan, 1985): 243–64; J. Jessen et al., "The Informal Work of Industrial Workers: Present Situation, Trend Prognosis and Policy Implications," in *The Unofficial Economy: Consequences and Perspectives in Different Economic Systems*, ed. Sergio Alessandrini and Bruno Dallago (Aldershot, UK: Gower, 1987): 271–82; Colin C. Williams and Jan Windebank, "Social Polarization of Households in Contemporary Britain: A 'Whole Economy' Perspective," *Regional Studies* 29, no. 8 (December 1995): 723–28.

3. Note the similarity to the conditions that underwrite the entrepreneurial, moonlighting activities of members of good job households. Those activities also require major investments before they create a financial profit.

4. Although an activity such as home construction would be hard to duplicate in an urban area, it should be remembered that extensive renovation of brownstones is a very common urban phenomenon.

5. The fact that good work is being eroded does not undercut this point. As long as individuals hold on to good work, they can believe that they have the security that kind of employment used to offer.

6. Twenty-four percent of each group of households lived in rental units. Among good job households, only one family had an arrangement whereby they could exchange services for cash payments. A more substantial proportion of bad job households (27 percent) made these kinds of arrangements.

7. For each individual self-provisioning activity, bad job households had slightly higher rates than did good job households: growing vegetables (73 percent versus 69 percent), changing oil in car (86 percent versus 81 percent), gathering or cutting wood for fuel (60 percent versus 31 percent), growing or raising meat (23 percent versus 18 percent), and plowing the driveway (71 percent versus 56 percent). The only difference that achieves statistical significance (.05 level) is that for gathering or cutting wood for fuel.

8. Much feminist literature has demonstrated that the "leisured" housewife was anything but leisured, that she engaged in a wide variety of "productive" and "reproductive" activities that were crucial to the survival of her family. See, for example, DiLeonardo's discussion of "kin work" (Michelle DiLeonardo, "The Female World of Cards and Holidays: Women, Families and the Work of Kinship," *Signs* 12 [1987]: 440–53), Bose's analysis of the undercount of women's employment (Christine Bose, "Devaluing Women's Work: The Undercount of Women's Employment in 1900 and 1980," in *Hidden Aspects of Women's Work*, ed. Christine Bose, Roslyn Feldberg, and Natalie Sokoloff [New York: Praeger, 1987]: 95–115), and Smith's description of the variety of unwaged activities engaged in by her mother (Joan Smith, "The Way We Were: Women and Work," *Feminist Studies* 8, no. 2 [Summer 1982]: 437–56).

9. Joan Smith, "All Crises Are Not the Same: Households in the United States During Two Crises," in *Work Without Wages: Comparative Studies of Domestic Labor and Self-Employment*, ed. Jane L. Collins and Martha Giminez (Albany: State University of New York Press, 1990): 128–41; Cornelia Butler Flora, "The New Poor in Midwestern Farming Communities," in *Rural Poverty in America*, ed. Cynthia M. Duncan (New York: Auburn House, 1992): 202–11.

10. Among households in which men were unemployed, Wheelock noted that while there was some "level of additional domestic economy activity," it was well below that which economists see as being possible. Wheelock explains that the gap between what unemployed men actually do and what others believe they should do may "in part be explained by a lack of the necessary equipment and materials for replacing market purchases with domestic activities, and [by] some evidence of disinvestment in consumer durables amongst the sample households." Jane Wheelock, "Capital Restructuring and the Domestic Economy: Family Self Respect and the Irrelevance of 'Rational Economic Man,' " *Capital and Class*, no. 41 (Summer 1990): 118.

11. Among high-income households, the difference between single-earner

households and dual-earner households in the extent to which they engage in self-provisioning is statistically significant at the .05 level or higher.

12. Jessen et al., "The Informal Work of Industrial Workers: Present Situation, Trend Prognosis and Policy Implications."

13. Although here too there is more self-provisioning when there are two workers than when there is but one (23 percent versus 9 percent), the differences are not as large as they are among bad job households (a difference of 14 percent versus a difference of 27 percent), and they do not achieve statistical significance.

14. Among both high-income and low-income good job households, the difference between households with a moonlighter and those without a moonlighter in the extent to which they engage in self-provisioning is statistically significant at the .05 level or higher.

15. In fact, the particular activities that rise dramatically with moonlighting (changing oil in one's car, snowplowing) are precisely those activities that accompany the kind of entrepreneurial moonlighting found among men in these households. That is, car repair on the side equips one to accomplish one's own car repair, and landscaping and lawn mowing businesses equip one to take care of the snow piled in one's own driveway.

16. In addition to the points we note below, Jessen et al. argue that "whenever skilled handiwork is concerned, workers first of all think that they are competent to do the job themselves. This often leads to a deep-rooted distrust of the skilled handiwork offered on the formal market." They note as well that it is "characteristic for workers to think in terms of their working capacity instead of their buying capacity" (Jessen et al., "The Informal Work of Industrial Workers: Present Situation, Trend Prognosis and Policy Implications": 275).

17. There were no differences between good job households and bad job households in the degree to which they engaged in individual practices of inter-household exchange. For each of the following, bad job households are listed before good job households: received vegetables (20 percent versus 23 percent), received oil change (2 percent versus 1 percent), received wood for fuel (5 percent versus 5 percent), received meat (10 percent versus 8 percent), and someone plowed the driveway (6 percent versus 9 percent).

18. Pahl found patterns not dissimilar to our own; that is, he found that those who were busy did more for others, but he did not explore what was done *for* them (R. E. Pahl, *Divisions of Labour* [Oxford; UK: Basil Blackwell, 1984]). What we find with respect to this issue is a kind of polarization among the good job households themselves. See also Lorna McKee, "Households During Unemployment: The Resourcefulness of the Unemployed," in *Give and Take in Families: Studies in Resource Distribution*, ed. Julia Brannen and Gail Wilson (Boston: Allen & Unwin, 1987): 96–116.

19. McKee argues that "there are cultural norms which emphasize the reciprocity of relationships within families and those which dictate the value of autonomy and 'standing on your own two feet.' " McKee also suggests that "the research interview may provide a particular kind of representation of relationships and there will always be limitations to network research which relies only on the account of one informant in that network" (McKee, "Households During Unemployment: The Resourcefulness of the Unemployed": 100).

20. Stack (*All Our Kin* [New York: Harper & Row, 1975]) describes a family that frees itself from the interpersonal bonds of the networks that support that population in order to achieve upward mobility. See our discussion below of good job and bad job households that seek to shed responsibility to relatives who make too many demands.

21. Martin D. Lowenthal, "The Social Economy in Urban Working-Class Communities," in *The Social Economy of Cities*, ed. G. Gappert and H. Rose (Beverly Hills, CA: Sage, 1975): 460. Young and Wilmott anticipated that these arrangements would decline with employment (Michael Young and P. Willmott, *Family and Kinship in East London* [London: Penguin, 1957]).

22. Our respondents say that barter usually occurs between individuals whose skills and services already have been accorded a monetary value and that it entails the exchange of dissimilar items. The more casual exchange of babysitting for babysitting or of "favors" (I'll mow your lawn because I have the lawn mower out and I am in a beneficent mood and next week you reciprocate by bringing over a bowl of string beans) is not considered barter.

23. Wellman argued similarly about the use of social networks among blue-collar workers in East York, a residential, densely settled area of Toronto (Barry Wellman, "Domestic Work, Paid Work and Net Work," in *Understanding Personal Relationships: An Interdisciplinary Approach*, ed. Steve Duck [Beverly Hills, CA: Sage, 1985]: 159–91).

24. Martin D. Lowenthal, "The Social Economy in Urban Working-Class Communities." For an argument that network relationships are reinforced through exchanges of favors, see Margaret Grieco, *Keeping It in the Family: Social Networks and Employment Chance* (London: Tavistock, 1987): 177.

25. Marcel Mauss, *The Gift: Forms and Functions of Exchange in Archaic Societies* (Glencoe, IL: The Free Press, 1954); Marshall D. Sahlins, *Stone-Age Economics* (Chicago: Aldine-Atherton, 1972). This trust may be especially important when both sides are engaged in illegal activities insofar as they are being concealed for tax purposes. (One woman told an interviewer about the barter arrangements of her husband and subsequently called to make sure that we would not be writing anything that would reveal the source of that information.) Networks also create the good will that ensures that someone will not make a fuss about illegal zoning practices. Tom Hubbard, a member of a good job household, smoothed over conflicts—even at risk of a financial loss—to avert the consequences of ill feeling:

> I would rather keep peace with the neighbors and the friends and the relatives than start up an argument over $20 or something. But, at least 95 percent of your neighbors or friends or whatnot ask you how much do I owe you, what do you want for that. The ones that you have to let slide are the ones that have already decided they're not going to pay you. I had one one time that I had to rebuild the carburetor on his truck and by the time I was all done he hands me a six-pack of Mountain Dew and says, "Here you go. Thanks a lot." It was like that $2.39 six-pack of Mountain Dew was supposed to pay for my two hours of working on his carburetor. That's one of those things you have to let slide because otherwise it's World War III by the time you get done. And you have to be concerned—especially with this type of work [when] you're working at home—with keeping the neighbors happy. You have to, because otherwise they take your livelihood away from you. It's very simple, with the zoning boards. It's real easy to do.

26. Janet Finch, *Family Obligations and Social Change* (Cambridge, MA: Polity, 1989); Lydia Morris, "Informal Aspects of Social Divisions," *International Journal of Urban and Regional Research* 18, no. 1 (March 1994): 112–26.

27. McKee argues from her research on unemployed workers that "The pressure to return or repay kindness with kindness, help with help, was clearly appreciated by even those families who reported little aid stemming from the outside . . . being on the receiving end can have negative or unwelcome consequences for the individual. Some couples prefer to be free of such obligations" (McKee, "Households During Unemployment: The Resourcefulness of the Unemployed": 108–9). Similarly, Wallace and Pahl write "The norm of reciprocity becomes a burden when it is not possible to reciprocate without fear of the consequences" (Claire Wallace and Ray Pahl, "Polarisation, Unemployment and All Forms of Work," in *The Experience of Unemployment*, ed. Sheila Allen [Basingstoke, UK: Macmillan, 1986]: 127).

28. Morris notes that this greater reliance on family rather than friends has further consequences with respect to employment—that is, once one has narrowed one's "circle," one has fewer opportunities to find work of any kind and especially good work (Morris, "Informal Aspects of Social Divisions"). This is, of course, the argument that Wilson makes when he speaks of an "underclass." One need not go to that extreme to make a similar point. William Julius Wilson, *The Truly Disadvantaged: The Inner City, the Underclass, and Public Policy* (Chicago: University of Chicago Press, 1987).

29. This does not mean that members of these households absolutely avoid barter within their principal activities of self-employment. What it does mean is that they do *not* barter when that income is necessary to sustain the household.

30. Although we will expand on this point in Chapter 5, we note here that this cost is not borne evenly within a household. Because women are largely responsible for managing the household's income, the unpredictable cash flow burdens them much more than it does their husbands. It is their husbands, however, who much more frequently decide when to barter, for how much, and with what results. In fact, men's bartering often disrupts and circumvents their wives' budget plans.

31. Wheelock found that households in which men were unemployed did *not* receive more from family and friends than they had before; she also found that households in which men were unemployed centered their informal exchanges far more on relatives than on neighbors and friends (Wheelock, "Capital Restructuring and the Domestic Economy: Family Self Respect and the Irrelevance of 'Rational Economic Man' "). See also McKee, "Households During Unemployment: The Resourcefulness of the Unemployed."

32. For example, in their investigation of life in Schuyler County, New York, Levitan and Feldman found frequent examples of families living together, generally, although not invariably, in response to some kind of crisis. Unlike our sample, their survey revealed that half of the households they interviewed did not fit within the norm of the one- or two-generational nuclear family or the single householder. Lois Levitan and Shelley Feldman, "For Love or Money: Nonmonetary Economic Arrangements among Rural Households in Central

New York," in *Household Strategies*, Research in Rural Sociology and Development 5, ed. Daniel C. Clay and Harry K. Schwarzweller (Greenwich, CT: JAI, 1991): 149–72.

33. Quotation is from ibid., p. 161. The random survey was a telephone survey. A household that consisted of two separate nuclear families would show up as a single, albeit nonnuclear, household. However, unless the "host" family already fit our criteria—two adults living together as partners, each eligible for labor force participation, at least one member employed in formal waged work—we would not include the household at all. Even if the "host" family fit our criteria, we would get most of the information about that host family and not the other current members of that household; that is, each household would not be interviewed separately, and therefore we would not obtain information about why there was an atypical family.

34. A recent newspaper article in an area newspaper noted the rise in "specialty" farming—llamas, emu, donkeys. That article also noted that few could make a living off this endeavor and that in most families at least one—and often both—adults held down full-time jobs that effectively supported the agricultural activity.

CHAPTER 5

1. In a circular manner, that lower status in the family has also been viewed as the source of constraints on women's workplace involvement. For a classic exposition of this viewpoint, see Heidi Hartmann, "Capitalism, Patriarchy, and Job Segregation by Sex," *Signs* 1, no. 3, pt. 2 (1976): 137–67. A plethora of studies examines women's labor force experiences in contrast to those of men, with special attention to the household configuration and how that shapes women's employment. A number of historical studies have shown that economic structure and household composition interact—in very complex ways—to determine who goes "out to work" and who makes contributions to the household in other ways. See, for example, Alice Kessler-Harris, *Out to Work: A History of Wage-Earning Women in the United States* (New York: Oxford University Press, 1982); Louise A. Tilly and Joan W. Scott, *Women, Work and Family* (New York: Holt, Rinehart, and Winston, 1978); Christine Bose, "Dual Spheres," in *Analyzing Gender*, ed. Beth Hess and Myra Marx Ferree (Newbury Park, CA: Sage, 1987): 267–87. For more contemporary studies that look at the interplay between the broader economy and domestic constraints as determinants of women's work experiences, see Myra Marx Ferree, "Beyond Separate Spheres: Feminism and Family Research," *Journal of Marriage and the Family* 52 (November 1990): 866–84; Elizabeth Berger, "The Economic Context of Labor Allocation," *Journal of Family Issues* 12, no. 2 (June 1991): 140–57; Barbara Zsembik and Chuck Peek, "The Effect of Economic Restructuring on Puerto Rican Women's Labor Force Participation in the Formal Sector," *Gender and Society* 8, no. 4 (December 1994): 525–40; Dana V. Hiller and William W. Philliber, "The Division of Labor in Contemporary Marriage: Expectations, Perceptions and Performance," *Social Problems* 33, no. 3 (February 1986): 191–201.

For some work on U.S. nonmetropolitan women that attempts to distinguish between the impact of the household and that of the broader labor market opportunities, see Janet L. Bokemeier and Ann R. Tickamyer, "Labor Force Experiences of Nonmetropolitan Women," *Rural Sociology* 50, no. 1 (1985): 51–73; Ann R. Tickamyer and Janet Bokemeier, "Sex Differences in Labor-Market Experiences," *Rural Sociology* 53, no. 2 (1988): 166–89.

In an interesting discussion of these issues, Bradley points out that the relationship between women's employment opportunities and their labor force participation does not go just one way: "Women's paid employment . . . has also been an important influence on the past restructuring of jobs: jobs are created in the light of availability of female labour and its requirements" (Harriet Bradley, "Work, Home and the Restructuring of Jobs," in *The Changing Experience of Employment: Restructuring and Recession*, ed. Kate Purcell, Stephen Wood, Alan Waton, and Sheila Allen [Houndsmill, Basingstoke, Hampshire, UK: Macmillan in association with the British Sociological Association, 1986]: 112).

2. By focusing on "customary" gender patterns of difference and hierarchy, we do not mean to convey that we condone either the practices on which they rest or their outcomes. Rather, we simply assume that those patterns constitute a social reality in which individuals have deep investments. After all, we are dealing here with white men and white women who might well have expected the privileges those patterns have conferred in the past.

One question that is sure to arise is that of "agency": Is gender recreated through the efforts of individuals—both men and women alike—to maintain the privileges "traditional" gendered patterns offer? Well, yes and no. In what follows, the logic of our argument is that the household strategies that emerge in the two sets of households do so in response to broader economic pressures. Having said as much, we acknowledge as well that particular aspects of these strategies—who goes to work when but one worker can be sustained, who engages in moonlighting, what self-provisioning activities and interhousehold exchanges are initiated and by whom—are decisions shaped at least in part by attempts to reinvigorate traditional gendered patterns and relationships. (In fact, it is precisely at moments of change that these decisions—what can be understood as the work of "doing gender"—become visible rather than taken for granted. See Ferree, "Beyond Separate Spheres: Feminism and Family Research": 869; Judith Gerson and Kathy Peiss, "Boundaries, Negotiations, Consciousness: Reconceptualizing Gender Relations," *Social Problems* 32 (1985): 317–31. As we show below, the structure of the good job household strategy both builds on and allows for that reinvigoration. In contrast, the circumstances of bad job households offer a greater challenge to the "usual" enactment of gender.

3. The labor force participation of women in good job households is almost as high as that of men (90 percent versus 98 percent) and considerably higher than the average rates for married women with a husband present in the county (65 percent). Within dual-earner good job households, women work more intensively than is the norm for the area: 77 percent of women in good job households work full time, in comparison with 65 percent of women in the county.

4. Numerous studies shows that women are more likely than men to spend

their "personal" money on the household. See Lourdes Beneria and Martha Roldan, *Crossroads of Class and Gender: Industrial Homework, Subcontracting, and Household Dynamics in Mexico City* (Chicago: University of Chicago Press, 1987); Lydia Morris, "Local Social Networks and Domestic Organisations: A Study of Redundant Steel Workers and Their Wives," *Sociological Review* 33, no. 2 (1985): 327–42.

5. In Chapter 4, we noted that among bad job households, trading substituted for self-provisioning as a kind of ersatz entrepreneurial activity. Like the true entrepreneurial moonlighting found among good job households, trading is predominantly a male activity.

6. Cockburn noted that there is much ideology about what technology is considered appropriate to women (e.g., sewing machines) and what is appropriate to men (e.g., power drills) (Cynthia Cockburn, *Machinery of Dominance: Women, Men and Technical Know-How* [London: Pluto Press, 1985]). Luxton as well argues that men do more of the jobs in the home that involve machinery (Meg Luxton, "Two Hands for the Clock: Changing Patterns in the Gendered Division of Labour in the Home," in *Through the Kitchen Window: The Politics of Home and Family*, 2d, enlarged ed., ed. Sedef Arat-Koc, Meg Luxton, and Harriet Rosenberg [Toronto: Garamond, 1990]: 39–55). See also Barbara L. Marshall, *Engendering Modernity: Feminism, Social Theory and Social Change* (Boston: Northeastern University Press, 1994).

7. In an interesting analysis of the allocation of money within marriage, Jan Pahl suggests that whether or not men engage in these activities might have something to do with other aspects of household "politics." In those households where men generally turn over all their earnings to their wives, they are less likely to moonlight (because they cannot keep those earnings) than when they provide their wives with an allowance and then keep their "extra" earnings for themselves. Pahl also argues that wage increases are viewed less positively by men than are bonuses because the former simply go to household expenses, whereas the latter may be defined as the man's personal spending money (Jan Pahl, "The Allocation of Money and the Structuring of Inequality Within Marriage," *Sociological Review* 31, no. 2 [1983]: 237–62). See also Gail Wilson, "Money: Patterns of Responsibility and Irresponsibility in Marriage," in *Give and Take in Families*, ed. Julia Brannen and Gail Wilson (Boston: Allen & Unwin, 1987): 136–54.

8. Women who do industrial homework (which in our sample was almost exclusively women in bad job households) do often involve their husbands—as well as other family members—in that labor.

9. We should note that in what follows we focus on that group of households in which men moonlight and even more specifically on that group of households in which men do that moonlighting through entrepreneurial activity. We do so for three reasons. First, as noted above, among those we interviewed in the *nonrandom* survey—where we believe we received more "honest" answers—moonlighting was far more common than it was among the *random* sample of good job households as a whole (and far more common than national averages would predict). Hence, we have reason to believe that among *working-class* men in good job households, moonlighting comes very close to being the

norm. Second, data from our research as well as the national data on moonlighting suggest that moonlighting is, at least in part, a response to economic restructuring. Third, and this point is not unrelated to the previous one, moonlighting has risen dramatically within the recent past; it is a growing phenomenon.

10. Harris argues that male networks might be special sites for the reinforcement of gender identity. Hence, Harris argues, those who spend a considerable amount of time in their networks will be discouraged from reorienting their domestic lives (C. C. Harris, *Redundancy and Recession in South Wales* [Oxford, UK: Blackwell, 1987]: 138).

11. Women also take on a set of tasks that require less physical strength: "I'm usually the one with the paintbrush. I do most of the stuff in the house except when it comes to the carpentry end of it. I did most of the painting, planting, that kind of stuff"; "I did stuff like putting on molding, staining, woodworking, sanding, various little things here and there."

12. The nature of women's self-employment also may make barter less likely. For example, women who participate in commission sales cannot barter with customers. Women—like Ellen Woodward—often do child care, which is less likely to involve barter than other kinds of self-employment for several reasons: It is time-bound and thus cannot be offered on weekends or "off" hours, and it is usually negotiated with women and thus with others who are themselves poorly positioned to engage in barter (Margaret K. Nelson, *Negotiating Care: The Experience of Family Day Care Providers* [Philadelphia: Temple University Press, 1990]).

13. Wheelock shows that *men* do more of this sort of caregiving when they are unemployed (Jane Wheelock, "Capital Restructuring and the Domestic Economy: Family Self Respect and the Irrelevance of 'Rational Economic Man' " *Capital and Class*, no. 41 [Summer 1990]: 103–41). For evidence that women who are employed outside the home decrease the amount of time spent on giving help to family members in providing transportation and other assistance, see "Time Available Does Not Determine Amount of Help Going to Family," *The Division of the Social Sciences Reports, University of Chicago*, no. 15 (Autumn 1995): 1–2.

14. See Nelson, *Negotiating Care: The Experience of Family Day Care Providers* (p. 90) for a discussion of this kind of "naturalization" in women's skills with respect to child care. See also A. Fuentes and B. Ehrenreich, *Women in the Global Factory* (New York: Institute for New Communications, 1983); Beneria and Roldan, *Crossroads of Class and Gender: Industrial Homework, Subcontracting, and Household Dynamics in Mexico City*.

15. Tupperware parties are a superb example of this blurring. They build on the idea of mixing sociability and income. Justine J. Green and Joan D'Aiuto, "A Case Study of Economic Distribution Via Social Networks," *Human Organization* 36, no. 3 (Fall 1977): 309–15; Elayne Rapping, "Tupperware and Women," *Radical America* 14, no. 6 (November/December 1980): 39–49; Pam Weisz, "Times Sure Have Changed When Tupperware Is Cool," *Brandweek* (July 11, 1994): 28; Tom Dunkel, "The Tupperware Lady Is an MBA," *Working Woman* 20, no. 4 (April 1995): 44–52.

16. In an interesting historical analogy, Osterud notes that in the nineteenth century in the area in which she conducted research, women did not make sharp divisions between work that was done for pay and work that was done cooperatively or as part of a reciprocal exchange.

> Women exchanged information and shared labor more extensively in sewing than they did in any other kind of work. Sometimes kinswomen worked cooperatively; sometimes one woman employed another. This was a continuum rather than a dichotomy, however, and in practice the two were often almost indistinguishable. Women sometimes paid their relatives for assistance, while neighbors sometimes helped one another freely with the expectation that eventually the favor would be returned. The same woman who was employed on one project might herself hire help for another. (Nancy Grey Osterud, *Bonds of Community: The Lives of Farm Women in Nineteenth-Century New York* [Ithaca, NY: Cornell University Press, 1991]: 188–9)

She did not find the same continuum among men. Osterud also offers a historical explanation for some of the patterns we have observed surrounding the naturalization of women's skills but not those of men:

> [T]he gender division of labor intersected with capitalist expansion to produce substantial asymmetries in men's and women's relationship to the market.... [C]ommercialization penetrated those farm operations for which men were responsible more rapidly and deeply than it did for those for which women were responsible ... the gender division of labor corresponded to a significant degree with the distinction between commodity and subsistence production. By capitalist criteria women's work was less valuable than men's work. (Ibid, p. 209)

17. Fuentes and Ehrenreich, *Women in the Global Factory*; Beneria and Roldan, *Crossroads of Class and Gender: Industrial Homework, Subcontracting, and Household Dynamics in Mexico City*; Osterud, *Bonds of Community: The Lives of Farm Women in Nineteenth-Century New York*.

18. In 1990, according to the census, more than half (58.7 percent) of fabricators, assemblers, inspectors, and samplers in Coolidge County were women even though they were but 46 percent of the labor force.

19. According to the 1990 census, only 25.6 percent of those filling positions as farm workers and related occupations in Coolidge County were women.

20. For an interesting discussion of the ways in which men seek to reestablish "masculinity" in work that is "degendered," see Robin Leidner, "Serving Hamburgers and Selling Insurance: Gender, Work, and Identity in Interactive Service Jobs," *Gender and Society* 5, no. 2 (June 1991): 154–77. For discussions of similar issues, see Ian Miles, "Consequences of the Changing Sexual Division of Labor," *Annals of the American Academy of Political and Social Science* 522 (July 1992): 92–103; Cynthia Cockburn, *In the Way of Women: Men's Resistance to Sex Equality in Organizations* (London: Macmillan Education, 1991).

21. In fact, almost half of all husbands in bad job households achieve a designation as primary worker because they are the *only* worker in the household; by way of contrast, only 15 percent of husbands in good job households rely on employment alone rather than the quality of employment for that designation.

22. Of course, not all men—and not even all white men—did earn those wages. See Martha May, "The Historical Problem of the Family Wage: The

Ford Motor Company and the Five Dollar Day," *Feminist Studies* 8, no. 2 (Summer 1982): 399–424; Martha May, "Bread Before Roses: American Workingmen, Labor Unions and the Family Wage," in *Women, Work and Protest: A Century of U.S. Women's Labor History*, ed. Ruth Milkman (Boston: Routledge and Kegan Paul, 1985): 1–21; Colin Creighton, "The 'Family Wage' as a Class-Rational Strategy," *The Sociological Review* 44, no. 2 (May 1996): 204–24.

23. An objection could be raised that in fact what we are finding is a set of "traditional" women who prefer the homemaker role. Perhaps. But we do have to question why this preference is located so strongly in one group of households rather than another. Often, it seemed to us that a stated preference for being home with the children, for being a housewife, served to rationalize a forced choice.

24. For a study that considers how attitudes and expectations concerning employment are shaped by households, see Hiller and Philliber, "The Division of Labor in Contemporary Marriage: Expectations, Perceptions and Performance."

25. Joseph H. Pleck, "Men's Power with Women, Other Men, and Society: A Men's Movement Analysis," in *Men's Lives*, ed. Michael S. Kimmel and Michael A. Messner (Boston: Allyn and Bacon, 1995): 11. See also the discussion of the rise and fall of the breadwinner role for men in Jesse Barnard, "The Good-Provider Role: Its Rise and Fall," in *Men's Lives*, ed. Michael S. Kimmel and Michael A. Messner (Boston: Allyn and Bacon, 1995): 149–63.

26. Brannen and Moss note that women's accounts suggest that they engaged in a mental accounting procedure of whether "it's worth my while working." They argue as well that because couples see the expenses of employment as coming out of women's earnings, "this charge on their earnings is one way in which women's financial contribution to the household is marginalized" (Julia Brannen and Peter Moss, "Dual Earner Households: Women's Financial Contributions after the Birth of the First Child," in *Give and Take in Families*, ed. Julia Brannen and Gail Wilson [Boston: Allen & Unwin, 1987]: 95). See also Joy Parr, "Re-Thinking Work and Kinship in a Canadian Hosiery Town, 1910–1950," *Feminist Studies* 13 (1987): 137–62; Viviana Zelizer, "The Social Meaning of Money: 'Special Monies,' " *American Journal of Sociology* 95, no. 2 (September 1989): 342–77; Viviana A. Zelizer, *The Social Meaning of Money: Pin Money, Paychecks, Poor Relief, and Other Currencies* (Princeton, NJ: Princeton University Press, 1997).

27. For a discussion of how women make these choices, see Kathleen Gerson, *Hard Choices: How Women Decide about Work, Career, and Motherhood* (Berkeley and Los Angeles: University of California Press, 1985).

28. This is hardly surprising. In Coolidge County, similar to elsewhere in the United States, 85.9 percent of men but only 64.7 percent of women worked thirty-five hours a week or more in 1990.

29. Harris, *Redundancy and Recession in South Wales*: 138.

CHAPTER 6

1. Harriet Presser, "Shift Work among American Women and Child Care," *Journal of Marriage and the Family* 48 (1986): 551–64; Geraldine Pratt and Susan Hanson, "On the Links Between Home and Work: Family-Household Strategies in a Buoyant Labor Market," *International Journal of Urban and Regional Research* 15, no. 1 (March 1991): 55–74.

2. It is not surprising, in fact, that we find high degrees of participation in these various activities—even across traditional divides. Hiller and Philliber's research suggests that although men and women do not want to give up their own gender roles, they are willing to participate in the traditional roles of the opposite sex (Dana V. Hiller and William W. Philliber, "The Division of Labor in Contemporary Marriage: Expectations, Perceptions and Performance," *Social Problems* 33, no. 3 [February 1986]: 191–201).

3. For a discussion of the significance of planning, see Marjorie DeVault, *Feeding the Family: The Social Organization of Caring as Gendered Work* (Chicago: University of Chicago Press, 1991).

4. Ibid.

5. We might note that even if housework is women's choice as a way to enact gender, we have to ask how it happens that housework is recreated as a primary mechanism for that enactment. In addition, some analyses of women's choice about housework focus on the issue of autonomy gained through an engagement in housework, but as we showed above, women might also lose some autonomy when men have a vested interest in the homes they have constructed and in the furnishing of those homes.

6. Arlie Hochschild, *The Second Shift* (New York: Avon Books, 1989): 221. For similar findings, see also Julie Brines, "Economic Dependency, Gender, and the Division of Labor at Home," *American Journal of Sociology* 100, no. 3 (November 1994): 652–88; Julia A. Heath and W. David Bourne, "Husbands and Housework: Parity or Parody?" *Social Science Quarterly* 76, no. 1 (March 1995): 195–202; Janeen Baxter, "Power Attitudes and Time: The Domestic Division of Labor," *Journal of Comparative Family Studies* 23, no. 2 (Summer 1992): 165–82; B. F. Kiker and Ying Chu Ng, "A Simultaneous Equation Model of Spousal Time Allocation," *Social Science Research* 19, no. 2 (June 1990): 132–52. For studies that did not find these relationships between command of resources and the time a husband contributes to the household, see Shelley Coverman, "Explaining Husband's Participation in Domestic Labor," *Sociological Quarterly* 26 (1985): 81–97; Shelley Coverman, "Women's Work Is Never Done: The Division of Domestic Labor," in *Women: A Feminist Perspective*, ed. Jo Freeman (Mountain View, CA: Mayfield, 1989): 356–68.

7. We might also acknowledge that our study—as well as Hochschild's—depends on relatively small numbers of cases. Drawing on even fewer case studies, Pahl reported that for a man who was employed part time and who spent his "nonwork" time gardening (and preserving), decorating the home, and selling plants, it was those informal activities that impinged on the gender division of household labor (R. E. Pahl, "Employment, Work and the Domestic Division

of Labour," *International Journal of Urban and Regional Research* 4, no. 1 [1994]: 12).

8. For a discussion of women's sense of failure and frustration when family meals disappear, see DeVault, *Feeding the Family: The Social Organization of Caring as Gendered Work.*

9. The negotiation of reduced rates also differentially affects men and women because it is most common with respect to child care, an area in which women take primary responsibility. Although both parties to a child care relationship might believe that the negotiated fee completes the transaction, child care providers frequently expect more than they are receiving, and they are especially likely to have these expectations when they are giving a friend or relative a "break" (Margaret K. Nelson, *Negotiating Care: The Experience of Family Day Care Providers* [Philadelphia: Temple University Press, 1990]).

10. In both sets of households, women generally assumed responsibility for paying routine bills.

11. If both men and women have mechanisms for negotiating informal assistance, almost invariably women alone handle negotiations with the state. In some cases, state support is more profitable and reliable than the support that might come from a male partner; some women easily make this exchange. For a discussion that views the state as patriarchal, taking over from men's individual powers in familial matters, see Carol Brown, "Mothers, Fathers and Children: From Private to Public Patriarchy," in *Women and Revolution*, ed. Lydia Sargent (Boston: South End, 1981): 239–67.

12. For a discussion of the central importance of meals, see DeVault, *Feeding the Family: The Social Organization of Caring as Gendered Work.*

13. Brumberg introduces the term "grazing," albeit with reference to more "affluent city dwellers" (Joan Jacobs Brumberg, *Fasting Girls: The History of Anorexia Nervosa* [Penguin, 1989]).

14. For material that links violence to economic marginality, see Christine Alder, "Violence, Gender and Social Change," *International Social Science Journal* 44, no. 2 (May 1992): 267–76.

CHAPTER 7

1. During the in-depth interviews, respondents were asked both what they expected of themselves in relation to employment *and* what they expected their employers to offer in return. The questions took a quite simple form and were parallel: "What kind of obligations does an employer owe to the workers?" and "What kind of obligations does an employee owe to the workplace?"

2. Even more particularly, we were asking questions at a specific moment. The predominant responses we describe below may have been a reaction to what has been termed the 1990–91 recession. For discussions of this recession, see Randy E. Ilg, "Long-Term Unemployment in Recent Recessions," *Monthly Labor Review* 117, no. 6 (June 1994): 12–15. Ilg argues that "long-term joblessness as a percent of the labor force did not expand quite as rapidly from 1989 to 1992 as it had in the two earlier major recessionary periods" (p. 14), and he attributes this to the slow pace of job growth as well as the fact that a larger

proportion of those who were unemployed were in the 35-to-44-year-old age group and thus faced quite different problems than would unemployed youth. For a discussion of men's and women's distinct experiences during the recent recession, see William Goodman, Stephen Antczak, and Laura Freeman, "Women and Jobs in Recessions: 1969–1992," *Monthly Labor Review* 116, no. 7 (July 1993): 26–35.

3. Michael B. Katz, *The Undeserving Poor: From the War on Poverty to the War on Welfare* (New York: Pantheon, 1989); Herbert J. Gans, *The War Against the Poor: The Underclass and Antipoverty Policy* (New York: Basic Books, 1995); Joel F. Handler, *The Poverty of Welfare Reform* (New Haven, CT: Yale University Press, 1995); Mimi Abramovitz, *Regulating the Lives of Women: Social Welfare Policy from Colonial Times to the Present*, rev. ed. (Boston: South End, 1996).

4. An *American Prospect* article ("Bidding for Your Job," *The American Prospect*, no. 23 [Fall 1995]: 96–97), drawing on information from *Newsweek*, reports that "corporate restructuring has proved the assumption wrong that a loyal employee can work a lifetime for a company" (96). The article describes how employees are trained in writing resumes and in selling themselves and then offered an opportunity to bid on a reduced number of positions in the firm. Often, in fact, those who are higher paid are forced to bid *for their own jobs* against employees who are younger and willing to work for less.

5. June Nash ("Global Integration and Subsistence Insecurity," *American Anthropologist* 96, no. 1 [March 1994]: 7–30) found similar attitudes among the workers she interviewed.

6. For an article that argues that companies that have downsized experience decreased morale and commitment among "survivors," see Dawn Anfuso, "Save Jobs: Strategies to Stop the Layoffs," *Personnel* 75, no. 6 (June 1996): 68.

7. We understand full well that the true family wage was as much ideology as it was reality—at least for vast portions of the U.S. working class—but these are white workers, and many of them entered the labor force at a time when manufacturing in their county was booming. Much of this early manufacturing did, indeed, pay high wages as well as offer the benefits that attended those high wages.

8. Although women were less likely than men to hold the expectation of supporting a family on their earnings alone, women did sometimes express disappointment at the fact that because they were working they were unable to provide the kind of family life that their parents had provided for them, that they were unable to maintain a "traditional" family. But they did not believe it is the employer's responsibility to provide wages sufficient to prevent this:

INTERVIEWER: What are your expectations of working at a job? Do you feel that an employer should pay people so that each person can work one job in a family, or even better that there's only one person who has to work full time?

RESPONDENT: That's not realistic. I feel very fortunate in that my mother was home. When I got off the school bus, my mother was home waiting for me. My kids were latchkey kids. I feel very badly about that. My older daughter had the key and she knew the rules and everything, and that's sort of too bad, it's kind of a void in your family life when there's not a mother waiting there. We'd have to really have a drastic change to be able to afford doing that, or do with less. And I don't see society doing that.

INTERVIEWER: Do you feel that an employer should make the effort?
RESPONDENT: Like, what do you mean? Give them more money? No.

9. See Nash, "Global Integration and Subsistence Insecurity": 24. For an analysis that links individualism to a respect for community, see Nancy A. Naples, "Contradictions in Agrarian Ideology: Restructuring Gender, Race, Ethnicity, and Class," *Rural Sociology* 59, no. 1 (Spring 1994): 132.

10. Charles F. Sabel, *Work and Politics: The Division of Labor in Industry* (Cambridge, UK: Cambridge University Press, 1982).

11. In the last several decades, Vermont has not been a strong union state (see Chapter 1). (Recently, there have been some new efforts on the part of unions to make headway in Vermont. They have recorded some successes.) It is hard to know what stands behind the lack of union activity. In their discussions of the possibility of a union at the work site, some good job workers indicated that fear rather than disinterest was the overriding motivation for rejecting that idea: "If you breathe the word 'union,' you might not be working there long." In fact, one union had approached workers at Sterling. Supervisors were quickly instructed on how to handle this threat:

> I understand last week that some people in the shop were approached by union people. Last week or the week before . . . I just heard some scuttlebutt about it. I received an 88 supervisor training. We had a section on union. It wasn't like, "no they don't want unions here," it's like "Hell, no we don't want unions here."

For good reviews of attitudes toward unions, see Jack Fiorito, Daniel Gallagher, and Charles Greer, "Determinants of Unionism: A Review of the Literature," in *Research in Personnel and Human Resources Management*, vol. 4, ed. K. Rowland and G. Ferris (Greenwich, CT: JAI, 1986): 269–306; Daniel B. Cornfield and Hyunhee Kim, "Socioeconomic Status and Unionization Attitudes in the United States," *Social Forces* 73, no. 2 (December 1994): 521–32.

12. Juliet Schor, *The Overworked American* (New York: Basic Books, 1991).

13. Contrast this with Schor, who says that this is primarily consumerism that is driving these workers (Schor, *The Overworked American*).

Of course, motivation and a particular view of "leisure" time are relevant. As Jessen et al. note, "it is characteristic for workers to think in terms of their working capacity instead of their buying capacity. As opposed to a finite earned income, one's work potential is considered as a permanently available resource. It is limited by qualification and lack of production facilities rather than limited by time" (J. Jessen et al., "The Informal Work of Industrial Workers: Present Situation, Trend Prognosis and Policy Implications," in *The Unofficial Economy: Consequences and Perspectives in Different Economic Systems*, ed. Sergio Alessandrini and Bruno Dallago [Aldershot, UK: Gower, 1987]: 275).

14. Robin Leidner, "Serving Hamburgers and Selling Insurance: Gender, Work, and Identity in Interactive Service Jobs," *Gender and Society* 5, no. 2 (June 1991): 173. Similarly, Lillian Rubin argues,

> the issues unemployment raises are different for men and for women. For most women, identity is multi-faceted, which means that the loss of a job isn't equivalent to the loss of self. No matter how invested a woman may be in her work, no matter how much

her sense of self and competence are connected to it, work remains only one part of identity—a central part perhaps, especially for a professional woman, but still only a part. She's mother, wife, friend, daughter, sister—all valued facets of the self, none wholly obscuring the others. . . . For a man, however, work is likely to be connected to the core of self. Going to work isn't just what he does, it's deeply linked to who he is. Obviously, a man is also father, husband, friend, son, brother. But these are likely to be roles he assumes, not without depth and meaning, to be sure, but not self-defining in the same way as he experiences work. (Lillian B. Rubin, *Families on the Faultline: America's Working Class Speaks about the Family, the Economy, Race and Ethnicity* [New York: Harper Collins, 1994]: 104)

For others with the same point of view, see Marilyn Porter, "Time, the Life Course and Work in Women's Lives: Reflections from Newfoundland," *Women's Studies International Forum* 14, no. 1/2 (1991): 1–13; and Leslie Woodcock Tentler, *Wage-Earning Women: Industrial Work and Family Life in the United States, 1900–1930* (Oxford, UK: Oxford University Press, 1979).

In contrast, see Wheelock, who argues that women often worked even when it did not have an economic utility:

The popular conception of low paid female workers is that they are uncommitted to the labour market. This was certainly not the case for the majority of women in the sample: not merely were many prepared to work despite the disincentives of the benefit system and of low pay, but also hours worked and length of time in current job indicated a substantial commitment to the labour market. (Jane Wheelock, "Capital Restructuring and the Domestic Economy: Family Self Respect and the Irrelevance of 'Rational Economic Man.' " *Capital and Class*, no. 41 [Summer 1990]: 121)

Similarly, see Rose, as reported in Miles, who argues that "the great bulk—96 percent—of the difference in work values between women and men vanishes when nongendered factors such as skill, labor market, and occupation are held constant. He thus suggests that many more women will develop a strong 'masculine' work ethic once the conditions that force many women into low-skill part-time jobs such as skill deficits and lack of child-care provision, are alleviated" (Ian Miles, "Consequences of the Changing Sexual Division of Labor," *Annals of the American Academy of Political and Social Science* 522 [July 1992]: 96–97). Also see Burris, who discusses class differences (Beverly H. Burris, "Employed Mothers: The Impact of Class and Marital Status on the Prioritizing of Family and Work," *Social Science Quarterly* 72, no. 1 [March 1991]: 50–66).

15. See Arlie Russell Hochschild, *The Time Bind: When Work Becomes Home and Home Becomes Work* (New York: Metropolitan Books, 1997).

16. For those who believe there have been "improvements" in women's status recently, see Barbara Bergmann, *The Economic Emergence of Women* (New York: Basic Books, 1986); Victor Fuchs, *Women's Quest for Economic Equality* (Cambridge, MA: Harvard University Press, 1988). On the other hand, there are those who argue that economic restructuring has had more devastating effects on women. See Gerda R. Wekerle and Brent Rutherford, "The Mobility of Capital and the Immobility of Female Labor: Responses to Economic Restructuring," in *The Power of Geography: How Territory Shapes Social Life*, ed. Jennifer Wolch and Michael Dear (Boston: Unwin Hyman, 1989): 130–72.

17. Naples, "Contradictions in Agrarian Ideology: Restructuring Gender, Race, Ethnicity, and Class."

18. Many of these good job workers did talk about the necessity for health insurance. This is entirely consistent with their other attitudes: They believe that health insurance would free them from their waged work and enable them to enact their dreams of self-employment.

19. R. E. Pahl, "Some Remarks on Informal Work, Social Polarization and the Social Structure," *International Journal of Urban and Regional Research* 12, no. 2 (1988): 263–64. See also Spyros Missiakoulis, R. E. Pahl, and Peter Taylor-Gooby, "Households, Work and Politics: Some Implications of the Divisions of Labour in Formal and Informal Production," *International Journal of Sociology and Social Policy* 6, no. 3 (1986): 28–40.

20. These attitudes are very much like those described by Sabel when speaking of the advantages offered by what he calls the peasant worker:

> The peasant worker lives on the margin of the factory world. . . . His ambition is to leave it altogether. His ideas of dignity are certainly no less distinct than those of other workers; but his dealings with more settled workmates are so limited, his ambitions so distant from theirs, that his struggles are more likely to exaggerate than reconcile the differences between them. In taking a factory job, the peasant worker agrees to do an honest day's work for an honest day's pay, both conventionally defined. (Sabel, *Work and Politics: The Division of Labor in Industry*: 132).

21. This emphasis on treatment includes a stronger sense of a *personal* relationship between employer and employee. In an interesting discussion of working-class attitudes toward employers, Greenberg notes that women were apt to think their employers were more loyal than were men; he argues that the difference "reflects the greater tendency of these married women to work part-time or in small business" (Stanley B. Greenberg, "Private Heroism and Public Purpose," *The American Prospect* 28 [September/October 1996]: 38). Many of the men who worked in bad jobs also worked part time and in small business. Like the women Greenberg interviewed, men who had bad jobs shared with women the emphasis on a personal relationship.

22. Both of the workers quoted here held jobs with Wilson Contract Manufacturing. In vivid contrast to the assertion of the manager (see Chapter 1), they believed they should receive benefits.

23. For a discussion of how men redefine work to consider it "manly," see Leidner. She argues something quite similar to our point: "Job features that allow or require gender-appropriate behaviors are not necessarily welcomed, then, but work routines that prevent workers from enacting gender in ways that they are comfortable with are resented and may contribute to workers' decisions to limit their investments of energy, effort and self-definition in their jobs" (Leidner, "Serving Hamburgers and Selling Insurance: Gender, Work, and Identity in Interactive Service Jobs": 174).

24. Sometimes they focus as well on their ability to work themselves into another position: "I called him up and bothered him for like three weeks"; "I wasn't even in the initial bunch but I was persistent."

25. Bad job workers who might otherwise be expected to be more prounion because of lower socioeconomic status generally work in smaller settings where the possibility of unions seems less likely ("this place's not big enough for a union") and where, to some extent, because they rely on a personal relation-

ship with the employer, a union seems like a betrayal of trust and as only reducing the possibility of receiving the personalized respect they crave. On the
relationship between socioeconomic status and union attitudes, see Cornfield
and Kim, "Socioeconomic Status and Unionization Attitudes in the United
States."

Interestingly, the worker quoted above who pushed his employers until they
fired him saw his response as being analogous to the more collective orientation
of his father, who had used a union as a mechanism for challenging *his* employers:

> My dad started the union with the King City Police Department. He was president,
> he started King City's union, what, eighteen or nineteen years ago, and took a lot of
> grief for it. That's why he was never promoted. He was always a thorn in the chief's
> side, he says. He was always the main headache. He used to battle City Hall and stuff.
> He was there eighteen years and he never went beyond lieutenant. The guy that's
> chief now . . . didn't have as many years in as my dad. But he would always buck the
> system, a trouble maker. I guess he brought me up to be the same way. Like father,
> like son.

26. The belief that assistance is a measure of one's own failure has immediate
repercussions. Some women find their husbands especially resistant to getting
the help the family desperately needs. They then have to balance a husband's
pride against the acute needs of their children:

> We have needed to get assistance but I'd say it's half and half. My husband doesn't
> like to be on it too long . . . so we've gone without a lot of the times because of his
> pride. . . . We just started getting assistance this year in January. We had been on before
> but we had gone off for a couple of years. Food stamps and Medicaid for the children.
> It was mostly my decision. For the last year or two I've had to take a firm stand on
> my husband doing things to help take care of the kids. . . . Sometimes all we lived on
> was like macaroni or spaghetti. If we could afford cereal the kids would eat cereal for
> at least two meals a day. . . . Our children's teeth needed to be taken care of . . . and
> he was saying we don't have enough money to take them to the dentist. I said then
> either you're going to make the money to take them or we're going to get help or else.
> . . . I grew up on [assistance]. I got some criticism growing up but I got used to it. I
> don't feel ashamed. I feel good knowing that my family, the kids are getting more that
> they deserve.

CONCLUSION

1. Harry Braverman, *Labor and Monopoly Capital: The Degradation of
Work in the Twentieth Century* (New York: Monthly Review Press, 1974).

2. We argue quite differently here from Hertz, who, although she suggests
that self-sufficiency "remains a vital element of the American Dream," also argues that among the dual-*career* couples she interviewed, "self-sufficiency takes
the form of control over the quantity and the quality of the things they consume." Among *our* sample of dual-*earner* couples in good job households, consumption appeared far less important—and far less significant to the goal of
self-sufficiency—than actual control over, and engagement in, producing and
maintaining many of the goods and services on which their domestic life depended. In addition, by actually becoming involved in moonlighting, at least
some individuals within these households became not simply employees, but

entrepreneurs themselves. Rosanna Hertz, "Dual-Career Couples and the American Dream: Self-Sufficiency and Achievement," *Journal of Comparative Family Studies* 22, no. 2 (Summer 1991): 260.

3. Throughout this study, we have focused on goods and services produced by the household and goods and services exchanged with other households outside a formal market rather than on consumption practices in the formal market. We did find, however, that bad job households sometimes substitute careful (and sometimes not so careful) consumption for the activity of self-provisioning. Even careful consumption, however, can become a problem in households that cannot afford to buy in bulk or coordinate the household activities to take advantage of savings.

4. In part, we have made the same kind of polarization argument as Pahl and Wallace did: "The more adults in a relatively affluent household, the more work will be done. Households of higher status not only do more work for themselves, they are also more likely to get others to do work for them. Such households produce more and consume more, formally and informally. Hence, employment status is the key to participation in *all* forms of work, not simply to the formal economy. . . . Hence, we argue that on a number of frequently overlapping dimensions, there is a process of *polarization* between the busy, highly work-motivated households, generally well-off with multiple earners and potential household workers, and others who are at the opposite end of the scale" (R. E. Pahl and Claire Wallace, "Household Work Strategies in Economic Recession," in *Beyond Employment: Household, Gender and Subsistence*, ed. Nanneke Redclift and Enzo Mingione [New York: Basil Blackwell, 1985]: 219). Also see Colin C. Williams and Jan Windebank, "Social Polarization of Households in Contemporary Britain: A 'Whole Economy' Perspective," *Regional Studies* 29, no. 8 (December 1995): 723–28. Where our argument differs from that of others is in its focus on instability and change rather than polarization alone.

5. Robert D. Hershey, Jr., "New Jobs Surge, but Gains in Pay Are Only Modest," *New York Times* (March 8, 1997): A1, 25; Louis Uchitelle and N. R. Kleinfeld, "On the Battlefields of Business, Millions of Casualties," *New York Times* (March 3, 1996): A1, 26–29; Peter T. Kilborn, "In New Work World, Employers Call All the Shots," *New York Times* (July 3, 1995): A1, 7.

6. June Nash, "Global Integration and Subsistence Insecurity," *American Anthropologist* 96, no. 1 (March 1994): 24; Nancy A. Naples, "Contradictions in Agrarian Ideology: Restructuring Gender, Race, Ethnicity, and Class," *Rural Sociology* 59, no. 1 (Spring 1994): 132; Lester C. Thurow, "Can 19th Century Capitalism Work in 2013," *New Perspectives Quarterly* 13, no. 2 (Spring 1996): 14–17.

7. Thurow, "Can 19th Century Capitalism Work in 2013": 15.

8. "Global Workers Prefer Leisure," *USA Today* (April 1996): 8–9; Juliet B. Schor, "Economic Trend: More Willing to Give Up Pay for Additional Time Off," *Nieman Reports* 49, no. 3 (Fall 1995): 8–9; Jeremy Rifkin, *The End of Work: The Decline of the Global Labor Force and the Dawn of the Post-Market Era* (New York: G. P. Putnam's Sons, 1996).

9. Schor, "Economic Trend": 8.

10. John P. Robinson and Geoffrey Godbey, "Are Average Americans Really Overworked?," *The American Enterprise* 6, no. 5 (September/October 1995): 43.

11. The term comes from J. I. Gershuny and R. E. Pahl, "Work Outside Employment: Some Preliminary Speculations," *New University Quarterly* 34 (1979): 120–35.

12. As our conversations with men who had been laid off suggest, some of these individuals—recognizing that the employment that they had lost was a scarce commodity in the current world and finding that they could not match their former salaries and working conditions—actually acted on that dream and chose the route of self-employment. In doing so, they thrust their households into the potential disarray of bad job households.

We might add here that some of them actually reduce their desires for consumption and refer to themselves as plain folk who can get by on little. This is often a source of a perverse pride—but one that, like their lowered expectations of their employers in other spheres, serves the same ends.

13. Stanley B. Greenberg, "Private Heroism and Public Purpose," *The American Prospect* 28 (September/October 1996): 38–39.

14. Interestingly, we could argue, the stress on good treatment—while a serious and legitimate concern—might also represent a response to, or an acceptance of, the window dressing that accompanies service work's relationship with the consumer. Consumers are bombarded with corporate images that suggest happy workers who cooperate as a team. (For a discussion of the costs of this, see Arlie Russell Hochschild, *The Managed Heart: Commercialization of Human Feeling* [Berkeley and Los Angeles: University of California Press, 1983].) Those who end up with employment in these kinds of enterprises might believe it their right to be made happy, to be part of that cheerful team. Alternatively, we might consider "treatment" as a way of letting employers off the hook. What a dream come true for an employer to find employees who will accept this window dressing in place of cold cash or real benefits.

15. The workers we interviewed make a sharp distinction between entitlement and means-tested programs.

16. Greenberg, "Private Heroism and Public Purpose": 40.

17. Ibid.

APPENDIX

1. Additional interviews were collected that ultimately were not included because the respondent did not meet the criteria of our sample. In a very few cases, quotations from these interviews are used to illustrate specific points having to do with issues surrounding employment. This is done only when an individual in the sample population was employed in the *same* workplace and held a similar attitude.

2. We reinterviewed one woman who previously had been interviewed with her husband. We also reinterviewed one woman who had lost employment shortly before our initial interview, to find out how she was doing and what employment decisions she had made. On several occasions, we were unable to

complete an interview in a single sitting, and we returned to finish at a later date.

3. Two interviews were conducted in eating establishments, and one was conducted in a subject's car.

4. The term comes from Arlie Hochschild, *The Second Shift* (New York: Avon Books, 1989).

5. In fact, the stress of conducting these interviews took its toll on our interview staff. One research assistant engaged us (and others) in long discussions of the legitimacy of "using" people as objects of sociological study; she subsequently decided to enroll in graduate school in sociology. Another interviewer, after training, conducted one interview and decided that she could do no more. Yet another, as she got better at her work, found it increasingly difficult because she was more engaged with, and concerned about, those she interviewed.

6. We stratified the county by town because it includes a range of kinds of locations, including hills and valleys, and towns and villages.

7. One respondent, uneasy about some of the questions that had been asked, called Middlebury College to find out more about the survey. The public relations officer, not aware that the Sociology Department was sponsoring such a survey, informed the local newspapers that residents should not respond to questions from individuals claiming to be affiliated with the college. The college subsequently issued a retraction of that notice. Only twenty-three interviews remained to be completed at the time of the notice; the response rate for the nights following that notice was not considerably lower than it had been earlier in the process.

8. John F. Stinson, Jr., "Multiple Jobholding up Sharply in the 1980's," *Monthly Labor Review* 113, no. 7 (July 1990): 3–10.

9. Joan Smith and Jamie Sudler, "A Postscript on Method," in *Creating and Transforming Households*, ed. Joan Smith and Immanuel Wallerstein (Cambridge, UK: Cambridge University Press, 1992): 263–72.

10. Lois Levitan and Shelley Feldman, "For Love or Money: Nonmonetary Economic Arrangements among Rural Households in Central New York," in *Household Strategies*, Research in Rural Sociology and Development 5, ed. Daniel C. Clay and Harry K. Schwarzweller (Greenwich, CT: JAI, 1991): 149–72.

11. See, for example, J. I. Gershuny and R. E. Pahl, "Work Outside Employment: Some Preliminary Speculations," *New University Quarterly* 34 (1979): 120–35; Enzo Mingione, "Social Reproduction of the Surplus Labour Force: The Case of Southern Italy," in *Beyond Employment: Household, Gender and Subsistence*, ed. Nanneke Redclift and Enzo Mingione (New York: Basil Blackwell, 1985): 14–54; R. E. Pahl and Claire Wallace, "Household Work Strategies in Economic Recession," in *Beyond Employment: Household, Gender and Subsistence*, ed. Nanneke Redclift and Enzo Mingione (New York: Basil Blackwell, 1985): 189–228.

12. See Pahl's discussion of the distinction between self-provisioning and do-it-yourself activities. R. E. Pahl, "The Restructuring of Capital, the Local Political Economy and Household Work Strategies," in *Social Relations and*

Spatial Structures, ed. D. Gregory and J. Urry (Basingstoke, UK: Macmillan, 1985): 243–64.

13. For example, Wheelock first distinguishes between the "formal economy" (identified as such because it is measured) and an unmeasured or "complementary economy" which she divides into a marketed (irregular sector) and a fully nonmarketed sector which she terms the "social economy." This latter is again divided into a household sector (interhousehold activity) and a domestic sector (intrahousehold activity) (Jane Wheelock, "Capital Restructuring and the Domestic Economy: Family Self Respect and the Irrelevance of 'Rational Economic Man,'" *Capital and Class*, no. 41 [Summer 1990]: 132). One problem with this classification scheme is that it makes a distinction between a "marketed" sector and a pure "social economy." Our evidence in the Introduction (where we discuss Bruce Sharp and his snowplow) suggests that these distinctions are not so easily made. See also Leif Jensen, Gretchen T. Cornwell, and Jill L. Findeis, "Informal Work in Nonmetropolitan Pennsylvania," *Rural Sociology* 60, no. 1 (Spring 1995): 91–107.

A somewhat different categorization is found in the analysis of Pahl and Wallace, who distinguish between "inter-household labor relations," and "intra-household self-provisioning" (Pahl and Wallace, "Household Work Strategies in Economic Recession"). Although this approach more closely parallels our own, in their analysis Pahl and Wallace neither analyze the full range of "inter-household labor relations" nor analyze fully the terms of those relations. First, they ask respondents primarily about the work that they *do for other people* (they asked "if there are any jobs that you do outside your home, for other people?") rather than focusing on activities that were done *for* them. As such, although they can tell us who does—and who does not—*offer* this kind of informal assistance to others in their social networks, they cannot tell us about who *receives* this assistance. As Mingione has noted, "reciprocal or voluntary unpaid activities . . . involve one household spending some of its time to ensure the survival of another; *they therefore belong to the reproduction pattern of the receiver rather than the provider*" (Enzo Mingione, *Fragmented Societies: A Sociology of Economic Life Beyond the Market Paradigm* (Oxford, UK: Basil Blackwell, 1991): 81; emphasis added).

It is not just that these activities "belong to the reproduction pattern" of one household rather than another: What is significant about these activities is that they take place within a social network and thus involve a *relationship* among and between households. Levitan and Feldman make a related point about Mingione's (earlier) work: "[B]y describing this 'work [which is] not exchanged for income' as 'deductions from the time of one household in favor of another,' he creates the impression of a parasitic drain on resources rather than a symbiotic enhancement of mutual potential, and belies . . . the multidimensionality of social networks within which such labor is shared" (Levitan and Feldman, "For Love or Money: Nonmonetary Economic Arrangements among Rural Households in Central New York": 154).

In fact, we might argue, some of these activities have but a minimal role in a household's "reproduction pattern." In some cases, their importance might be essentially symbolic, as for instance when activities are designed to create or shore up a social relationship that can be called on for material resources at a later point in time. Clearly this is exactly what Stack describes in her often cited book (Carol Stack, *All Our Kin* [New York: Harper & Row, 1975]).

14. Levitan and Feldman, "For Love or Money: Nonmonetary Economic Arrangements among Rural Households in Central New York": 151. The fascination with these kinds of activities—consider, for example, how often Stack's *All Our Kin* is cited or how much writing in anthropology has been directed toward discussions of the "gift"—inheres precisely in this combination of motivations, rewards, and costs. (The fascination might as well inhere in the futile hope [on the part of conservative and liberal politicians alike] that these arrangements can substitute for stable infrastructure support mechanisms. We need only recall Bush and his "thousand points of light" or the diatribes against big government in more recent political debates.) We might note as well that in spite of a rich body of theoretical material (Marcel Mauss, *The Gift: Forms and Functions of Exchange in Archaic Societies* [Glencoe, IL: The Free Press, 1954]; Marshall D. Sahlins, *Stone-Age Economics* [Chicago: Aldine-Atherton, 1972]), relatively few ethnographic studies explore the role of these relationships within white, rural communities. For exceptions, see Rhoda Halperin, *The Livelihood of Kin: Making Ends Meet "The Kentucky Way"* (Austin: University of Texas Press, 1990); Levitan and Feldman, "For Love or Money: Nonmonetary Economic Arrangements among Rural Households in Central New York." Fewer yet explore their differences by class and employment status. For exceptions, see Pahl and Wallace, "Household Work Strategies in Economic Recession"; Lydia Morris, "Domestic Labour and Employment Status among Married Couples: A Case Study in Hartlepool," *Capital and Class* 49 (Spring 1993): 37–52; Wheelock, "Capital Restructuring and the Domestic Economy: Family Self Respect and the Irrelevance of 'Rational Economic Man.' " Moreover, many studies focus on the household that *offers* goods and services rather than on the household that *receives* them. As such, these studies fail to explore the extent to which such assistance can become an aspect of a household's survival strategy. There is, however, a growing body of quantitative literature on social support that examines frequency across a variety of variables. See, for example, David J. Eggebeen and Dennis P. Hogan, "Giving Between Generations in American Families," *Human Nature* 1, no. 3 (1990): 211–32; Dennis P. Hogan, Ling-Xin Hao, and William L. Parish, "Race, Kin Networks, and Assistance to Mother-Headed Families," *Social Forces* 68, no. 3 (March 1990): 797–812; T. M. Cooney and P. Uhlenberg, "Support from Parents over the Life Course: The Adult Child's Perspective," *Social Forces* 71, no. 1 (1992): 63–84; D. Hogan, David J. Eggebeen, and Clifford C. Clogg, "The Structure of Intergenerational Exchange in American Families," *American Journal of Sociology* 98, no. 6 (May 1993): 1428–58; Mary Benin and Verna M. Keith, "The Social Support of Employed African American and Anglo Mothers," *Journal of Family Issues* 16, no. 3 (May 1995): 275–97.

The combination of elements that characterize nonmonetary exchanges might well discourage researchers from either counting or assigning a simple economic value to such arrangements. Not only is it often unclear what measure of value should be applied, but because of the complexities that invariably surround them, these exchanges also cannot easily be taken out of their specific context for the purpose of quantifying. Although we did count one of these, we remain aware that counting distorts the texture and meaning of these kinds of relationships. For a good critique of quantifying with respect to this kind of exchange, see Emily K. Abel, *Who Cares for the Elderly?* (Philadelphia: Temple University Press, 1990). See also McKee, who suggests that "the research interview may provide a particular kind of representation of relationships and there will always be limitations to network research which relies only on the account of one informant in that network" (Lorna McKee, "Households During Unemployment: The Resourcefulness of the Unemployed," in *Give and Take in Families: Studies in Resource Distribution*, ed. Julia Brannen and Gail Wilson [Boston: Allen & Unwin, 1987]: 100).

Bibliography

Abel, Emily K. *Who Cares for the Elderly?* Philadelphia: Temple University Press, 1990.

Abel, Emily K., and Margaret K. Nelson. *Circles of Care: Work and Identity in Women's Lives.* Albany: State University of New York Press, 1990.

Abramovitz, Mimi. *Regulating the Lives of Women: Social Welfare Policy from Colonial Times to the Present.* Rev. ed. Boston: South End, 1996.

Aglietta, Michel. *A Theory of Capitalist Regulation: The U.S. Experience.* London: Calmann-Levy, 1976.

Alder, Christine. "Violence, Gender and Social Change." *International Social Science Journal* 44, no. 2 (May 1992): 267–76.

Allen, Sheila. "Production and Reproduction: The Lives of Women Homeworkers." *The Sociological Review* 31, no. 4 (November 1983): 649–65.

Allen, Sheila, and Carol Wolkowitz. *Homeworking: Myths and Realities.* Basingstoke, UK: Macmillan Education, 1987.

Amott, Teresa. *Caught in the Crisis: Women and the U.S. Economy Today.* New York: Monthly Review Press, 1993.

Anfuso, Dawn. "Save Jobs: Strategies to Stop the Layoffs." *Personnel Journal* 75, no. 6 (June 1996): 66–69.

Barkley, David. *Economic Adaptation: Alternatives for Nonmetropolitan Areas.* Boulder, CO: Westview, 1993.

Barnard, Jesse. "The Good-Provider Role: Its Rise and Fall." In *Men's Lives,* ed. Michael S. Kimmel and Michael A. Messner, 149–63. Boston: Allyn and Bacon, 1995.

Barnett, Rosalind C., and Caryl Rivers. *She Works/He Works: How Two-Income Families Are Happier, Healthier, and Better-Off.* San Francisco: HarperSanFrancisco, 1996.

"Basket Maker Lays Off Workers." *Rutland Herald Daily* (May 23, 1996): 18.

Baxter, Janeen. "Power Attitudes and Time: The Domestic Division of Labor." *Journal of Comparative Family Studies* 23, no. 2 (Summer 1992): 165–82.

Beneria, Lourdes, and Martha Roldan. *Crossroads of Class and Gender: Industrial Homework, Subcontracting, and Household Dynamics in Mexico City.* Chicago: University of Chicago Press, 1987.

Benin, Mary, and Verna M. Keith. "The Social Support of Employed African American and Anglo Mothers." *Journal of Family Issues* 16, no. 3 (May 1995): 275–97.

Benincasa, Robert. "Vermont Income Down $2,700." *Burlington Free Press* (September 30, 1997): 1A, 9A.

Berger, Elizabeth. "The Economic Context of Labor Allocation." *Journal of Family Issues* 12, no. 2 (June 1991): 140–57.

Berger, Suzanne, and Michael J. Piore. *Dualism and Discontinuity in Industrial Societies.* Cambridge, UK: Cambridge University Press, 1980.

Bergmann, Barbara. *The Economic Emergence of Women.* New York: Basic Books, 1986.

———. *Saving Our Children from Poverty: What the United States Can Learn from France.* New York: Russell Sage Foundation, 1996.

Berk, Sarah F. *The Gender Factory: The Apportionment of Work in American Households.* New York: Plenum, 1985.

Bernat, G. Andrew, Jr., and Martha Frederick. *Rural America and the Changing Structure of Manufacturing: Spatial Implications of New Technology and Organization. A Conference Proceedings.* Washington, DC: U.S. Department of Agriculture, Economic Research Service, Agriculture and Rural Economy Division, 1993.

"Bidding for Your Job." *The American Prospect*, no. 23 (Fall 1995): 96–97.

Bluestone, Barry. "Is Deindustrialization a Myth? Capital Mobility Versus Absorptive Capacity in the U.S. Economy." *Annals of the American Academy of Political and Social Science* 475 (1984): 39–51.

Bluestone, Barry, and Bennett Harrison. *The Deindustrialization of America.* New York: Basic Books, 1982.

Bokemeier, Janet L., and Ann R. Tickamyer. "Labor Force Experiences of Nonmetropolitan Women." *Rural Sociology* 50, no. 1 (1985): 51–73.

Boris, Eileen. "Regulating Industrial Homework: The Triumph of 'Sacred Motherhood.'" *Journal of American History* 71, no. 4 (March 1985): 745–63.

———. "Homework and Women's Rights: The Case of the Vermont Knitters, 1980–1985." *Signs* 13, no. 1 (1987): 98–120.

———. *Home to Work: Motherhood and the Politics of Industrial Homework in the United States.* New York: Cambridge University Press, 1994.

Boris, Eileen, and Cynthia M. Daniels, eds. *Homework: Historical and Contemporary Perspectives on Paid Labor at Home.* Urbana: University of Illinois Press, 1989.

Bose, Christine. "Devaluing Women's Work: The Undercount of Women's Employment in 1900 and 1980." In *Hidden Aspects of Women's Work*, ed. Christine Bose, Roslyn Feldberg, and Natalie Sokoloff, 95–115. New York: Praeger, 1987.

———. "Dual Spheres." In *Analyzing Gender*, ed. Beth Hess and Myra Marx Ferree, 267–87. Newbury Park, CA: Sage, 1987.

Bourdieu, Pierre. "Marriage Strategies as Strategies of Social Reproduction." In *Family and Society: Selections from Annales*, 118–44. Baltimore: Johns Hopkins University Press, 1976.

Boyd, Monica, Mary Ann Mulvihill, and John Myles. "Gender, Power and Post-industrialism." *Canadian Review of Sociology and Anthropology* 28, no. 4 (1991): 407–36.

Bradley, Harriet. "Work, Home and the Restructuring of Jobs." In *The Changing Experience of Employment: Restructuring and Recession*, ed. Kate Purcell, Stephen Wood, Alan Waton, and Sheila Allen, 95–113. Houndsmill, Basingstoke, Hampshire, UK: Macmillan in association with the British Sociological Association, 1986.

Brannen, Julia, and Peter Moss. "Dual Earner Households: Women's Financial Contributions after the Birth of the First Child." In *Give and Take in Families*, ed. Julia Brannen and Gail Wilson, 75–95. Boston: Allen & Unwin, 1987.

Braus, Patricia. "Dual Incomes Cushion Job Seekers." *American Demographics* 21 (October 1991): 2.

Braverman, Harry. *Labor and Monopoly Capital: The Degradation of Work in the Twentieth Century*. New York: Monthly Review Press, 1974.

Bravo, Ellen. *Wage Replacement and Family Leave: Is It Necessary? Is It Feasible?* Cleveland: 9 to 5 Working Women Education Fund, 1992.

Brines, Julie. "Economic Dependency, Gender, and the Division of Labor at Home." *American Journal of Sociology* 100, no. 3 (November 1994): 652–88.

Brown, Carol. "Mothers, Fathers and Children: From Private to Public Patriarchy." In *Women and Revolution*, ed. Lydia Sargent, 239–67. Boston: South End, 1981.

Brumberg, Joan Jacobs. *Fasting Girls: The History of Anorexia Nervosa*. New York: Penguin, 1989.

Burris, Beverly H. "Employed Mothers: The Impact of Class and Marital Status on the Prioritizing of Family and Work." *Social Science Quarterly* 72, no. 1 (March 1991): 50–66.

Castells, Manuel, and Alejandro Portes. "World Underneath: The Origins, Dynamics, and Effects of the Informal Economy." In *The Informal Economy: Studies in Advanced and Less Developed Countries*, ed. Alejandro Portes, Manuel Castells, and Lauren A. Benton, 11–40. Baltimore: Johns Hopkins University Press, 1989.

Cattan, Peter. "Childcare Problems: An Obstacle to Work." *Monthly Labor Review* 114, no. 10 (October 1991): 3–9.

Chayanov, A. V. *The Theory of Peasant Economy*. Madison: University of Wisconsin Press, 1986.

Cheadle, Bruce. "More Canadians Moonlighting." *Halifax Daily News* (June 2, 1994): 28.

———. "Moonlighting on the Rise." *Ottawa Citizen* (June 2, 1995): B8.

Christensen, Kathleen. *Women and Home-Based Work: The Unspoken Contract*. New York: Henry Holt and Company, 1987.

Clay, Daniel C., and Harry K. Schwarzweller, eds. *Household Strategies*. Research in Rural Sociology and Development, vol. 5. Greenwich, CT: JAI, 1991.

Cockburn, Cynthia. *Machinery of Dominance: Women, Men and Technical Know-How*. London: Pluto, 1985.

———. *In the Way of Women: Men's Resistance to Sex Equality in Organizations*. London: Macmillan Education, 1991.

Cole, William, and Bichaka Fayissa. "The Urban Subsistence Labor Force: Toward a Policy-Oriented and Empirically Accessible Taxonomy." *World Development* 19, no. 7 (July 1991): 779–89.

Cooke, Kenneth. "The Withdrawal from Paid Work of the Wives of Unemployed Men: A Review of Research." *Journal of Social Policy* 16 (1987): 371–82.

Cooney, T. M., and P. Uhlenberg. "Support from Parents over the Life Course: The Adult Child's Perspective." *Social Forces* 71, no. 1 (1992): 63–84.

Corcoran, M., L. Datcher, and G. J. Duncan. "Most Workers Find Jobs Through Word of Mouth." *Monthly Labor Review* 103, no. 8 (August 1980): 33–36.

Core, Françoise. "Women and the Restructuring of Employment." *The OECD Observer*, no. 186 (February/March 1994): 4–11.

Cornfield, Daniel B., and Hyunhee Kim. "Socioeconomic Status and Unionization Attitudes in the United States." *Social Forces* 73, no. 2 (December 1994): 521–32.

County Business Patterns, Vermont. Washington, DC: U.S. Department of Commerce, Bureau of the Census, various years.

Coverman, Shelley. "Explaining Husband's Participation in Domestic Labor." *Sociological Quarterly* 26 (1985): 81–97.

———. "Women's Work Is Never Done: The Division of Domestic Labor." In *Women: A Feminist Perspective*, ed. Jo Freeman, 356–68. Mountain View, CA: Mayfield, 1989.

Creighton, Colin. "The 'Family Wage' as a Class-Rational Strategy." *The Sociological Review* 44, no. 2 (May 1996): 204–24.

Crispell, Diane. "Dual Disparity." *American Demographics* 11, no. 9 (September 1989): 16–17.

Crow, Graham. "The Use of the Concept of 'Strategy' in Recent Sociological Literature." *Sociology* 23, no. 1 (February 1989): 1–24.

Curran, Sara, and Donald Tomaskovic-Devey. "Uneven Development in North Carolina? Job Quality Differences Between Local and Nonlocal Firms." *Rural Sociology* 56, no. 4 (Winter 1991): 680–89.

Dabelko, David D., and Robert J. Sheak. "Employment, Subemployment and the Feminization of Poverty." *Sociological Viewpoints* 8 (Fall 1992): 31–66.

Dallago, Bruno. *The Irregular Economy*. Aldershot, UK: Dartmouth, 1990.

Davis, Mike. *Prisoners of the American Dream*. London: Verso, 1986.

DeVault, Marjorie. *Feeding the Family: The Social Organization of Caring as Gendered Work*. Chicago: University of Chicago Press, 1991.

"Digital Strands 350 Workers by Closing South Burlington Plant." *Burlington Free Press* (October 30, 1992): 1A.

DiLeonardo, Michelle. "The Female World of Cards and Holidays: Women, Families and the Work of Kinship." *Signs* 12 (1987): 440–53.

Drabenstott, Mark, Mark Henry, and Lynn Gibson. "The Rural Economic Policy Choice." In *Rural America in Transition*, ed. Mark Drabenstott and Lynn Gibson, 59–84. Kansas City, MO: Federal Reserve Bank of Kansas City, Research Division, 1988.

Duncan, Cynthia M. "Persistent Poverty in Appalachia: Scarce Work and Rigid Stratification." In *Rural Poverty in America*, ed. Cynthia M. Duncan, 111–33. New York: Auburn House, 1992.

Dunkel, Tom. "The Tupperware Lady Is an MBA." *Working Woman* 20, no. 4 (April 1995): 44–52.

Edin, Kathryn, and Laura Lein. *Making Ends Meet: How Single Mothers Survive Welfare and Low-Wage Work*. New York: Russell Sage Foundation, 1997.

Eggebeen, David J., and Dennis P. Hogan. "Giving Between Generations in American Families." *Human Nature* 1, no. 3 (1990): 211–32.

Falk, William W., and Thomas A. Lyson. "Rural America in the Industrial Policy Debate." In *Rural Policies for the 1990's*, ed. C. Flora and J. Christenson, 8–21. Boulder, CO: Westview, 1991.

"Families Now Run Faster to Catch Up with Dream." *Boston Globe* (April 30, 1995) : A1.

Ferman, Louis A., Stuart Henry, and Michele Hoyman. "Issues and Prospects for the Study of Informal Economies: Concepts, Research Strategies and Policy." *Annals of the American Academy of Political and Social Science* 493 (1987): 154–72.

Ferree, Myra Marx. "Beyond Separate Spheres: Feminism and Family Research." *Journal of Marriage and the Family* 52 (November 1990): 866–84.

Finch, Janet. *Family Obligations and Social Change*. Cambridge, MA: Polity, 1989.

Findeis, Jill. "Utilization of Rural Labor Resources." In *Economic Adaptation*, ed. David Barkley, 50–68. Boulder, CO: Westview, 1993.

Fiorito, Jack, Daniel Gallagher, and Charles Greer. "Determinants of Unionism: A Review of the Literature." In *Research in Personnel and Human Resources Management*, vol. 4, ed. K. Rowland and G. Ferris, 269–306. Greenwich, CT: JAI, 1986.

Fitchen, Janet M. "On the Edge of Homelessness: Rural Poverty and Housing Insecurity." *Rural Sociology* 57, no. 2 (Summer 1992): 175–93.

———. "Rural Poverty in the Northeast: The Case of Upstate New York." In *Rural Poverty in America*, ed. Cynthia M. Duncan, 177–200. New York: Auburn House, 1992.

Flaim, Paul O., and Ellen Sehgal. "Displaced Workers of 1979–83: How Well Have They Fared?" *Monthly Labor Review* 108, no. 6 (June 1985): 3–18.

Flora, Cornelia Butler. "The New Poor in Midwestern Farming Communities." In *Rural Poverty in America*, ed. Cynthia M. Duncan, 202–11. New York: Auburn House, 1992.

Flora, Cornelia Butler, and Jan L. Flora. "Entrepreneurial Social Infrastructure:

A Necessary Ingredient." *Annals of the American Academy of Political and Social Science* 529 (September 1993): 48–58.

Foegen, J. H. "A Sad but Needed Change." *Business and Society Review*, no. 87 (Fall 1993): 14–15.

Fortin, Nicole M., and Thomas Lemieux. "Institutional Changes and Rising Wage Inequality: Is There a Linkage?" *Journal of Economic Perspectives* 11, no. 2 (Spring 1997): 75–96.

Fuchs, Victor. *Women's Quest for Economic Equality*. Cambridge, MA: Harvard University Press, 1988.

Fuentes, A., and B. Ehrenreich. *Women in the Global Factory*. New York: Institute for New Communications, 1983.

Gallie, Duncan. *In Search of the New Working Class*. Cambridge, UK: Cambridge University Press, 1978.

Gans, Herbert J. *The War Against the Poor: The Underclass and Antipoverty Policy*. New York: Basic Books, 1995.

Gardner, Jennifer M. "Worker Displacement: A Decade of Change." *Monthly Labor Review* 118, no. 4 (April 1995): 45–57.

Gardner, Jennifer M., and Diane E. Herz. "Working and Poor in 1990." *Monthly Labor Review* 115, no. 12 (December 1992): 20–28.

"G. E. Lays Off 122 at Rutland Plants." *Burlington Free Press* (February 28, 1993): 5B.

Gershuny, J. I., and R. E. Pahl. "Work Outside Employment: Some Preliminary Speculations." *New University Quarterly* 34 (1979): 120–35.

Gerson, Judith, and Kathy Peiss. "Boundaries, Negotiations, Consciousness: Reconceptualizing Gender Relations." *Social Problems* 32 (1985): 317–31.

Gerson, Kathleen. *Hard Choices: How Women Decide about Work, Career, and Motherhood*. Berkeley and Los Angeles: University of California Press, 1985.

"Global Workers Prefer Leisure." *USA Today* (April 1996): 8–9.

Goodman, William, Stephen Antczak, and Laura Freeman. "Women and Jobs in Recessions: 1969–1992." *Monthly Labor Review* 116, no. 7 (July 1993): 26–35.

Gorhan, Lucy. "The Growing Problem of Low Earnings in Rural Areas." In *Rural Poverty in America*, ed. Cynthia M. Duncan, 21–39. New York: Auburn House, 1992.

———. "Changing Employment, Earnings, and Skill Requirements in Manufacturing: The Implications for Rural Workers." In *Rural America and the Changing Structure of Manufacturing: Spatial Implications of New Technology and Organization. A Conference Proceedings*, ed. G. Andrew Bernat, Jr., and Martha Frederick, 142–47. Washington, DC: U.S. Department of Agriculture, Economic Research Service, Agriculture and Rural Economy Division, 1993.

Gottschalk, Peter. "Inequality, Income Growth and Mobility: The Basic Facts." *Journal of Economic Perspectives* 11, no. 2 (Spring 1997): 21–40.

Gottschalk, Peter, and Robert Moffitt. "The Growth of Earnings Instability in the U.S. Labor Market." *Brookings Papers on Economic Activity* 2 (1994): 217–72.

Granovetter, Mark S. *Getting a Job: A Study of Contacts and Careers.* Cambridge, MA: Harvard University Press, 1974.

Green, Justine J., and Joan D'Aiuto. "A Case Study of Economic Distribution Via Social Networks." *Human Organization* 36, no. 3 (Fall 1977): 309–15.

Greenberg, Stanley B. "Private Heroism and Public Purpose." *The American Prospect* 28 (September/October 1996): 34–40.

Grieco, Margaret. *Keeping It in the Family: Social Networks and Employment Chance.* London: Tavistock, 1987.

Gringeri, Christina E. "Inscribing Gender in Rural Development: Industrial Homework in Two Midwestern Communities." *Rural Sociology* 58, no. 1 (Spring 1993): 30–52.

———. *Getting By: Women Homeworkers and Rural Economic Development.* Lawrence: University Press of Kansas, 1994.

Guttmann, P. "Are the Unemployed, Unemployed?" *Financial Analysts Journal* 34, no. 1 (1978): 26–29.

Halperin, Rhoda. *The Livelihood of Kin: Making Ends Meet "The Kentucky Way."* Austin: University of Texas Press, 1990.

Handler, Joel F. *The Poverty of Welfare Reform.* New Haven, CT: Yale University Press, 1995.

Hanson, Susan, and Geraldine Pratt. "Dynamic Dependencies: A Geographic Investigation of Local Labor Markets." *Economic Geography* 68, no. 4 (October 1992): 373–405.

Harding, Philip, and Richard Jenkins. *The Myth of the Hidden Economy: Towards a New Understanding of Economic Activity.* Philadelphia: Open University Press, 1989.

Hareven, Tamara. *Family Time and Industrial Time: The Relationship Between the Family and Work in a New England Industrial Community.* New York: Cambridge University Press, 1982.

Harris, C. C. *Redundancy and Recession in South Wales.* Oxford, UK: Blackwell, 1987.

Harrison, Bennett. *Lean and Mean: The Changing Landscape of Corporate Power in the Age of Flexibility.* New York: Basic Books, 1994.

Harrison, Bennett, and Barry Bluestone. *The Great U-Turn: Corporate Restructuring and the Polarizing of America.* New York: Basic Books, 1988.

Hartmann, Heidi. "Capitalism, Patriarchy, and Job Segregation by Sex." *Signs* 1, no. 3, pt. 2 (1976): 137–67.

Hayghe, Howard V. "Family Members in the Work Force." *Monthly Labor Review* 113, no. 3 (March 1990): 14–19.

Hayghe, Howard V., and Suzanne Bianchi. "Married Mothers' Work Patterns: The Job-Family Compromise." *Monthly Labor Review* 117, no. 6 (June 1994): 24–30.

Heath, Julia A., and W. David Bourne. "Husbands and Housework: Parity or Parody?" *Social Science Quarterly* 76, no. 1 (March 1995): 195–202.

Hershey, Robert D., Jr., "New Jobs Surge, but Gains in Pay Are Only Modest." *The New York Times* (March 8, 1997): 1A, 25.

Hertz, Rosanna. "Dual-Career Couples and the American Dream: Self-

Sufficiency and Achievement." *Journal of Comparative Family Studies* 22, no. 2 (Summer 1991): 247–63.

Hiller, Dana V., and William W. Philliber. "The Division of Labor in Contemporary Marriage: Expectations, Perceptions and Performance." *Social Problems* 33, no. 3 (February 1986): 191–201.

Hochschild, Arlie. *The Managed Heart: The Commercialization of Human Feeling*. Berkeley and Los Angeles: University of California Press, 1983.

———. *The Second Shift*. New York: Avon Books, 1989.

———. *The Time Bind: When Work Becomes Home and Home Becomes Work*. New York: Metropolitan Books, 1997.

Hofferth, Sandra. "Employer Benefits and Parental Leave Policies in the U.S." Paper presented at the annual meeting of the American Sociological Association, Washington, DC, August 1990.

Hofferth, Sandra L., April Brayfield, Sharon Deich, and Pamela Holcomb. *National Child Care Survey, 1990: A National Association for the Education of Young Children Study*. Washington, DC: Urban Institute Press, 1991.

Hogan, D., David J. Eggebeen, and Clifford C. Clogg. "The Structure of Intergenerational Exchange in American Families." *American Journal of Sociology* 98, no. 6 (May 1993): 1428–58.

Hogan, Dennis P., Ling-Xin Hao, and William L. Parish. "Race, Kin Networks, and Assistance to Mother-Headed Families." *Social Forces* 68, no. 3 (March 1990): 797–812.

Hoyman, Michele. "Female Participation in the Informal Economy: A Neglected Issue." *Annals of the American Academy of Political and Social Science* 493 (September 1987): 64–82.

Humphries, Jane. "Women's Employment in Restructuring America: The Changing Experience of Women in Three Recessions." In *Women and Recession*, ed. Jill Rubery, 15–47. London: Routledge & Kegan Paul, 1988.

Ilg, Randy E. "Long-Term Unemployment in Recent Recessions." *Monthly Labor Review* 117, no. 6 (June 1994): 12–15.

Jensen, Joan M. "Cloth, Butter and Boarders: Women's Household Production for the Market." *The Review of Radical Political Economics* 12, no. 2 (Summer 1980): 14–23.

Jensen, Leif, Gretchen T. Cornwell, and Jill L. Findeis. "Informal Work in Nonmetropolitan Pennsylvania." *Rural Sociology* 60, no. 1 (Spring 1995): 91–107.

Jessen, J., W. Slebel, C. Slebel-Rebell, U.-J. Walther, and I. Weyrather, "The Informal Work of Industrial Workers: Present Situation, Trend Prognosis and Policy Implications." In *The Unofficial Economy: Consequences and Perspectives in Different Economic Systems*, ed. Sergio Alessandrini and Bruno Dallago, 271–82. Aldershot, UK: Gower, 1987.

"Job Loss of 30 Workers When Goodyear Plant in Windsor Closes Down." *Rutland Herald Daily* (November 7, 1986): A7.

Kamerman, Sheila B., and Alfred J. Kahn. *Family Policy: Government and Families in Fourteen Countries*. New York: Columbia University Press, 1978.

———. *Child Care, Family Benefits and Working Parents: A Study of Comparative Policy*. New York: Columbia University Press, 1981.

Kassab, Cathy, A. E. Luloff, and Fred Schmidt. "The Changing Impact of Industry, Household Structure, and Residence on Household Well-Being." *Rural Sociology* 60, no. 1 (Spring 1995): 67–90.

Katz, Michael B. *The Undeserving Poor: From the War on Poverty to the War on Welfare.* New York: Pantheon, 1989.

Kessler-Harris, Alice. *Out to Work: A History of Wage-Earning Women in the United States.* New York: Oxford University Press, 1982.

Kiker, B. F., and Ying Chu Ng. "A Simultaneous Equation Model of Spousal Time Allocation." *Social Science Research* 19, no. 2 (June 1990): 132–52.

Kilborn, Peter T. "In New Work World, Employers Call All the Shots." *New York Times* (July 3, 1995): A1, 7.

Knapp, Tim. "Rust in the Wheatbelt: The Social Impacts of Industrial Decline in a Rural Kansas Community." *Sociological Inquiry* 65, no. 1 (February 1995): 47–66.

Komarovsky, Mirra. *Blue-Collar Marriage.* New York: Random House, 1967.

Kotz, David M. "Household Labor, Wage Labor, and the Transformation of the Family." *Review of Radical Political Economics* 26, no. 2 (June 1994): 24–56.

Leach, Belinda, and Anthony Winson. "Bringing 'Globalization' Down to Earth: Restructuring and Labour in Rural Communities." *The Canadian Review of Sociology and Anthropology* 32, no. 3 (1995): 341–64.

Lee, Don. "Employees Get Real Workout." *Los Angeles Times* (September 4, 1995): A1.

Leidner, Robin. "Serving Hamburgers and Selling Insurance: Gender, Work, and Identity in Interactive Service Jobs." *Gender and Society* 5, no. 2 (June 1991): 154–77.

Levitan, Lois, and Shelley Feldman. "For Love or Money: Nonmonetary Economic Arrangements among Rural Households in Central New York." In *Household Strategies*, Research in Rural Sociology and Development 5, ed. Daniel C. Clay and Harry K. Schwarzweller, 149–72. Greenwich, CT: JAI, 1991.

Levy, Frank. *Dollars and Dreams.* New York: Russell Sage Foundation for the National Committee for Research on the 1980 Census, 1987.

Levy, Frank, and Richard C. Michel. *The Economic Future of American Families: Income and Wealth Trends.* Washington, DC: The Urban Institute Press, 1991.

Lichter, Daniel T. "The Underemployment of American Rural Women: Prevalence, Trends and Spatial Inequality." *Journal of Rural Studies* 5, no. 2 (1989): 199–208.

Lichter, Daniel T., and David J. Eggebeen. "Child Poverty and the Changing Rural Family." *Rural Sociology* 57, no. 2 (Summer 1992): 151–72.

Lichter, Daniel T., Gail M. Johnston, and Diane K. McLaughlin. "Changing Linkages Between Work and Poverty in Rural America." *Rural Sociology* 59, no. 3 (1994): 395–415.

Lichter, Daniel T., and Diane K. McLaughlin. "Changing Economic Opportunities, Family Structure, and Poverty in Rural Areas." *Rural Sociology* 60, no. 4 (Winter 1995): 688–706.

Lipietz, Alain. *Mirages and Miracles: The Crises of Global Fordism.* London: Verso, 1987.

Livingston, Joy, and Elaine McCrate. *Women and Economic Development in Vermont: A Study for the Governor's Commission on Women.* Montpelier, VT: Governor's Commission on the Status of Women, 1993.

Lobao, Linda M., and Michael D. Schulman. "Farming Patterns, Rural Restructuring, and Poverty: A Comparative Regional Analysis." *Rural Sociology* 56, no. 4 (Winter 1991): 565–602.

Lorber, Judith. *Paradoxes of Gender.* New Haven, CT: Yale University Press, 1994.

Lowenthal, Martin D. "The Social Economy in Urban Working-Class Communities." In *The Social Economy of Cities,* ed. G. Gappert and H. Rose, 447–69. Beverly Hills, CA: Sage, 1975.

Luxton, Meg. "Two Hands for the Clock: Changing Patterns in the Gendered Division of Labour in the Home." In *Through the Kitchen Window: The Politics of Home and Family,* 2d, enlarged ed., ed. Sedef Arat-Koc, Meg Luxton, and Harriet Rosenberg, 39–55. Toronto: Garamond, 1990.

Lyson, T., and W. Falk, eds. *Forgotten Places: Uneven Development in Rural America.* Lawrence: University Press of Kansas, 1993.

MacPherson, Alan. "Service-to-Manufacturing Linkages among Small- and Medium-Sized Firms: Prospects for Rural Industrialization." In *Rural America and the Changing Structure of Manufacturing: Spatial Implications of New Technology and Organization. A Conference Proceedings,* ed. Andrew G. Bernat, Jr., and Martha Frederick, 55–68. Washington, DC: U.S. Department of Agriculture, Economic Research Service, Agriculture and Rural Economy Division, 1993.

Madrick, Jeff. "In the Shadows of Prosperity." *New York Review of Books* (August 14, 1997): 40.

Marks, N. F., and S. S. McLanahan. "Gender, Family Structure, and Social Support among Parents." *Journal of Marriage and the Family* 55 (May 1993): 481–93.

Marshall, Barbara L. *Engendering Modernity: Feminism, Social Theory and Social Change.* Boston: Northeastern University Press, 1994.

Massey, Doreen. *Spatial Divisions of Labor: Social Structures and the Geography of Production.* New York: Methuen, 1984.

Mauss, Marcel. *The Gift: Forms and Functions of Exchange in Archaic Societies.* Glencoe, IL: The Free Press, 1954.

Maxwell, Nan L. "Changing Female Labor Force Participation: Influences on Income Inequality and Distribution." *Social Forces* 68, no. 4 (June 1990): 1251–66.

May, Martha. "The Historical Problem of the Family Wage: The Ford Motor Company and the Five Dollar Day." *Feminist Studies* 8, no. 2 (Summer 1982): 399–424.

———. "Bread Before Roses: American Workingmen, Labor Unions and the Family Wage." In *Women, Work and Protest: A Century of U.S. Women's*

Labor History, ed. Ruth Milkman, 1–21. Boston: Routledge and Kegan Paul, 1985.

McCrate, Elaine, and Joan Smith. "When Work Doesn't Work: The Failure of Current Welfare Reform." Economics Department, University of Vermont, 1996.

McGranahan, David A. "Rural Workers in the National Economy." In *Rural Economic Development in the 1980's: Prospects for the Future*, ed. David H. Brown, 29–75. Washington, DC: Agriculture and Rural Economy Division, Economic Research Service, U.S. Department of Agriculture, 1988.

———. "Rural America in the Global Economy: Socioeconomic Trends." *Journal of Research in Rural Education* 10, no. 3 (Winter 1994): 139–48.

McKee, Lorna. "Households During Unemployment: The Resourcefulness of the Unemployed." In *Give and Take in Families: Studies in Resource Distribution*, ed. Julia Brannen and Gail Wilson, 96–116. Boston: Allen & Unwin, 1987.

McMath, Robert. "Niche Marketing Is the Buzzword as Manufacturers Polish Their Pitch." *Brandweek* (January 17, 1994): 36–37.

Merrill, Michael. "Cash Is Good to Eat: Self-Sufficiency and Exchange in the Rural Economy of the United States." *Radical History Review* 4 (Winter 1977): 42–71.

Michelotti, Kopp. "Multiple Jobholders in May 1975." *Monthly Labor Review* 98, no. 11 (November 1975): 56–61.

Miles, Ian. "Consequences of the Changing Sexual Division of Labor." *Annals of the American Academy of Political and Social Science* 522 (July 1992): 92–103.

Miller, James P. "Small and Midsize Enterprise Development: Prospects for Nonmetropolitan Areas." In *Economic Adaptation: Alternatives for Nonmetropolitan Areas*, ed. David L. Barkley, 89–104. Boulder, CO: Westview, 1993.

Miller, S. M. "The Pursuit of Informal Economies." *Annals of the American Academy of Political and Social Science* 493 (September 1987): 26–35.

———. *Fragmented Societies: A Sociology of Economic Life Beyond the Market Paradigm*. Oxford, UK: Basil Blackwell, 1991.

Mingione, Enzo. "Social Reproduction of the Surplus Labour Force: The Case of Southern Italy." In *Beyond Employment: Household, Gender and Subsistence*, ed. Nanneke Redclift and Enzo Mingione, 14–54. New York: Basil Blackwell, 1985.

Missiakoulis, Spyros, R. E. Pahl, and Peter Taylor-Gooby. "Households, Work and Politics: Some Implications of the Divisions of Labour in Formal and Informal Production." *International Journal of Sociology and Social Policy* 6, no. 3 (1986): 28–40.

Moch, Leslie Page, Nancy Folbre, Daniel Scott Smith, Laurel L. Cornell, and Louise A. Tilly. "Family Strategy: A Dialogue." *Historical Methods* 20, no. 3 (Summer 1987): 113–25.

Morgan, David H. J. "Strategies and Sociologists: A Comment on Crow." *Sociology* 23, no. 1 (February 1989): 25–29.

Morris, Lydia. "Local Social Networks and Domestic Organisations: A Study of Redundant Steel Workers and Their Wives." *Sociological Review* 33, no. 2 (1985): 327–42.

———. "Domestic Labour and Employment Status among Married Couples: A Case Study in Hartlepool." *Capital and Class* 49 (Spring 1993): 37–52.

———. "Informal Aspects of Social Divisions." *International Journal of Urban and Regional Research* 18, no. 1 (March 1994): 112–26.

Naples, Nancy A. "Contradictions in Agrarian Ideology: Restructuring Gender, Race, Ethnicity, and Class." *Rural Sociology* 59, no. 1 (Spring 1994): 110–35.

Nash, June. "Global Integration and Subsistence Insecurity." *American Anthropologist* 96, no. 1 (March 1994): 7–30.

Nelson, Margaret K. *Negotiating Care: The Experience of Family Day Care Providers*. Philadelphia: Temple University Press, 1990.

Oakley, Ann. *The Sociology of Housework*. New York: Pantheon, 1974.

Oberhauser, Ann M. "Gender and Household Economic Strategies in Rural Appalachia." *Gender, Place and Culture* 2, no. 1 (1995): 51–70.

O'Hare, William P. *The Rise of Poverty in Rural America*. Washington, DC: Population Reference Bureau, 1988.

Osterud, Nancy Grey. *Bonds of Community: The Lives of Farm Women in Nineteenth-Century New York*. Ithaca, NY: Cornell University Press, 1991.

Pahl, Jan. "The Allocation of Money and the Structuring of Inequality Within Marriage." *Sociological Review* 31, no. 2 (1983): 237–62.

Pahl, R. E. *Divisions of Labour*. Oxford, UK: Basil Blackwell, 1984.

———. "The Restructuring of Capital, the Local Political Economy and Household Work Strategies." In *Social Relations and Spatial Structures*, ed. D. Gregory and J. Urry, 243–64. Basingstoke, UK: Macmillan, 1985.

———. "Does Jobless Mean Workless?: Unemployment and Informal Work." *Annals of the American Academy of Political and Social Science* 493 (September 1987): 36–46.

———. "Some Remarks on Informal Work, Social Polarization and the Social Structure." *International Journal of Urban and Regional Research* 12, no. 2 (1988): 247–67.

———. "Employment, Work and the Domestic Division of Labour." *International Journal of Urban and Regional Research* 4, no. 1 (1994): 1–20.

Pahl, R. E., and Claire Wallace. "Household Work Strategies in Economic Recession." In *Beyond Employment: Household, Gender and Subsistence*, ed. Nanneke Redclift and Enzo Mingione, 189–228. New York: Basil Blackwell, 1985.

Parr, Joy. "Re-Thinking Work and Kinship in a Canadian Hosiery Town, 1910–1950." *Feminist Studies* 13 (1987): 137–62.

Passell, Peter. "Benefits Dwindle along with Wages for the Unskilled." *New York Times* (June 14, 1998): A1, 28.

Peace and Justice Center. *The Job Gap Study: Phase II: Livable Wage Jobs: The Job Gap*. Burlington, VT: Author, May 1987.

Pennar, Karen, and Christopher Farrell. "Notes from the Underground Economy." *Business Week* (February 15, 1993): 98–101.

Phillips, Kevin. *The Politics of Rich and Poor: Wealth and the American Electorate in the Reagan Aftermath*. New York: Harper Perennial, 1990.

Piore, Michael J., and Charles F. Sabel. *The Second Industrial Divide: The Possibilities for Prosperity*. New York: Basic Books, 1984.

Pleck, Joseph H. "Men's Power with Women, Other Men, and Society: A Men's Movement Analysis." In *Men's Lives*, ed. Michael S. Kimmel and Michael A. Messner, 5–12. Boston: Allyn and Bacon, 1995.

Plunkert, Lois M. "The 1980's: A Decade of Job Growth and Industry Shifts." *Monthly Labor Review* 113, no. 9 (September 1990): 3–16.

Porter, Marilyn. "Time, the Life Course and Work in Women's Lives: Reflections from Newfoundland." *Women's Studies International Forum* 14, no. 1–2 (1991): 1–13.

Porterfield, Shirley. "Service Sector Offers More Jobs, Lower Pay." *Rural Development Perspectives* (June-September 1990): 2–7.

Portes, Alejandro, Manuel Castells, and Lauren A. Benton, eds. *The Informal Economy: Studies in Advanced and Less Developed Countries*. Baltimore: Johns Hopkins University Press, 1989.

Portes, Alejandro, and Saskia Sassen-Koob. "Making It Underground: Comparative Material on the Informal Sector in Western Market Economies." *American Journal of Sociology* 93 (1987): 30–61.

Pratt, Geraldine, and Susan Hanson. "On the Links Between Home and Work: Family-Household Strategies in a Buoyant Labor Market." *International Journal of Urban and Regional Research* 15, no. 1 (March 1991): 55–74.

Presser, Harriet. "Shift Work among American Women and Child Care." *Journal of Marriage and the Family* 48 (1986): 551–64.

———. "Shift Work and Child Care among Young Dual-Earner American Parents." *Journal of Marriage and the Family* 50, no. 1 (February 1988): 133–48.

Pugliese, Enrico. "The Three Forms of Unemployment." *Social Research* 54, no. 2 (Summer 1987): 303–17.

Rapping, Elayne. "Tupperware and Women." *Radical America* 14, no. 6 (November/December 1980): 39–49.

Rasmussen, Wayne D., and Douglas F. Bowers. "Rural America in the Twentieth Century." In *Rural America in Transition*, ed. Mark Drabenstott and Lynn Gibson, 1–14. Kansas City, MO: Federal Reserve Bank of Kansas City, Research Division, 1988.

Regets, Mark. "Labor Supply in the Naval Reserve." Ph.D. diss., State University of New York at Binghamton, 1989.

Reskin, Barbara, and Irene Padavic. *Women and Men at Work*. Thousand Oaks, CA: Pine Forge, 1994.

Riche, Martha Farnsworth. "Fiscal Attraction." *American Demographics* 10, no. 7 (July 1988): 19.

Rifkin, Jeremy. *The End of Work: The Decline of the Global Labor Force and the Dawn of the Post-Market Era*. New York: G. P. Putnam's Sons, 1996.

Roberts, Bryan R. "Household Coping Strategies and Urban Poverty in Comparative Perspective." In *Urban Life in Transition*, Urban Affairs Annual

Reviews 9, ed. Marc Gottdiener and C. C. Pickvance, 135–68. Newbury Park, CA: Sage, 1991.

———. "Informal Economy and Family Strategies." *International Journal of Urban and Regional Research* 18, no. 1 (March 1994): 6–21.

Robinson, John P., and Geoffrey Godbey. "Are Average Americans Really Over-worked?" *The American Enterprise* 6, no. 5 (September/October 1995):43.

Rose, Stephen J. *Declining Job Security and the Professionalizaion of Opportunity*. Research Report 94-04. Washington, DC: National Commission for Employment Policy, 1995.

Rosen, Ellen Israel. *Bitter Choices: Blue-Collar Women in and out of Work*. Chicago: University of Chicago Press, 1987.

Rubin, Lillian B. *Families on the Faultline: America's Working Class Speaks about the Family, the Economy, Race and Ethnicity*. New York: Harper-Collins, 1994.

Rubin, Rose M., and Bobye J. Riney. *Working Wives and Dual-Earner Families*. New York: Praeger, 1995.

Sabel, Charles F. *Work and Politics: The Division of Labor in Industry*. Cambridge, UK: Cambridge University Press, 1982.

Sahlins, Marshall D. *Stone-Age Economics*. Chicago: Aldine-Atherton, 1972.

Sassen-Koob, Saskia. "New York City's Informal Economy." In *The Informal Economy: Studies in Advanced and Less Developed Countries*, ed. Alejandro Portes, Manuel Castells, and Lauren A. Benton, 60–78. Baltimore: Johns Hopkins University Press, 1989.

Schiff, Lenore, and John Labate. "Labor Force Mysteries: The Working Poor and the Underground Economy." *Fortune* (August 24, 1992): 22.

Schor, Juliet. *The Overworked American*. New York: Basic Books, 1991.

———. "Economic Trend: More Willing to Give Up Pay for Additional Time Off." *Nieman Reports* 49, no. 3 (Fall 1995): 8–9.

Scott, Joan Wallach. *Gender and the Politics of History*. New York: Columbia University Press, 1988.

Singelmann, Joachim. "Will Rural Areas Still Matter in the 21st Century? (or) Can Rural Sociology Remain Relevant?" *Rural Sociology* 61, no. 1 (Spring 1996): 143–58.

Smith, Dorothy. "Women's Inequality and the Family." In *Families and Work*, ed. Naomi Gerstel and Harriet Engel Gross, 23–54. Philadelphia: Temple University Press, 1987.

Smith, Gavin. "Towards an Ethnography of Idiosyncratic Forms of Livelihood." *International Journal of Urban and Regional Research* 18, no. 1 (1994): 71–87.

Smith, Joan. "The Way We Were: Women and Work." *Feminist Studies* 8, no. 2 (Summer 1982): 437–56.

———. "The Paradox of Women's Poverty: Wage-Earning Women and Economic Transformation." In *Women and Poverty*, ed. Barbara C. Gelpi, Nancy C. M. Hartock, Clare C. Novak, and Myra H. Strober, 121–40. Chicago: University of Chicago Press, 1986.

———. "Transforming Households: Working Class Women and Economic Crisis." *Social Problems* 35 (1987): 416–36.

———. "All Crises Are Not the Same: Households in the United States During Two Crises." In *Work Without Wages: Comparative Studies of Domestic Labor and Self-Employment*, ed. Jane L. Collins and Martha Giminez, 128–41. Albany: State University of New York Press, 1990.

Smith, Joan, and Jamie Sudler. "A Postscript on Method." In *Creating and Transforming Households*, ed. Joan Smith and Immanuel Wallerstein, 263–72. Cambridge, UK: Cambridge University Press, 1992.

Smith, Joan, and Immanuel Wallerstein. *Creating and Transforming Households*. Cambridge, UK: Cambridge University Press, 1992.

Soga, Aki. "Beating the Bad-Job Trap: Family Struggles to Regain a Dream." *Burlington Free Press* (October 9, 1995): A1.

Spalter-Roth, Roberta M., and Heidi I. Hartmann. *Unnecessary Losses: Costs to Americans of the Lack of Family and Medical Leave*. Washington, DC: Institute for Women's Policy Research, 1990.

Stack, Carol. *All Our Kin*. New York: Harper & Row, 1975.

Statistical Abstract of the United States. Washington, DC: Government Printing Office, various years.

Stinson, John F., Jr., "Multiple Jobholding up Sharply in the 1980's." *Monthly Labor Review* 113, no. 7 (July 1990): 3–10.

Storper, Michael, and Richard Walker. *The Capitalist Imperative: Territory, Technology, and Industrial Growth*. London: Basil Blackwell, 1989.

Swanson, Linda L., and Margaret A. Butler. "Human Resource Base of Rural Economies." In *Rural Economic Development in the 1980's: Prospects for the Future*, ed. David H. Brown, 159–200. Washington, DC: Agriculture and Rural Economy Division, Economic Research Service, U.S. Department of Agriculture, 1988.

Swinnerton, Kenneth A., and Howard Wial. "Is Job Stability Declining in the U.S. Economy?" *Industrial and Labor Relations Review* 48, no. 2 (1995): 293–98.

Tentler, Leslie Woodcock. *Wage-Earning Women: Industrial Work and Family Life in the United States, 1900–1930*. Oxford, UK: Oxford University Press, 1979.

Thurow, Lester C. "Can 19th Century Capitalism Work in 2013." *New Perspectives Quarterly* 13, no. 2 (Spring 1996): 14–17.

Tickamyer, Ann R., and Janet Bokemeier. "Sex Differences in Labor-Market Experiences." *Rural Sociology* 53, no. 2 (1988): 166–89.

Tickamyer, Ann R., and Cynthia M. Duncan. "Poverty and Opportunity Structure in Rural America." *Annual Review of Sociology* 16 (1990): 67–86.

Tienda, Marta. "Industrial Restructuring in Metropolitan and Nonmetropolitan Labor Markets: Implications for Equity and Efficiency." In *Symposium on Rural Labor Markets: Research Issues*, ed. Molly S. Killian, Leonard E. Bloomquist, Shelly Pendleton, and David A. McGranahan, 33–70. Washington, DC: U.S. Department of Agriculture, September 1986.

Tilly, Chris. *Short Hours, Short Shrift, Cause and Consequence of Part-Time Work*. Washington, DC: Economic Policy Institute, 1990.

———. *Half a Job*. Philadelphia: Temple University Press, 1996.

Tilly, Louise A., and Joan W. Scott. *Women, Work and Family*. New York: Holt, Rinehart, and Winston, 1978.

"Time Available Does Not Determine Amount of Help Going to Family." *The Division of the Social Sciences Reports, University of Chicago*, no. 15 (Autumn 1995): 1–2.

Tolbert, Charles M., and Thomas A. Lyson. "Earnings Inequality in the Nonmetropolitan United States: 1967–1990." *Rural Sociology* 57, no. 4 (Winter 1992): 494–511.

Uchiltelle, Louis, and N. R. Kleinfield. "On the Battlefields of Business, Millions of Casualties." *New York Times* (March 3, 1996): A1, 26–29.

U.S. Department of Commerce. *County and City Data Book*. Washington, DC: U.S. Department of Commerce, Economics and Statistics Administration, Bureau of the Census, 1994.

Vermont Department of Employment and Training. *1994 Employment and Wages*. Montpelier, VT: Department of Employment and Training, Labor Market Information Sector, October 1995.

———. *Vermont Labor Market Bulletin. Statewide and Labor Market Area; 3rd Quarter, 1995*. Montpelier, VT: March 1996.

———. *Vermont Labor Market*. Montpelier, VT: Author, June 1997.

———. *Vermont UI Covered Employment and Wages*. Montpelier, VT: July 1997.

Vermont Department of Social and Rehabilitation Services. *Journal for Family Day Care Homes*. Montpelier, VT: Division of Licensing and Registration, 1989.

Veum, Jonathan R., and Philip M. Gleason. "Child Care: Arrangements and Costs." *Monthly Labor Review* 114, no. 10 (October 1991): 10–17.

Wallace, Claire, and Ray Pahl. "Polarisation, Unemployment and All Forms of Work." In *The Experience of Unemployment*, ed. Sheila Allen, 116–49. Basingstoke, UK: Macmillan.

Wallerstein, Immanuel, and Joan Smith. "Households as an Institution of the World Economy." In *Creating and Transforming Households*, ed. Joan Smith and Immanuel Wallerstein, 3–23. Cambridge, UK: Cambridge University Press, 1992.

Weisz, Pam. "Times Sure Have Changed When Tupperware Is Cool." *Brandweek* (July 11, 1994): 28.

Wekerle, Gerda R., and Brent Rutherford. "The Mobility of Capital and the Immobility of Female Labor: Responses to Economic Restructuring." In *The Power of Geography: How Territory Shapes Social Life*, ed. Jennifer Wolch and Michael Dear, 130–72. Boston: Unwin Hyman, 1989.

Wellman, Barry. "Domestic Work, Paid Work and Net Work." In *Understanding Personal Relationships: An Interdisciplinary Approach*, ed. Steve Duck, 159–91. Beverly Hills, CA: Sage, 1985.

Wells, Jennifer. "This Thing Called 'Outsourcing' Has Your Job." *Maclean's* (September 30, 1996): 46–49.

Western, Bruce. *Between Class and Market: Postwar Unionization in the Capitalist Democracies*. Princeton, NJ: Princeton University Press, 1997.

Wheelock, Jane. "Capital Restructuring and the Domestic Economy: Family Self

Respect and the Irrelevance of 'Rational Economic Man.' " *Capital and Class*, no. 41 (Summer 1990): 103–41.

Williams, Colin C., and Jan Windebank. "Social Polarization of Households in Contemporary Britain: A 'Whole Economy' Perspective." *Regional Studies* 29, no. 8 (December 1995): 723–28.

Wilson, Gail. "Money: Patterns of Responsibility and Irresponsibility in Marriage." In *Give and Take in Families*, ed. Julia Brannen and Gail Wilson, 136–54. Boston: Allen & Unwin, 1987.

Wilson, William Julius. *The Truly Disadvantaged: The Inner City, the Underclass, and Public Policy*. Chicago: University of Chicago Press, 1987.

———. *When Work Disappears: The World of the New Urban Poor*. New York: Random House, 1996.

Wolff, Edward N. *Top Heavy: A Study of the Increasing Inequality of Wealth in America*. New York: The Twentieth Century Fund Press, 1995.

Young, Michael, and P. Willmott. *Family and Kinship in East London*. London: Penguin, 1957.

Zelizer, Viviana A. "The Social Meaning of Money: 'Special Monies.' " *American Journal of Sociology* 95, no. 2 (September 1989): 342–77.

———. *The Social Meaning of Money: Pin Money, Paychecks, Poor Relief, and Other Currencies*. Princeton, NJ: Princeton University Press, 1997.

Zsembik, Barbara, and Chuck Peek. "The Effect of Economic Restructuring on Puerto Rican Women's Labor Force Participation in the Formal Sector." *Gender and Society* 8, no. 4 (December 1994): 525–40.

Index

African Americans: dual-earner households, 45; interhousehold exchanges, 51, 219n21; labor market, 17; moonlighting, 47, 217n13; women in paid employment, 214–15n1
Age: effect on choice of survival strategy, 62, 67
Agriculture: in Coolidge County, 18, 19, 20
Ajax, 26–27; benefits, 27, 205n26; employees, 27, 224–25n12; outsourcing, 31–32, 206n33; temporary workers, 31; unions in, 206n32; wages, 27, 205n26
Amalgamated Clothing and Textile Workers Union, 206n32
American Enterprise Institute, 181
Ayer, Lucy, 81, 190
Ayer, Pete, 81, 88, 91, 190

Badger, Barbara, 77–79, 80, 113–15, 170, 178
Badger, Ernie, 77–79, 80, 114–15
Bad jobs: in Coolidge County, 2, 33, 36–37, 39; definition of, 9–10, 202n30; degendered, 129–30, 135, 167, 179, 244n23; growth in, 2, 14–18, 176, 185; instability of, 15, 167–68, 177; lack of benefits, 3, 15–16, 36–37, 72, 166, 221–22n29; layoffs, 76–79; recruitment for, 224–25n12; in service sector, 16–17, 35, 176, 204n13, 247n14; treatment of employees, 166–67, 168–70, 183, 244n21, 247n14; in Vermont, 2. See also Employment; Good jobs
Bad job households: "bad" cycle, 76–79, 116; characteristics, 57–58; commuting patterns, 133, 134; consumption decisions, 246n3; definition of, 10; differences among individual families in group, 61–62; division of labor, 140–41, 144, 146, 147–51, 153–54, 179–80; dual-earner strategy, 65–68, 69, 70–71, 72–73, 74, 131, 132–33, 177; effects of job loss, 76–79; financial resources, 55, 153–54; former good job households, 58–62, 75, 77–79, 98–99, 221n28; gender differences in earnings, 120, 129, 131; gender differences in employment patterns, 120; gender roles, 118–19, 129–39, 179–80; interhousehold exchanges, 54, 55, 107, 108–9, 110–14, 177–78; internal tensions, 153–54; job instability, 54–55, 65–66, 72, 73–74; labor force participation, 55, 68, 133; lack of resources for entrepreneurial moonlighting, 88–89, 90, 105, 226–27n19; lack of resources for self-provisioning, 62–63; meals, 148–49; moonlighting, 53–54, 82–83, 84–87, 91, 93–94, 134–36, 170; networks, 77; part-time jobs, 55, 65, 133–34, 222nn2, 3; political attitudes, 170–71, 183–84; routine self-provisioning, 54, 100, 101–4, 106–7; self-employment, 79, 80–81; similarities to good job households, 176–77, 184; single-earner strategy, 68, 73, 77, 101, 131–32, 137; strategies chosen, 3, 53–54, 59–60, 116, 176–78; substantial self-provisioning, 98–99; time management, 91; trading activities, 91–93, 136–37, 183, 228n27; unstable patterns, 64–65, 147–48. See also Good job households; Households
Barter: in bad job households, 110, 112–13, 126, 138; in Coolidge County, 51, 107, 108; definition of, 11, 50,

Compositor: Binghamton Valley Composition
Text: 10/13 Sabon
Display: Sabon
Printer: Maple-Vail Book Manufacturing Group
Binder: Maple-Vail Book Manufacturing Group